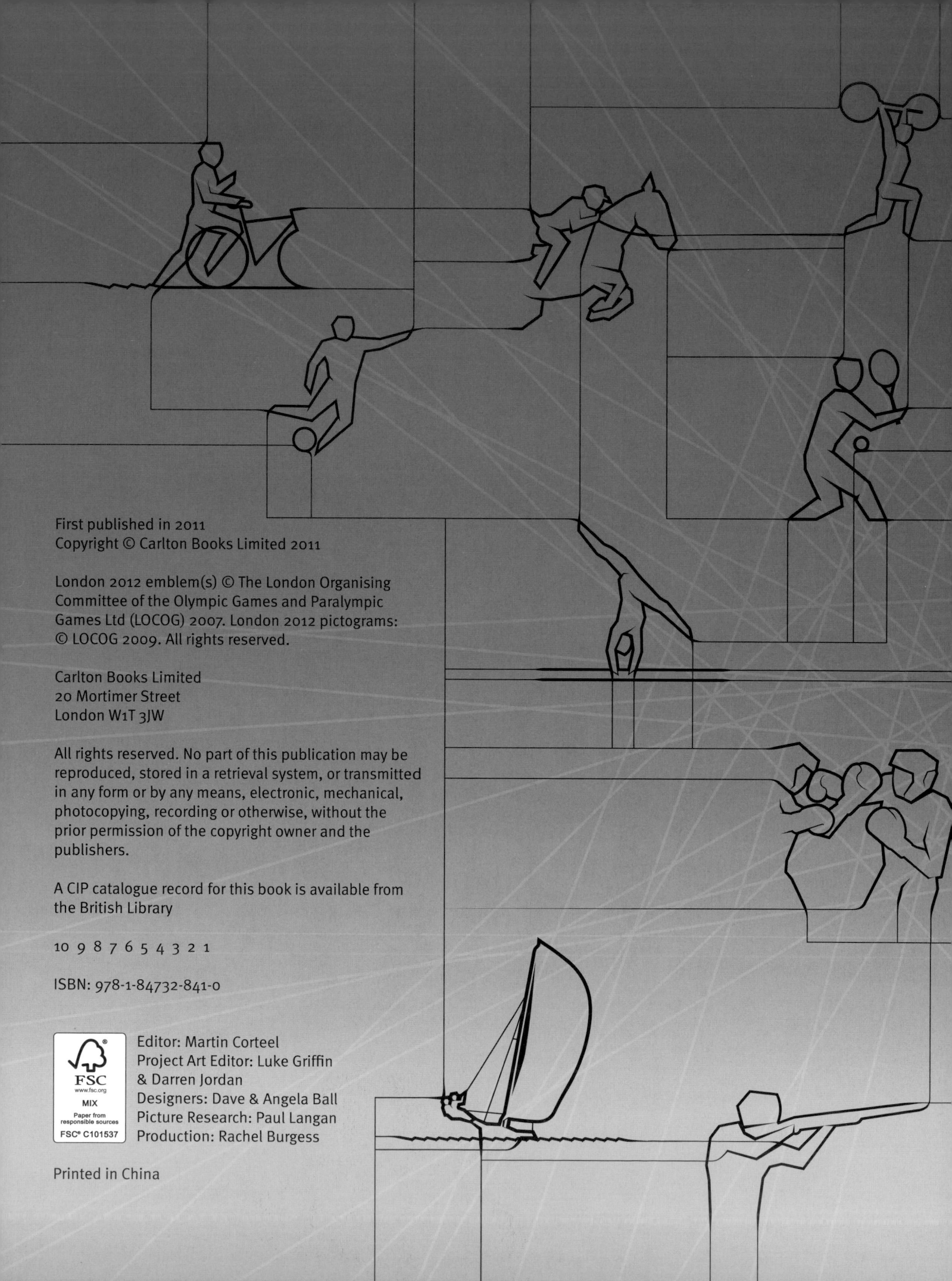

First published in 2011
Copyright © Carlton Books Limited 2011

London 2012 emblem(s) © The London Organising
Committee of the Olympic Games and Paralympic
Games Ltd (LOCOG) 2007. London 2012 pictograms:
© LOCOG 2009. All rights reserved.

Carlton Books Limited
20 Mortimer Street
London W1T 3JW

A CIP catalogue record for this book is available from
the British Library

10 9 8 7 6 5 4 3 2 1

ISBN: 978-1-84732-841-0

Editor: Martin Corteel
Project Art Editor: Luke Griffin
& Darren Jordan
Designers: Dave & Angela Ball
Picture Research: Paul Langan
Production: Rachel Burgess

Printed in China

OLYMPIC AND WORLD RECORDS 2012

**AN OFFICIAL LONDON 2012
OLYMPIC GAMES PUBLICATION**

KEIR RADNEDGE

CARLTON

Contents

Introduction

The date 6 July 2005 is etched in history in the annals of British sport. That was the day when Jacques Rogge, President of the International Olympic Committee, revealed to the world that the Host City for the 2012 Olympic Games would be … 'London!'

Nine cities had bid, initially. One year before the final decision Havana, Istanbul, Leipzig and Rio de Janeiro were eliminated from the process. That left London, Madrid, Moscow, New York and Paris.

Four rounds of voting were needed at the 117th IOC Session in Singapore. The city receiving fewest votes was eliminated each time. Moscow fell first, then New York City, then Madrid. London emerged triumphant in the last round, pipping Paris at the post by a margin of just four votes.

A vision of legacy for the youth of tomorrow was one of the most persuasive arguments proclaimed by a bid team led by Lord Coe and supported by the last-minute lobbying of the then Prime Minister, Tony Blair.

On another historic date – 27 July 2012 – London thus becomes the first city to host the Games on three occasions: after 1908 and the so-called 'Austerity Games' of 1948.

No sports event on the planet – perhaps, no event of any sort – compares with the Olympic Games and Paralympic Games. Its unique status lies not only in the drama of high-level, simultaneous competition in so many and varied sports in close proximity but in the link with antiquity which inspired Pierre de Coubertin … and in the ideals which the Olympic Movement seeks to spread worldwide through sport's inspirational, unifying medium.

But 'London pride' is more than a spirit of defiance or a song title or a plant. It is represented in the transformation of the East End of the city by the Olympic Park, a triumph over the pessimism of those who had doubted whether British sport would ever attract a major event.

Winning the Olympic Games for London inspired other cities and sports federations to bring their own events 'home'; it helped fire Great Britain's athletes to their remarkable medals haul in Beijing in 2008; and it will bring the world to London to join the party in 2012.

The first modern Olympic Games were held in 1896 in Athens. This book recounts the achievements of heroes and heroines from that day to this. But it is only the story, so far. Another chapter is about to be written …

← *Usain Bolt breezes to victory in the men's 100m Final at Beijing 2008.*

← ← *Contents (clockwise from top left): Carl Lewis, Isabell Werth, Teofilo Stevenson, Daley Thompson, Im Dong-Hyun, Matthias Steiner, Steve Redgrave, Steffi Graf, Nadia Comaneci, Lionel Messi, Chris Hoy and Michael Phelps.*

← ← ← *Front endpaper: The Opening Ceremony at the Beijing 2008 Games.*

Chapter One
Olympic Games heritage

The history of the Olympic Games dates back to 776 BC. That was when the Ancient Greeks held sporting contests on a plain above a village in the Peloponnese called Olympia. These Olympic Games grew from a single event to widespread popularity across the city states of Greece. They lasted until AD 393, when they were discontinued by decree of the Roman Emperor Theodosius, who considered them a pagan festival.

In the years after the Franco-Prussian war of 1871, a young Frenchman called Pierre de Coubertin travelled to England and the United States. There he saw the growth of competitive sport in schools, colleges and clubs and decided that sporting competition would be beneficial not only for his country and its youth in particular but for others throughout the world.

In 1894, still only 31, he gathered like-minded men from across the world at the University of the Sorbonne in Paris, founded the International Olympic Committee and persuaded them to revive the Olympic Games. The first games of the modern era were scheduled for Athens in 1896.

These were modest beginnings. Fewer than 250 athletes took part from a dozen nations and all were men. Since then the Games have overcome many obstacles to become the greatest sporting show on earth. De Coubertin, who died in 1937, would have been amazed to see just how much his brainchild has grown.

When the Olympic Flame burned in Beijing in 2008, nearly 11,000 competitors from 204 countries were present. Almost half the competitors were women, and in all there were a staggering 303 gold medal events in 28 sports.

The Olympic Flame flares out above the Bird's Nest Stadium in Beijing before the close of the historic 2008 Summer Games. This was the first time they had ever taken place in China.

Olympic Games stadiums

The word 'stadium' takes its name from the ancient length of the same name in Latin. This was the length of the track or the equivalent of 180 metres. At the Olympic Games of antiquity held in Olympia, sporting contests took place in conjunction with a religious festival. The stadium was next door to the temple.

⬆ *The White City Stadium in west London was the all-purpose venue for the 1908 Olympic Games.*

Athens 1896 and 2004

The centrepiece of the 1896 Games was the Panathenaic Stadium, a marble structure built in the fourth century BC. Greek benefactor Georgios Averof paid for the renovation. Shaped almost like a horseshoe, with spectators seated on three sides, the running track featured tight turns at either end. To the delight of the crowd, Spiridon Louis of Greece came home to win the first Olympic Marathon. At the 2004 Games, the stadium again staged the finish of the Marathon, as well as Archery.

⬇ *Crowds gather for the Opening Ceremony at the Panathenaic Stadium in Athens ahead of the 1896 Games, the first of the modern era.*

London 1908

The organisers of the London 1908 Olympic Games did not have to pay for the stadium. It was built in White City, West London, by the company organising an Anglo-French exhibition on the same site. In exchange for a percentage of the gate receipts they accepted the costs of construction and the specifications laid down by Olympic Games chief Lord Desborough. The Great Stadium, as it was known at the time, featured cycling and running tracks and even a swimming pool on the infield. It offered a legacy ahead of its time and, later known as the White City Stadium, was used for athletics, rugby league, football, speedway and even greyhound racing before it finally closed in the mid-1980s.

Los Angeles 1932 and 1984

The Los Angeles Memorial Coliseum was built in the early 1920s to honour the fallen in the First World War. It staged the Games first in 1932 and again in 1984, when a jet-powered rocket man began the proceedings. Some 84 pianists played Gershwin's Rhapsody in Blue before Ronald Reagan became the first incumbent American president to open the Games. Carl Lewis made the stage his own during the following days with four gold medals. The Games ended with a spectacular light show finale featuring a spaceman who bade farewell.

London 1948

Wembley owner Sir Arthur Elvin did his bit for the Olympic Games effort in 1948 by offering his stadium to the Organising Committee. He reasoned that staging the Games would be a great advertisement for Wembley. King George VI declared the Games open, 26 years after he had laid the first foundation stone at the start of construction. Dutch housewife Fanny Blankers-Koen dominated the headlines, winning four gold medals on a cinder track. Wembley also held medal matches in Hockey and Football, Show Jumping and even a demonstration match in Lacrosse.

Munich 1972

Munich's Olympiastadion, built for the 1972 Games, has a futuristic roof made of self-cleaning acrylic glass plates. With a surface area of 75,000 square metres, it offers a unique and dramatic tented effect. Two years after the Games the stadium was used for the 1974 World Cup final, and it has also hosted three European Cup finals

Barcelona 1992

The Estadi Montjuic in Barcelona was built on a hill overlooking the city with the 1936 Olympic Games in mind. However, Barcelona lost out to Berlin in the IOC vote in 1931. When the city was finally chosen to host the 1992 Olympic Games, the interior was completely renovated, while the impressive facade was maintained.

Helsinki 1952

The stadium used for the 1952 Games in Helsinki pays homage to Finland's magnificent heritage in athletics. Visitors are welcomed by a giant statue of the great long-distance runner Paavo Nurmi, the 'Flying Finn'. He lit the Olympic Flame in the stadium at the start of the Games. The stadium also hosted the inaugural World Athletics Championships in 1983.

Berlin 1936

A giant bell tolled above Berlin's Olympic Stadium to welcome the world to the 1936 Olympic Games. Designed by Werner March, the stadium was monumental in design and held more than 100,000 in its heyday. The first Olympic Flame brought by relay from Olympia burned here. Adolf Hitler declared the Games open, but the star was Jesse Owens, who won four gold medals on the track below. The stadium formed part of an overall sports complex. The Olympic swimming pool was next door and vast gymnastic displays were held on the Maifeld, an arena behind the stadium.

← *Adolf Hitler, accompanied by International Olympic Committee members, arrives at the Berlin Olympic Stadium to open the 1936 Games.*

Melbourne 1956

Melbourne Cricket Ground was the main centre for the 1956 Olympic Games and hosted Athletics, the Football final and a demonstration event in Australian Rules Football. Originally built in 1853 as a base for the Melbourne Cricket Club, it staged the first cricket Test match between Australia and England in 1877 and is also home to Australian Rules Football, Rugby Union and Rugby League.

Beijing 2008

Immediately dubbed the 'Bird's Nest' by locals and visitors alike, Beijing's Olympic Stadium was five years in the making and was constructed using 45,000 tonnes of steel. During the Games, it held 91,000 and was used for Athletics and the men's Football final. A complex system of steel wires above the stadium made possible some spectacular displays, none more so than when gymnast Li Ning soared through the air to light the Olympic Flame on the stadium roof.

⬇ *Built at a cost of US$423 million, the Bird's Nest Stadium was the magnificent focal point of the 2008 Games in Beijing.*

Atlanta 1996

The stadium used for the 1996 Centennial Games in Atlanta was built with the future in mind. It held 85,000 and incorporated a series of underground passages to allow for dramatic set pieces during the Opening Ceremony. World champion boxer Evander Holyfield brought the flame through one of these tunnels to reach the stage, and later Muhammad Ali appeared to light the Olympic Flame on a free-standing tower outside the stadium itself! After the Games the entire arena was rebuilt as a baseball park for the Atlanta Braves, and the running track was given to a local university.

Host Cities

Twenty-two cities on five of the world's continents have had the honour of hosting an Olympic Games with four cities – Athens (1896, 2004), Paris (1900, 1924), London (1908, 1948) and Los Angeles (1932, 1984) having hosted the spectacle on two occasions. In 2012, London will become the first city in history to become a three-time Olympic Games Host City.

Longest games

The London 1908 Olympic Games were the longest in history. They began on 27 April at Queen's Club, in West Kensington, when Evan Baillie Noel won the first gold medal in Racquets. They came to an end on the last day of October, when England won the Hockey final. They included a strange mixture of events including Ice Skating, Motor Boating, Lacrosse, Rugby Union and even Tug of War.

Political change

Berlin was awarded the 1936 Games five years earlier, before the Nazis came to power. A bitter critic of the Olympic Movement, Adolf Hitler later tried to hijack the Games for political gain. His theories of racial superiority were confounded by the exploits of American Jesse Owens, who won four gold medals and forged a life-long friendship with his German rival in the Long Jump, 'Luz' Long. For the first time full results from every event were set down.

Heading down south

Melbourne in 1956 was the first southern hemisphere city to stage the Olympic Games. Never before had an Olympic Games begun in November. They became known as 'The Friendly Games' despite a tense Cold War political backdrop as a result of the Suez crisis and the Hungarian uprising. The sporting competition launched the career of Australian swimmer Dawn Fraser, who dominated the women's 100m Freestyle over the next three Olympic Games.

Doubling up

Paris was the first city to host the Olympic Games twice. In 1900 they were run in conjunction with the Paris Exhibition and were, to a certain extent, overshadowed by the fun of the fair. They lasted five months but were surrounded by confusion over what were official events. The Games returned in 1924 and are associated with the story of British athletes Eric Liddell and Harold Abrahams, later celebrated in the Oscar-winning film *Chariots of Fire*.

Stockholm stand-in

Stockholm was thrust into the Olympic spotlight for the second time in 1956. Australian quarantine laws prevented the transit of horses to Melbourne, the designated Host City, so the equestrian events were held earlier in the year in the Swedish capital. They took place in the stadium that had been used for the 1912 Games. Gymnast Karin Lindberg was chosen to light the Olympic Flame, becoming the first woman to do so.

↑ *Colonel Frank Wheldon receives the gold medal on behalf of the victorious British Eventing team at Stockholm in 1956.*

Hiroshima remembered

The 1964 Games in Tokyo were the first held in Asia. Tokyo had been designated as Host City for 1940 before the war intervened. The Olympic Flame was lit by Yoshinori Sakai, born in Hiroshima the day the atom bomb was dropped. These were the first Games to be televised by satellite. The traditional Japanese sport of Judo was included on the programme for the first time, but to the dismay of the host nation the blue riband open category was won by the giant Dutchman, the late Anton Geesink.

← *Hiroshima survivor Yoshinori Sakai about to light the Olympic Flame in Tokyo in 1964.*

Beating the boycott

In the build-up to the 1980 Games in Moscow, the International Olympic Committee struggled to prevent a western boycott. The United States chose to stay away as a protest against the Soviet invasion of Afghanistan, along with Canada, Japan and the Federal Republic of Germany. Great Britain did compete, but British chef de mission Dick Palmer marched alone in the Opening Ceremony carrying the Olympic Flag. Other nations also competed under the IOC flag or that of their National Olympic Committee.

⬆ Dick Palmer, Great Britain's chef de mission, marches alone at the Opening Ceremony of the boycott-hit 1980 Games in Moscow.

Altitude advantage

In 1968, Mexico City became the first Central American city to stage the Games. Athletes from altitude prospered in the distance events. Kenyans Kip Keino (men's 1500m) and Naftali Temu (men's 10,000m) and Ethiopian Mamo Wolde in the men's Marathon all took gold. The Track events also produced a world record harvest: Jim Hines (men's 100m) Tommie Smith (men's 200m), Lee Evans (men's 400m) and, most famously, Bob Beamon in the men's Long Jump.

Harmony breakthrough

Seoul unexpectedly beat the Japanese city of Nagoya to win the 1988 nomination. At the time Korea had only hosted one World Championship event (in shooting), but the Games proved a great success. Some 149 nations marched in the Opening Ceremony, the last at a Summer Games to be held in daylight. The 'Games of Harmony' were the first in 12 years to be attended by both the Soviet Union and the United States. Soviet gymnast Vladimir Artemov won four gold medals, in Horizontal Bars, Parallel Bars, All-Around Individual and Team Combined exercises.

More than a games

Barcelona finally won the right to stage the Olympic Games in 1992, some 60 years after having bid first. These proved spectacular Games from the moment Paralympic archer Antonio Rebollo lit the Olympic Flame with a burning arrow. The home crowds were delighted by the men's 1500m success of Fermin Cacho on the track, and across town Spain won Football gold at the iconic Nou Camp Stadium with a team including Barcelona's own Pep Guardiola.

When and where

1896	Athens (6–15 April)
1900	Paris (20 May – 25 October)
1904	St Louis (1 July – 23 November)
1908	London (27 April – 31 October)
1912	Stockholm (5 May – 22 July)
1916	Berlin – not held
1920	Antwerp (23 April – 12 September)
1924	Paris (4 May – 27 July)
1928	Amsterdam (17 May – 12 August)
1932	Los Angeles (30 July – 14 August)
1936	Berlin (1–16 August)
1940	Tokyo – not held
1944	London – not held
1948	London (29 July – 14 August)
1952	Helsinki (19 July – 3 August)
1956	Melbourne (22 November – 8 December)*
1960	Rome (25 August – 11 September)
1964	Tokyo (10–24 October)
1968	Mexico City (12–27 October)
1972	Munich (26 August – 10 September)
1976	Montreal (17 July – 1 August)
1980	Moscow (19 July – 3 August)
1984	Los Angeles (28 July – 12 August)
1988	Seoul (17 September – 2 October)
1992	Barcelona (25 July – 9 August)
1996	Atlanta (20 July – 4 August)
2000	Sydney (16 September – 1 October)
2004	Athens (13–29 August)
2008	Beijing (8–24 August)

*Stockholm for Equestrian events (10–17 June)

⬅ Spain gave the home crowd cause for cheer when they beat Poland 3–2 in the men's Football Final to take gold at the 1992 Games.

Famous firsts

Twenty-six Olympic Games held in the modern era (since 1896) and the numerous editions of the Ancient Games – held in Greece, normally on a four-yearly basis, between 776BC and 393AD (when they were suppressed by Theodosius I in an attempt to impose Christianity on the region) – have produced numerous landmarks. Here is a selection of the most significant of them.

How it began

A heat of the men's 100m was the first event to be held at the first Olympic Games of the modern era in 1896. American Frank Lane was the first to cross the line. The first gold medal to be decided came in the men's Triple Jump. Harvard student James Connolly had made the trip to Athens against the advice of the dean at his university but returned home with the first-ever gold medal awarded at the Games. He later ran for Congress, but without success.

← *American athlete James Connolly holds the distinction of winning the first-ever Olympic Games gold medal, in the men's Triple Jump at Athens in 1896.*

All-round winner

American Eddie Eagan was the first man to win Summer and Winter gold medals. In 1920 he boxed his way to Light Heavy Weight gold at the Summer Games in Antwerp. He then studied law at Yale and also at Oxford, but returned to the Olympic arena to make history as part of the US Four-man Bobsleigh team that won gold at the 1932 Winter Games at Lake Placid.

Out in front

The first recorded Olympic champion was a man called Coroebus. He lived close to Olympia in the province of Elis and won the stadion race over a distance of approximately 180 metres in 776 BC. A baker by profession, he received an olive branch for his trouble and could be described as the first celebrity chef.

Oath of respect

The Olympic Oath was taken first at the Antwerp 1920 Games by the Belgian fencer Victor Boin. A journalist and member of the organising committee, Boin had previously represented his country in Water Polo and Swimming. He grasped the Belgian national flag as he swore the Oath, promising to respect the rules. Since 1984 the Olympic Flag has been used in the Opening Ceremony instead of a national flag, and an anti-doping clause has been added. An Oath for judges was introduced in 1972.

↑ *Belgian fencer Victor Boin (centre) becomes the first athlete in history to swear the Olympic Oath, introduced for the first time at the 1920 Games.*

Women's breakthrough

Great Britain's Charlotte Cooper was the first woman to win an Olympic gold medal. She beat the local favourite Hélène Prévost to win the women's Tennis Singles at the Paris 1900 Olympic Games. She added a second gold with Reggie Doherty in the Mixed Doubles. Cooper won the women's singles title at Wimbledon on five occasions and lived to the grand old age of 96.

← *Five-time Wimbledon champion Charlotte Cooper added to her legend when she won the Tennis Singles title at the 1900 Games to become the first female gold-medal winner.*

Cultural competition

Competitions for artists were introduced for the first time at the Stockholm 1912 Olympic Games, making it possible to win a gold medal for painting, sculpture, music, literature and even architectural design. Olympic founding father Baron Pierre de Coubertin won a prize for his 'Ode to Sport'. He submitted his entry under the pseudonyms George Hohrod and M. Eschbach. The artistic contests were discontinued following the London 1948 Games, but art and music are now included in the Cultural Olympiad, which runs in conjunction with the Games.

Ice in summer

The first gold medals for Ice Skating were awarded at the London 1908 Olympic Games. Florence 'Madge' Syers won the women's competition and skated to a bronze in the Pairs with her husband Edgar. Sweden's Ulrich Salchow was the winner of the men's competition. Figure Skating was also held at the Antwerp 1920 Olympic Games, but from 1924 it was included in the Winter Olympic Games.

Teenager's vision

A letter by a Chinese Australian teenager called John Ian Wing prompted one of the enduring traditions of the Olympic Movement. He wrote to the organisers of the Melbourne 1956 Olympic Games with his idea for the Closing Ceremony: 'The march I have in mind is different from the Opening. War, politics and nationality will be forgotten if the world could be made as one nation. They must not march but walk freely and wave to the public.' Games organisers arranged the parade of athletes as he had suggested. Ever since, competitors have entered the arena at the Closing Ceremony without distinction of nationality, creed or colour. Wing did not attend any of the events in Melbourne and was identified only many years later. He was guest of honour at the Closing Ceremony at the Sydney 2000 Olympic Games.

All in the swim

The long-distance Swimming events held in Beijing were not the first Olympic events held in open water. In 1896 all racing was held in the bay of Piraeus and, in 1900, competition even took place in the River Seine. Swimming was not held in an indoor pool until the 1948 Games in London.

Benoit's Marathon

Joan Benoit of the United States became the first woman to win an Olympic gold medal for the Marathon. The event was not introduced until the 1984 Olympic Games in Los Angeles. Organisers had included an 800m race for women at the 1928 Games in Amsterdam, but this was considered unsuccessful. As a result, women did not compete at any distance over 200m until the 1964 Games in Tokyo.

↖ *Joan Benoit won the first women's Marathon to be held at the Games, in Los Angeles in 1984, in a time of 2:24:52 – more than a minute ahead of her closest rival.*

↑ *Nadia Comaneci's perfection earned not only top marks but also headlines around the world.*

Comaneci perfection

Nadia Comaneci was only 14 when she flew off the Parallel Bars to execute a perfect landing on the first day of competition in Gymnastics in 1976 in Montreal. The judges awarded her a perfect ten. Her routine during the Team Competition established her as the star of the Games. She received a further ten on Balance Beam and achieved the same score five times more en route to three individual gold medals.

Famous gold medal hauls

Thousands of athletes have achieved their dream of competing at the Olympic Games over the years, some of them have entered Games folklore by winning a gold medal and a select few (220) have achieved legendary status by striking gold on at least three occasions. The following can be considered to be among the greatest Olympians of all time.

⬆ *Emile Zatopek won men's 5000m, 10,000m and the Marathon gold at Helsinki 1952.*

⬆ *Larissa Latynina won nine gold medals at three Olympic Games.*

Ewry's standing start

In the early Games, jump events from a standing start were included on the roster and Ray Ewry was a master at it, winning the Standing High Jump, Standing Long Jump and Standing Triple Jump at the 1900 and 1904 Games and the Standing High Jump and Long Jump in 1908. His eight gold medals are a record for a field event athlete.

The unique Zatopek

Czechoslovak Emil Zatopek had already served notice of his ability as a long-distance runner by winning men's 10,000m gold in 1948 in London, but it was in Helsinki in 1952 that he carved his name in the history books. Zatopek retained his 10,000m title and completed the long-distance track double with victory over 5000m. Only three days later, he took part in his first Marathon and won it. In one single week he had raced four times over a total distance of some 62 kilometres. He remains the only athlete in history to win all three long-distance events at a single Olympic Games.

Lucky nine for Larissa

Over three Olympiads, from 1956 to 1964, Ukrainian-born Larissa Latynina dominated women's Gymnastics. A member of the all-conquering Soviet team, individually she won four golds in Melbourne in 1956, including the blue riband All-Around title which she retained four years later. Her ninth and final gold came with the USSR team in 1964. She also won a further five bronze and four silver medals, and her 18 Olympic medals remain a record. In her entire Olympic career she finished outside the medals in only one event.

Captain Canada

Canadian showjumper Ian Millar began his Olympic career in Munich in 1972 but had to wait until his ninth Olympic Games before he won a medal. Still going strong in 2008, aged 61, he was a member of the Canadian silver medal winners in the Team Jumping event held in Hong Kong.

History man Phelps

No man has enjoyed more success at the Olympic Games than Michael Phelps. He had already written his name in the annals of world swimming before he competed at Beijing in 2008. He eclipsed the feat of fellow American Mark Spitz with eight golds at a single Olympiad, all but one set in world record times and all set before lunch — making him the ultimate morning person. The magical eight was completed in the men's 4 x 100m Medley Relay. In Athens he had already stormed to victory in six events to bring his career tally to 14. He has also won two bronze medals.

⬉ *Michael Phelps collected gold medals at a record rate at Athens and Beijing. To date he has won 14 of them – no athlete has won more.*

Time after time

Fencer Aladar Gerevich won his first gold as a member of Hungary's Sabre team at Los Angeles 1932. Twenty-eight years later, aged 50, he was the senior member of the Hungary team that took gold in Rome. It was the sixth time he had stood on the medal rostrum as part of a team and he also won the Individual Sabre at London 1948. His wife and son were also Olympic medallists.

Pole Vault breakthrough

Pole-vaulter Wolfgang Nordwig from the German Democratic Republic soared to victory in 1972 in Munich. He beat world record-holder Bob Seagren of the United States and so ended the longest winning sequence in the Games. Nordwig was the first non-American to win medal since the event's introduction in 1896.

Twin triumph

Slovak canoeing twins Pavol and Peter Hochschorner formed an unbeatable partnership from their Olympic Games debut at Sydney 2000. They won three consecutive gold medals together in the Canoe Doubles Slalom, coached by their father Peter.

⬇ *It was a family affair for Pavol and Peter Hochschorner: the Slovak twins won three consecutive gold medals between 2000 and 2008.*

➡ *Lazlo Papp was Hungary's hat-trick hero.*

Hat-trick in the ring

Hungarian Lazlo Papp was the first boxer to win three consecutive gold medals at the Olympic Games. He beat home favourite John Wright to win the Middle Weight title at the London 1948 Games, then claimed further gold medals at Light Middle Weight in 1952 and 1956. Afterwards he was allowed to turn professional, a rarity in the communist era.

Redgrave's record

Sir Steve Redgrave's five gold medals in Olympic Rowing have given him legendary status. In 1984, he was a member of the Coxed Four that won Great Britain's first Rowing gold in 36 years. In 1988, he won gold in the Coxless Pairs partnered by Andy Holmes and then formed a powerful alliance with Matt Pinsent, eight years his junior. Together they won gold in the Coxed Pairs in 1992 and 1996. Both men were chosen for the Coxless Four in Sydney where, amid feverish speculation, Redgrave played his part to win a fifth consecutive gold at 38, a staggering feat in an endurance event. Redgrave was later knighted.

⬅ *Five gold medals at five consecutive Olympic Games between 1984 and 2000 brought Steve Redgrave both legendary status and a knighthood.*

Family fortunes

Italian brothers Piero and Raimondo D'Inzeo were the first men to compete together at eight consecutive Games. In 1948, older brother Piero competed in Showjumping and Raimondo in Eventing. They competed as team-mates in 1956, with Raimondo winning silver and Piero bronze plus a team silver. Raimondo went on to win Individual Jumping gold in 1960. The brothers' final appearance came at the 1976 Games. Between them they won 12 Olympic medals.

Four for Lewis

Carl Lewis emulated his countryman Jesse Owens by winning four gold medals at a single Games. At Los Angeles 1984, he took gold in the men's 100m, 200m, the 4 x 100m Relay and the Long Jump. Although his dominance in the sprints faded, his power in the Long Jump never waned and his victory at Atlanta 1996 gave him four consecutive titles, equalling the feat of discus thrower Al Oerter.

Opening Ceremonies

The ceremonial aspects of the Olympic Games set them apart from other international sports events, with the splendour of the Opening Ceremony helping to heighten the anticipation of the coming 16 days of sporting action.

Growth of the Games

When the first modern Olympic Games were staged in Athens in 1896, the Opening Ceremony featured competitors from 22 national Olympic committees. In London in 2012, it is expected that more than 200 nations will send competitors.

Parade of nations

The Olympic Charter demands that 'each delegation dressed in its official uniform must be preceded by a name-board bearing its name and must be accompanied by its flag'. The Charter's rules also determine the marching order for all Opening Ceremonies, with Greece, as the first home of the Games, given the honour of leading the parade. To bring a show to a suitable climax, the Charter stipulates that the country hosting the Games should always be the last to enter the stadium.

↑ *Queen Elizabeth II opens the 1976 Olympic Games.*

Speech-making

IOC rules not only expect there to be certain ceremonial speeches made at the Opening Ceremony; they even provide the precise wording that officials are supposed to use. This means that on the evening of 27 July 2012, in her Golden Jubilee year, Her Majesty Queen Elizabeth II will utter the words: 'I declare open the Games of London celebrating the 30th Olympiad of the modern era.' It will not be the first time that The Queen has made the speech at an Opening Ceremony. At Montreal, in 1976, Her Majesty declared the Games open and, mindful that she was in French-speaking Quebec, the first language that she used was French.

↑ *As is the custom, Greece – considered the mother nation of the Olympic Games – was handed the honour of leading the Parade of Nations at the Opening Ceremony at the 2008 Olympic Games in Beijing.*

The right flag

Olympic rules were re-written ahead of the Moscow 1980 Olympic Games to allow teams to march behind 'a' flag, rather than their national flag. The United States had called for a boycott of Moscow following the Soviet Union's invasion of Afghanistan – but the British Olympic Association defied its government's orders and let its athletes follow their own conscience about whether they should compete. As a result, the British team in Moscow marched behind the Olympic Flag, and the likes of Duncan Goodhew, Steve Ovett and Allan Wells never heard 'God Save the Queen' when they received their gold medals. Indeed, Seb Coe had to come back and win the men's 1500m for a second time in 1984 to have that experience.

Flag games

The Olympic Flag has been used at the Opening Ceremony in 1992 by the 'Unified Team' – comprising competitors from the states of the former Soviet Union – and by Timor-Leste in 2000. On other occasions, a special flag has been used by delegations, such as when the two Koreas marched together in Sydney in 2000 and again in Athens in 2004.

The Olympic Oath

The most solemn part of the ceremony is the Olympic Oath, introduced at the Antwerp 1920 Olympic Games. A similar oath was introduced for officials at the Munich 1972 Games. The Olympic Oath now reads: 'In the name of all competitors I promise that we shall take part in these Olympic Games, respecting and abiding by the rules which govern them, committing ourselves to a sport without doping and without drugs, in the true spirit of sportsmanship, for the glory of sport and the honour of our teams.'

Peace for pigeons...

The flame-lighting was formerly preceded by the release of a flock of doves or pigeons to signify peace. Since 1988, though, the bird release has taken place after the lighting of the Flame. This was decided, according to the IOC, 'following the unfortunate demise of several pigeons sitting on the edge of the Olympic cauldron'.

Big-budget productions

When Baron Pierre de Coubertin revived the Olympic Games at the end of the 19th century, he believed that such ceremonies would be an essential element for creating the correct atmosphere at the Games, with a strong acknowledgement towards the Games' roots in ancient Greece. However, writing nearly 30 years ago, Lord Killanin, another former president of the International Olympic Committee, expressed his concern at the tendency for Opening Ceremonies to feature ever more extravagant, big-budget productions: 'An unfortunate tradition has arisen for using the Opening Ceremony as a means of displaying national pride,' the Irishman wrote, 'with teams vying with each other for the most outstanding uniforms, especially now that women athletes are so prominent.' Killanin was writing after the Moscow 1980 Games but clearly could not have foreseen the Hollywood-style production, even including a man entering the Coliseum in Los Angeles using a James Bond jet-pack, staged at the Opening Ceremony for the 1984 Games ... to say nothing of the 1,000 perfectly synchronised drummers in Beijing.

↑ *Australian athlete Cathy Freeman finds herself centre stage as she lights the Olympic Flame at the climax of the Opening Ceremony at the 2000 Olympic Games in Sydney.*

Flaming climax

The ceremonial all leads to the biggest set-piece of the Opening Ceremony, the lighting of the Olympic Flame, which burns brightly over the stadium, and the Host City, signifying a two-week truce. The lighting of the Flame has seen some spectacular moments at recent Games: Muhammad Ali, winner of a Boxing gold medal in 1960, performed the task at Atlanta 1996; Cathy Freeman, seemingly standing in a shower of fire, was handed the honour of lighting the Flame at Sydney 2000; and, most spectacular of all, Spanish archer Antonio Rebollo sending his flaming arrow arcing into the Barcelona night sky in 1992.

← *A gold-medal winner at Rome 1960, Mohammad Ali was a hugely popular choice to light the Olympic Flame at the 1996 Olympic Games in Atlanta.*

Record breaks

It is unlikely that any future Olympic organisers will have the resources used for the Opening Ceremony at Beijing 2008, which is reported to have cost more than £70 million and featured 22,000 performers, 43,000 fireworks and a 16-tonne globe rising from the ground.

Closing Ceremonies

Steeped in protocol, the Closing Ceremony has become an both an integral, memorable and spectacular part of the Olympic Games. It climaxes with extinguishing the Olympic Flame, singing the Olympic Hymn and, finally, to the sound of a farewell song, the symbolic lowering of the Olympic Flag before it is carried out of the arena.

Eight for luck

At the 2008 Olympic Games in Beijing, London's Boris Johnson, in common with the receiving mayors of previous Host Cities all the way back to the Antwerp Games in 1920, waved the newly received Olympic Flag from side to side eight times, as required by tradition. Once the Olympic Flag was symbolically in London's hands, a short performance was staged within the vast Bird's Nest Stadium to offer the 100,000 spectators, and the world watching on TV, a taster of what London will have to offer. The show featured a bold red double-decker bus as the stage for a spectacular display by scores of dancers, many carrying umbrellas, plus Jimmy Page, from the rock group Led Zeppelin, playing guitar to accompany singer Leona Lewis, together with various sound clips from BBC radio and the folk tune 'Greensleeves', all rounded off by David Beckham kicking a football.

Closing rules

Many of the elements of the Closing Ceremonies are governed more by tradition than by International Olympic Committee rules. Usually flag bearers from each participating country enter the stadium in single file, and behind them march all of the athletes who have competed in the Games, not in strict team order – as the protocol of the Opening Ceremony demands – but mixed together informally. Certain key sports always used to be staged on the final day of the Games: the Individual Showjumping Grand Prix was often the centrepiece of the final day's action, the event sometimes event being staged in the main stadium. The final Athletics event to be run, with exhausted runners drifting into the stadium before the Closing Ceremony began, would be the men's Marathon. Perhaps because of the Marathon's close connections with the Olympics' Greek roots, the medal ceremony for the race is usually integrated into the Closing Ceremony.

Flag days

Flags play a massively significant part in the formalities of the Closing Ceremonies. One key part is the symbolic transfer, from the host city to the next hosts, of the Olympic Flag. For nearly 70 years, the flag used was the 'Antwerp Flag', so called because it had been presented to the IOC by the Belgian hosts at the 1920 Summer Games, where this part of the ceremony was introduced. This flag was used until the 1988 Games in Seoul, when the Korean organisers gave the IOC a near-identical replacement, known at the 'Seoul Flag'. The Winter Olympics have a similar ceremony at the end of the Games, where the 'Oslo Flag', presented to the IOC at the 1952 Winter Games, is used.

⬇ *The essential flags at the 2008 Games Closing Ceremony: Greece, the Olympic Flag, China (the host nation) and Great Britain (the next hosts).*

Handover Ceremony

The formality of handing over 'possession' of the Games from one Host City to the next was incorporated into the Closing Ceremony at the Montreal 1976 Games. A formal protocol governs the procedure, with the mayor of the Host City joining the President of the IOC on the rostrum and returning to him the Olympic Flag. The IOC President then places it in the hands and the trust of the mayor of the next Host City.

→ *London Mayor Boris Johnson waves the Olympic Flag at the Closing Ceremony at Beijing 2008.*

Ceremonial and oaths

Once all the athletes have entered the stadium, three national flags are hoisted on flagpoles, while the corresponding national anthems are played: the flag of Greece on the middle pole to honour the birthplace of the Olympic Games, the flag of the host country on the left-hand pole, and the flag of the country hosting the next Games on the right-hand pole. In 2012, this third flag will be that of Brazil, as Rio de Janeiro will host the 2016 Olympics.

Appointments and accolades at the Closing Ceremony

The Closing Ceremony is now used by the International Olympic Committee (IOC) to conclude some of the business it has conducted outside the sporting arenas. During the Games, all competitors are invited to elect new members of the IOC Athletes' Commission, the body that represents the competitors' views, and which comprises active or recently retired Olympians. On behalf of the athletes, one of these new members then presents a bouquet of flowers to a Games volunteer as a mark of tribute and gratitude for their work during the duration of the event.

Medal surge

At the early stagings of the modern Games at the beginning of the 20th century, all the medal presentations were staged at the Closing Ceremony. However, if this were to be done in London in 2012, with gold, silver and bronze medals to be handed out in more than 250 events across 26 sports, the medal presentations alone could last more than 12 hours.

The dying flame

After all the speeches, the time has finally come to end the Games, and as the IOC itself says, 'The last protocol element is undoubtedly the most moving.' The Olympic Flame, which will have been burning above the city for the previous 17 days, will slowly be extinguished while the Olympic Hymn plays and the Olympic Flag is lowered from its flagpole and carried from the stadium.

Last words

The flag-raising at the Closing Ceremony is followed by an address from the chairman of the host organising committee. In London, the IOC President will then formally close the Olympics by saying: 'I declare the Games of the 30th Olympiad closed and, in accordance with tradition, I call upon the youth of the world to assemble four years from now in Rio de Janeiro to celebrate the Games of the 31st Olympiad.'

← *International Olympic Committee President Jacques Rogge delivers his final address at the Closing Ceremony of the 2008 Olympic Games.*

Olympic Torch Relays

The modern Olympics maintain a link with the Games of Ancient Greece through the ceremonial Olympic Torch Relay, carrying the sacred flame from Olympia, the original site of the Games, to the Host City. There, the lighting of the cauldron, usually positioned high above the main stadium, signifies the precise moment when the Games truly begin.

Flame tradition

The ceremonial surrounding the Torch Relay is strictly controlled by the IOC and the Olympic Charter. Rule 55 of the Charter includes the statement: 'Like the messengers who proclaimed the sacred Olympic truce, the runners who carry the Olympic Flame carry a message of peace on their journey.'

⬆ *Greek actress Maria Nafpliotou (right) assumes the role of high priestess during the lighting ceremony at Ancient Olympia for the 2008 Games in Beijing.*

IOC fire

The International Olympic Committee says: 'In the context of the modern Games, the Olympic Flame represents the positive values that man has always associated with fire. The purity of the flame is guaranteed by the way it is lit using the sun's rays. The choice of Olympia as a starting point emphasises the link between the Ancient and Modern Games and underlines the profound connection between these two events.'

The ancient relay

When the Games were staged in Rome, Italy, in 1960, the Torch Relay was used to shine a spotlight on the two poles of classical civilisation: Athens and Rome. Lesser-known ancient sites in Greece and Italy were brought to the public's attention. For the first time, the relay was televised and the event was closely followed by the media.

The divine Flame

The Ancient Greeks considered fire a divine element and they maintained perpetual fires in front of their temples, including the one at Olympia, where they would stage sporting Games during a period of truce. Before each modern Games, the Flame is lit in a solemn ceremony at Olympia by 11 women representing vestal virgins. The Flame was originally lit using the rays of the sun, to ensure its purity, and a skaphia, the ancestor of the parabolic mirror used today for lighting the Olympic Flame.

The relay to the new world

In 1968, when Mexico City hosted the Games, the Torch Relay's journey retraced the steps of Christopher Columbus to the New World. The last runner on Spanish soil was Cristóbal Colón de Carbajal, a direct descendant of the great navigator. The Olympic Flame made a stop at the Great Pyramid of the Moon in Teotihuacan, where a 'New Fire' ceremony was held. In the Aztec tradition, this marked the end of a 52-year cycle, and the reappearance of the sun at dawn symbolised the renewal of the world.

Relight the fire

The fire ceremony was reintroduced at the modern Games for the first time in Amsterdam in 1928. The Torch Relay was first staged at the suggestion of Carl Diem, the head of the local organising committee for the 1936 Games staged in Berlin. Inspired by torch races that were held in Ancient Greek times, Diem suggested that a flame be lit in Olympia and transported to Berlin for what would be the first Olympic Torch Relay.

➔ *The final leg of a relay involving more than 3,000 runners comes to a close as the last Olympic Torch-bearer reaches Lustgarten in Berlin prior to the 1936 Games.*

The relay of peace

The 1948 Games saw a war-ravaged London take on the first Games for 12 years with a sense of peace and reconciliation, and a strong symbol of this was the Torch Relay. More than 1,400 Torchbearers were used, all on foot, carrying the Flame 3,365 kilometres from Olympia to London's Wembley Stadium, via Italy, Switzerland, France, Luxembourg and Belgium. In homage to the restorer of the Games, the relay passed through Lausanne, in Switzerland, and a ceremony was organised at Pierre de Coubertin's tomb in Bois-de-Vaux.

⬆ *British athlete John Mark lights the Olympic Flame at Wembley Stadium in 1948.*

Relay's hard slog

The last time the Torch Relay was conducted entirely on foot, without any flights or sea crossings, was for the 1980 Games in Moscow. Originally, the Torch Relay runners were mainly selected from local athletics clubs, but gradually celebrities and the general public have begun to participate. Each Games now designs its own, distinctive version of the Torch, and Torch-bearers can opt to buy the Torch after they have carried the Flame their set distance and transferred it to the next relay runner.

London's new relay

The 2012 Torch Relay will start on 18 May and last more than two months, reaching the stadium in East London's Olympic Park on 27 July some time after 12 minutes past eight in the evening – or 20:12, in the 24-hour clock. Around 3,000 runners will share in carrying the Torch 300 metres in the relay. The 2012 Torch Relay will tour the United Kingdom, visiting national heritage sites, venues with sporting significance, cultural festivals and many schools. The concept of an international relay was abandoned after problems during the 2008 run.

Novel conveyance

Traditionally, the Torch Relay was conducted entirely on foot. More recent Games have seen the Torch Relay use the pony express through the United States and a camel caravan across the Australian outback. As well as travelling by boat, some Torch Relays have even taken the Flame underwater. It has travelled faster than the speed of sound on Concorde, and the Torch has even been taken in to space by astronauts – twice. Before the 2008 Games in Beijing, the Torch Relay visited the summit of Mount Everest, the world's highest mountain.

Highlighting the Flame

The Torch Relay ends at the Opening Ceremony. The identity of the final carrier of the Torch is usually a closely guarded secret, revealed only as the Torch is passed to them. Over the years, it has become a tradition to let a famous athlete be the last runner in the Torch Relay. Paavo Nurmi, a hero of Finland with nine gold medals at the Games from the 1920s and 1930s, was an easy choice to light the cauldron at the Helsinki 1952 Games. On other occasions, the Olympic Flame has been lit by people who are not famous, but who symbolise the Games' ideals. At Tokyo 1964, the Games' organisers gave the Flame-lighting honour to runner Yoshinori Sakai, who had been born in Hiroshima on 6 August 1945, the day the atomic bomb exploded.

⬆ *Former Chinese gymnast Li Ning was handed the honour of lighting the Olympic Flame at the 2008 Games in Beijing.*

Games mascots

They may now be an integral part of the build-up to an Olympic Games and an ever-present feature during the event itself, but Games mascots are a relatively new phenomenon, with the first – a German dachshund called Waldi – appearing as recently as 1972. Here is a collection of the most memorable mascots to have appeared over the years.

Waldi the dachshund left his mark at the 1972 Games.

Wenlock and Mandeville

The London 2012 mascots, Wenlock and Mandeville, reflect the multi-media age of the 21st century, because they are much more than simple designs for a few cuddly toys: Wenlock and Mandeville have featured in a series of animated films and use social media, with both on Twitter and running their own Facebook pages. The names come from Much Wenlock, considered by many as the true birthplace of the modern Games, and Stoke Mandeville, home of the famous spinal injuries unit where the Paralympic movement began in 1948 – with the staging of the Stoke Mandeville Games.

First mascot

The Summer Olympic Games' first mascot – at Munich 1972 – was a cuddly, multi-coloured German dachshund named Waldi. His image appeared on posters, stickers, key-rings and mugs – all in the colours of the Olympic Rings. Four years earlier the 1968 Winter Games in Grenoble had presented a stylised skiing figure, known as Schuss. Although this was sometimes described as the first Games mascot, it was not produced by the French organisers and was therefore not officially recognised.

Wenlock and Mandeville will become two of the best-known faces not only in London but also around the world in 2012.

The reasoning

As with any major modern sporting event, Olympic Games mascots are now an integral part of the overall business plan. A key part of any Games budget is revenue from merchandise sales. London's organisers have targeted £1bn from Olympic and Paralympic Games retail sales, with significant sums expected to come directly from sales of Wenlock and Mandeville branded T-shirts, key-rings and other items.

Mascots with mini-movies

The mini-movies of Wenlock and Mandeville's life stories, which are downloadable from YouTube, are based on scripts created by the children's laureate, Michael Morpurgo. The author came up with the concept of the mascots being fashioned from two drops of molten steel spilt in the making of the last steel girder used in the Olympic Stadium. Foundry worker George picks up the drops of steel and fashions them into figures, which he then gives to his grandchildren. Magically brought to life by a rainbow, they turn somersaults for the children before flying off on the rainbow to journey round Great Britain and on towards the Games.

Memorable Misha

The Games have also produced some memorable 'characters': Misha, the bear adopted by the 1980 Moscow Games, showed the Russians to be engaged with the modernisation of the Games, and four years later Sam, the Los Angeles eagle, was very Disney-like in its styling and demeanour. A statue of Misha still stands inside the entrance to the Luzhniki sports complex in Moscow, which is dominated by the Olympic Stadium.

Missing the point

The least successful mascots of all time are generally thought to be Izzy, the cartoon character produced for the 1996 Centenary Games in Atlanta – the first Games mascot to be designed by computer – and the beaver Amik from Montreal 1976, who also did little to engage public sympathies.

➜ *Atlanta's luckless Izzy tried his best in 1996 … but will be remembered as one of the least successful Games mascots.*

↑ *Sydney went for a three-in-one mascot concept in 2000 with (from left to right) Ollie, Millie and Syd.*

Multiple mascots

The trend for multiple mascots, representing different aspects of the Olympic Games and Paralympic Games, was started in 2000, with Sydney's cartoon characters Syd, Millie and Olly – based on native Australian animals.

Who's who?

Munich 1972:	Waldi – a dachshund
Montreal 1976:	Amik – a beaver, its name coming from the American Indian Algonquian language
Moscow 1980:	Misha – a bear created by children's books illustrator Victor Chizikov
Los Angeles 1984:	Sam the Eagle – designed by Walt Disney
Seoul 1988:	Hodori – a friendly little tiger
Barcelona 1992:	Cobi – a dog
Atlanta 1996:	Izzy – a computer-generated fantasy figure
Sydney 2000:	Syd, Olly and Millie – based on a kookaburra, a platypus and an echidna, all native to Australia
Athens 2004:	Athena and Phevos – based on ancient dolls found at archeological sites in Greece. Athena was the goddess of wisdom and patron of the city of Athens, while Phevos was the god of light and music
Beijing 2008:	Beibei (blue fish), Jingjing (black panda), Huanhuan (red flame), Yingying (yellow antelope) and Nini (green swallow) – these five names together translated as 'Welcome to Beijing'
London 2010:	Wenlock and Mandeville – riveting robots

⬇ *Beijing's mascots were colourful characters that, assembled in the right order, spelled out a welcoming message.*

Chapter Two
Aquatics

The Aquatics programme at the Olympic Games consists of Swimming, Diving, Synchronised Swimming and Water Polo. Swimming has been a fundamental part since the first Games in 1896, when there were four men-only events, all of them Freestyle, held in the sea near Piraeus.

Swimming was first contested in a pool in 1908, and not until 1924 was the pool 50 metres in length, the official Olympic distance today. By 2008 there were 34 Swimming events, split evenly between the genders, 13 individual, three relays and one in open water.

The first Swimming champion was a Hungarian, Alfred Hajos, who won the 100m Freestyle. Swimmers have since become some of the most famous among Olympians, most notably the Americans, Michael Phelps, with his record 14 gold medals, and Mark Spitz, who won seven in 1972.

Events for women were first held in 1912, and again the first champion was in the 100m Freestyle, Australian Fanny Durack. Water Polo was added to the Olympic programme for men in 1900, but only after another century for women. Diving was added in 1904 for men and for women in 1912, and the latest aquatic addition, for women only, was Synchronised Swimming in 1984.

Russia's team make a sensational splash in perfect unison during the final of the free routine Synchronised Swimming event during the 2008 Olympic Games in Beijing.

Men's Diving

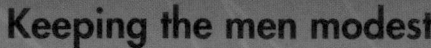

The first men's Diving event took place at the 1904 Olympic Games in St Louis, in which athletes contested Platform Diving and a plunge-for-distance event (in which competitors aimed to reach the furthest distance from a standing dive). Today, men compete in 10m Platform and 3m Springboard events – both in individual and, since 2000, synchronised competitions.

Keeping the men modest

It was not only the women divers who were made to cover up when competing. Regulations in 1920 decreed that men must wear 'cloth drawers' at least 6 centimetres wide at the hip. Their regulations covered the whole trunk and the legs down to the thighs with a hole only 7.5cm from the armpit for the arms.

↗ Sweden's Erik Adlerz, a Platform Diving silver medallist at the 1920 Games, models the discreet swimwear of the era.

The first perfect ten

The first perfect score of ten was awarded to the only man ever to win the 10m Platform at three straight Olympic Games, the Italian Klaus Dibiasi, and it was awarded for the last dive of a career spanning four Olympic Games. It won him the gold in 1976 by a margin of 23 points and made him the first man ever to score a total of more than 600 in a 10m Platform competition at the Olympic Games.

← Klaus Dibiasi from Italy set an unbeatable standard over four Olympic Games Diving events between Tokyo 1964 and Montreal 1976.

Degrees of difficulty

Typical tariffs for dives at the Games

3m Springboard / 10m Platform

Forward dive:	1.6 / 1.6
Forward somersault:	1.7 / 1.8
Forward 1½ somersault:	1.9 / 1.9
Forward 2½ somersault:	2.8 / 2.7
Forward 3½ somersault, pike:	3.1 / 3.0
Forward 4½ somersault, pike:	4.2 / 4.1
Back 2½ somersault:	- / 3.3
Back 4½ somersault, pike:	4.6 / 4.5
Reverse dive ½ twisty:	- / 2.1
Reverse 4½ somersault, pike:	- / 4.7

The marks out of 10 of the middle five of seven scoring judges are multiplied by the degree of difficulty laid down by FINA and divided by 0.6 (or, more simply, multiplied by five and divided by 3).

Courage worth gold for Louganis

Greg Louganis became the first man to win 3m Springboard and 10m Platform gold medals at two Olympic Games in Seoul in 1988. His victory was not without drama and extreme courage on his part. In a preliminary dive in the Springboard, a reverse 2½ somersault in the pike position, he hit his head on the board and landed clumsily. He was slightly concussed and needed four temporary sutures in the wound, but 35 minutes later he dived again.

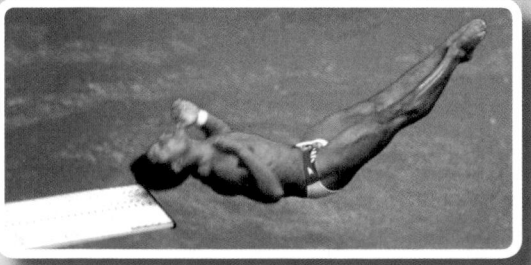

⬆ The moment when Greg Louganis hit the springboard at the 1988 Olympic Games in Seoul.

Back to square one...

The first diving championship was organised in Scotland in 1889, featuring a dive from the side and another from a height of 1.8 metres. The first national championship was held in 1895 at Highgate Ponds, in north London, where the country's first permanent diving stage (4.6m high) had been erected in 1893. Another 10m board was built, but was taken down after each staging of the competition, which ended in 1920.

Chinese fireworks

China's Hu Jia entered the 10m Platform Final at Sydney 2000 in the lead and kept it with a brilliantly executed back 3½ somersault which was awarded a maximum ten by all but one judge. However, with a very difficult back 3½ somersault pike, his compatriot Tian Liang scored 101.52 points, then the highest scoring dive in the Games' history. Both men finished with more than 700 points, a record, Tian winning by 11 points with his total of 724.53.

← China's Sun Shuwei was a teenage sensation who struck gold at the 1982 Games in Barcelona aged 16.

Pinkston sets a trend

Clarence 'Bud' Pinkston's gold medal in 10m Platform in 1920 began a run of seven successive victories for the United States that came to an end in 1956, when Mexican Joaquin Capilla Perez took gold. Americans won again in 1960 and 1964, which meant that they had won nine of the ten gold medals in a span of 44 years.

Fading meteor

Sun Shuwei, from Guangdong province in China, had a meteoric rise. He won the 10m platform at the Asian Games aged 14 in 1990, became world champion in 1991, and in 1992 set a world record for the most points earned on a single dive when he was awarded perfect tens on a reverse 3½ somersault tuck for a total of 102 points. The same year, aged 16, he took gold at Barcelona with some ease. That was his peak – he was never to compete at another Games. He missed selection in 1996 and was injured in 2000.

How the judges see it

Officials judge a dive on four phases – approach, take-off, technique and grace in the air and water entry. Each is scoring on a maximum of ten, the perfect score. The top- and bottom-marking judges' scores are tossed out and the remaining five determine the outcome. A spectator can guage how a diver has done by seeing how good the dive looks in the air and by how little it disturbs the water on entry.

Lee the master

Sammy Lee, an American of Korean parentage, was a doctor of medicine and a major in the US Army. He was also among the greatest authorities on diving technique in the sport's history. Lee was the first man to defend the 3m Springboard title at the Games successfully, winning in 1948 and 1952. Robert Webster, the second man to achieve the distinction, was coached by Lee. The third American man to do the double, Greg Louganis, was also coached by Lee.

→ Sammy Lee, a champion in his own right and, later, a champion coach.

The last ten champions

3m Springboard / 10m Platform
1972 Vladimir Vasin (Russia) / Klaus Diabasi (Italy)
1976 Philip Boggs (USA) / Klaus Diabasi (Italy)
1980 Aleksandr Portnov (Belarus) / Falk Hoffmann (GDR)
1984 Greg Louganis (USA) / Greg Louganis (USA)
1988 Greg Louganis (USA) / Greg Louganis (USA)
1992 Mark Lenzi (USA) / Sun Shuwei (China)
1996 Xiong Ni (China) / Dmitri Sautin (Russia)
2000 Xiong Ni (China) / Tian Liang (China)
2004 Peng Bo (China) / Hu Jia (China)
2008 He Chong (China) / Matthew Mitcham (Australia)

Women's Diving

Women's Diving has been part of the Olympic Games programme since Antwerp 1920. As is the case with the men, they compete in 10m Platform and 3m Springboard events, both as individuals and, since Sydney 2000, in synchronised events. Recent competitions have been dominated by Chinese divers.

Too young to dive?

Fu Mingxia was 11 when she won the 1990 Goodwill Games and only 12½ when she won the world title in 10m Platform in 1991. Shocked, FINA, the world body for diving, decreed a minimum age for Olympic competition of 14 years in the Olympic year. Although Fu qualified for the 1992 Games only narrowly, having turned 14 just 20 days before her 10m Platform Final, she won the gold medal by the most decisive margin in 60 years – and won again in 1996.

Like mother like daughter

Patricia McCormick was the first diver, man or woman, to win 3m Springboard and 10m Platform gold medals at two Olympic Games, in 1952 and 1956. Eighteen years later, at the Olympic Games in her home city of Los Angeles, her daughter Kelly missed out on gold in the 3m Springboard by just 3.24 points. Four years later she was to win another medal for the McCormick family, a 3m Springboard bronze.

Young and old

Aileen Riggin, of Newport, Rhode Island, won the first 3m Springboard gold medal, at Antwerp 1920. She was 14 years old and just 1.40 metres tall, the smallest competitor in the entire Games that year. She was diving into an outdoor moat of cold water and there were no hot showers for competitors, as there are today. It obviously did her no harm, because 82 years after her victory (aged 96) she won six age group titles at the World Masters Championships.

American hand-over

The United States dominated women's Diving from 1920 to 1956, but since China's return to the Olympic Games in 1984 in Los Angeles their women have reigned supreme. Zhou Jihong's gold medal in 10m Platform was China's only gold in that comeback Games, but Chinese women have since won the last six 3m Springboard titles, the only three synchronised golds contested and five of the last seven 10m Platform events. Their women won all four gold medals contested when the country hosted the 2008 Games in Beijing.

↖ *Double gold-medal winner Pat McCormick in action at Helsinki 1952.*

Doubling up

Synchronised Diving for pairs was introduced at Sydney 2000, effectively doubling the number of events. Nine judges, instead of seven, officiate, five looking for synchronisation and four for execution, two for each diver. The highest and lowest scores for both phases are discarded, the remainder added and then multiplied by the degree of difficulty. There are no preliminaries or semi-finals. Only eight pairs can qualify for the Olympic Games from major events in the previous year.

↗ *China's Chen Ruolin (front) and Wang Xin (back) put in a collection of gold medal-winning dives at the 2008 Games in Beijing.*

In the beginning...

Modern divers enter a depth of around 5 metres of water so perfectly filtrated that they can see the bottom, but swimming pools in the 19th century were too shallow to allow diving. Most diving was therefore done outdoors into deeper pools, often muddy and always cold. The first Diving competition for women at the Games, in 1920, was into a dark moat. 'I had a mental block,' said the winner, Aileen Riggin. 'It was about sticking in the mud at the bottom. I kept thinking, "The water is black and nobody would find me if I really got stuck down there."'

↑ *It was lucky 13 for American diver Marjorie Gestring in Berlin in 1936.*

The diving baby

Californian Marjorie Gestring is the youngest person in history to have won an individual gold medal in any sport. She was only 13 years 268 days old when she won the 3m Springboard in 1936, too young to compete under modern rules. Younger still was Dorothy Poynton, another American, when she won the 3m Springboard silver medal at 13 years 23 days in 1928. She went on to compete in three Games, winning the 10m Platform in 1932 and 1936.

Keeping it in the family

Elizabeth Becker and Clarence 'Bud' Pinkston are the most successful Diving couple in Olympic history. He won gold in the 10m Platform and silver in the 3m Springboard in 1920 and a bronze in 1924. At the latter Games, in Paris, he met Elizabeth Becker, another member of the US Diving team, who won gold in the 3m Springboard and silver in the 10m Platform. They married, had twins, and on their second birthday in 1928 she was back in Europe to win 10m Platform gold and 3m Springboard bronze in Amsterdam, making a family grand total of seven medals (two gold, two silver and three bronze).

Lucky break

Three-and-a-half months before the United States Olympic trials in 2000, Laura Wilkinson broke three bones in her right foot in training. The foot was in a cast for ten weeks, but a month after its removal she won selection for the US team. Incredibly, in Sydney six months after the accident, she won the gold medal in 10m Platform after entering the final round in fifth place and going on to beat Chinese diver Li Na by the slenderest of margins – 1.74 points.

No head for heights

Mary Ellen Clark won bronze at Barcelona 1992, diving from the 10-metre board, an exercise which means a body hits the water at 30mph. A year before the 1996 Games, however, she began to feel dizzy every time she dived, even from the 1m board. She was diagnosed with benign paroxysmal position vertigo and for nine months could not dive. After treatment including head swinging, neck collars and acupuncture, she returned to win bronze in 1996, aged 33, to become Diving's oldest medallist.

↑ *Mary Ellen Clark completed an amazing comeback from vertigo at Atlanta 1996 when she won bronze.*

The last ten champions

3m Springboard / 10m Platform
1972 Maxine King (USA) / Ulrika Knape (Sweden)
1976 Jennifer Chandler (US) / Elena Vaitsekovskaia (Russia)
1980 Irina Kalinina (Russia) / Martina Jaschke (GDR)
1984 Sylvie Bernier (Canada) / Zhou Jihong (China)
1988 Gao Min (China) / Xu Yanmei (China)
1992 Gao Min (China) / Fu Mingxia (China)
1996 Fu Mingxia (China) / Fu Mingxia (China
2000 Fu Mingxia (China) / Laura Wilkinson (USA)
2004 Guo Jingjing (China) / Chantelle Michell-Newbery (Australia)
2008 Guo Jingjing (China) / Chen Ruolin (China)

Men's Swimming

Swimming was one of the ten sports contested at the inaugural Olympic Games in 1896, with athletes competing in four events: the 50m Freestyle, 100m Freestyle, 500m Freestyle and, surprisingly, the 100m Freestyle for sailors. A part of the programme at every Games since, by 2008 the number of events for men had grown to 17.

The dead heat

Australian John Devitt was so certain he had lost the 100m Freestyle final in 1960 that he congratulated 'winner' Lance Larson and left the pool. But then confusion reigned. The two men's times were identical at 55.2 seconds – an Olympic record. Two first-place judges thought Devitt had won, but two second-place judges thought Devitt second, so of six judges three voted for Devitt, three for Larson. A head judge with a casting vote decided it for Devitt.

Ultimate victor

American teenager Michael Phelps had every chance of equalling Mark Spitz's record of seven gold medals when he went to Athens for the 2004 Games. But he gave up his place on the United States 4 x 100m Medley Relay team to Ian Crocker after beating him in the 100m Butterfly by just 0.04sec, so settled for six golds. In 2008 in Beijing, Phelps went one better by breaking Spitz's single Games record with eight gold medals, giving him 14 in all.

Not like father...

Swimming's first champion was Alred Hajos, a Hungarian who had become a good swimmer after his father drowned in the River Danube when Alred was 13. The competition in 1896 was held in the sea near Piraeus, with the water temperature only 13° Celsius, an incentive for quick swimming. He later also won the 1,200m Freestyle when rough conditions caused 3.5-metre waves. Some 28 years later he won a prize as an architect in the Olympic Art Contest.

↖ *Hungarian Alred Hajos was a double Olympic Games gold-medal winner: in Swimming at Athens 1896 and in Art at Paris 1924.*

Hollywood days

The Olympic swimming pool seemed to lead directly to Hollywood stardom between the two World Wars. First to take his swimming fame to the silver screen was Duke Kahanamoku, who made several silent moves, but more famous was Johnny Weissmuller, a winner of five gold medals in the 1920s who became the most popular of all Tarzans. Eleanor Holm, the 1932 Backstroke champion, later became Jane to another Tarzan, Olympic Decathlon champion Glenn Moore, while Buster Crabbe, the 1932 400m Freestyle champion, became Flash Gordon on screen.

↑ *Five-time Olympic Games gold medallist Johnny Weissmuller earned even greater fame as Tarzan in Hollywood's own golden era appearing in 36 films.*

➔ *The mighty wingspan of Germany's Michael Gross earned him not only his 'Albatross' nickname but also three Olympic Games gold medals and three world records.*

Gross the albatross

There was only one feature of the West German swimmer Michael Gross that was greater than his immense height of 2.01m (6ft 7in) – his arm-span. From fingertip to fingertip he measured 2.25 metres. He was nicknamed the 'Albatross', and he used his immense reach to win three gold medals in 1984 and 1988 and set three world records.

Magnificent seven

American Mark Spitz was anticipating a hat-full of gold medals in 1968, having won five at the previous year's Pan-American Games. He won just two, both from relays, and in his final race, the 200m Butterfly in which he held the world record, he finished last. Four years later, it was his first event and he won it in world record time. He went on to win seven gold medals, the first athlete in Olympic Games history to do so.

⬇ *Mark Spitz was the star of the show at Munich 1972, becoming the first Olympian in history to land a haul of seven gold medals at one Games.*

⬆ *There was a golden lining to a school accident for Britain's Duncan Goodhew when he won 100m Breaststroke gold at the 1980 Olympic Games in Moscow.*

Goodhew proves his point

Swimmers invariably wore tight-fitted rubber caps to reduce water drag from their hair. Some even shaved their heads. Duncan Goodhew, a dyslexic Briton, did not need anything artificial. He lost his hair permanently from the trauma of falling from a tree at his Sussex school when he was ten, thereafter suffering years of adolescent abuse. His determination to overcome his problems was channelled into swimming and he won 100m Breaststroke gold at the 1980 Games.

Golden reward for iceman ross

Richard Ross should not have taken part in the 400m Individual Medley at the Tokyo 1964 Olympic Games. Japanese doctors advised an immediate operation when he was stricken with severe appendicitis three days before his competition. The world record holder would not hear of it, nor would he accept their offer of pain-killing drugs. Instead his lower torso was packed in ice until the day of the race, when he emerged to win gold in a world record time.

➡ *Russia's Aleksandr Popov celebrates after winning gold in the 100m Freestyle at Barcelona 1992. He went on to win the 50m Freestyle as well to add to his gold-medal tally.*

Popov the marathon man

Aleksandr Popov, a 6ft 6in Russian, was a converted backstroke swimmer who remained at the top of the rankings at 100m Freestyle for a dozen years. His first great victory was at the 1991 European Championships, but it was at Barcelona 1992 that he drew gasps. His final 50 metres was the first sub-25-second length ever recorded. He won again in 1996, by which time he held the world record at 48.21, was second at Sydney 2000, and only missed out on the Athens 2004 final by a single place.

Apologetic champion

Rick Carey, a New Yorker, was so disgusted with the time that won him the 200m Backstroke gold medal in 1984 that he hung his head at the Victory Ceremony and expressed only anger. He had wanted to break his own world record. So vociferous was the criticism that greeted his attitude in the American press that Carey issued a formal public apology. 'I found it very difficult to smile when my performance didn't live up to my expectations,' he wrote.

Golden second chance

Duke Kahanamoku, a Hawaiian of royal ancestry, won the first two rounds of the 100m Freestyle at the 1912 Games in Stockholm comfortably but, like his two American team-mates, he believed himself through to the final. All three missed the semi-final round but were invited to swim off between them for two remaining final spots. Kahanamoku broke the world record to take one of them, and went on to win the final by two yards.

First black champion

Competitors of African origin were a rarity at one time in pools at the Olympic Games until, at Seoul 1988, Trinidad-born Anthony Nesty proved there was no reason for it. He won the 100m Butterfly, becoming the first person from the tiny South American country of Surinam, in which there was only one 50-metre pool, to win a medal at the Olympic Games in any sport.

⬆ *A moment of Olympic Games history as Surinam's Anthony Nesty becomes the first African-American athlete to win a Swimming gold medal.*

Breaststroke loopholes

The most complex of strokes has had many techniques over the last 100 years, with the rules being inexorably tightened. Many loopholes were exploited in earlier days. In the 1930s, American swimmers began bringing their arms back above the surface, until in 1952 this was recognised as a new, different stroke, butterfly. And then in the 1950s the Japanese began swimming under-water because it was faster, but this was banned in 1956.

Unbroken record

No swimmer had a record to match that of Tamas Darnyi, a Hungarian who had lost all sight in his left eye when he was hit by an icy snowball as a boy. Between 1985 and 1992 he never lost a race at either Individual Medley distance. During that time he set numerous world records and won the 200m and 400m titles at both the 1988 and 1992 Games. Two of his world records came in finals: the 200m Individual Medley in 1988 and the 400m Individual Medley in 1992.

⬇ *Hungary's Tamas Darnyi was unbeatable in Individual Medley over both 200m and 400m, winning four gold medals between 1988 and 1992.*

Unlucky asthmatic

Rick DeMont, 16, from California, had been taking medication for asthma since he was four years old and listed those medications on an official form when he qualified for the United States team for Munich 1972. When he woke with a wheeze on the eve of the final he took his usual drug Marax, and thought nothing of it. Later that day he won the 400m Freestyle final, and received the gold medal, but three days later was told he had failed a drug test. US team doctors had omitted to clear his drugs, an act they publicly acknowledged only 29 years later.

One for mum

Pablo Morales expected a gold medal at the 1984 Olympic Games. He held the world record at 100m Butterfly and broke it in the final, only for German Michael Gross to swim even faster. A relay gold and another individual silver came as scant consolation. In 1988, after failing to make the US team, he retired, but when his mother, Bianca, died of cancer in 1991 he vowed to win gold in her memory. He returned to competition eight months before the 1992 Games in Barcelona and went on to win the gold he missed out on in 1984.

Top ten nations by medals

	Nation	Gold	Silver	Bronze	Total
1.	United States	127	91	63	281
2.	Australia	31	31	36	98
3.	Japan	16	18	15	49
4.	Hungary	13	17	12	42
5.	Soviet Union	9	14	18	41
6.	Britain	9	11	14	34
7.	Germany	9	7	12	28
8.	Sweden	8	10	10	28
9.	Canada	6	7	10	23
10.	France	3	7	13	23

Boy winner in a man's world

Andrew Charlton was always known as 'Boy' because of his extreme youth when he made his name at 16, beating a great Swedish swimmer, Arne Borg. On the long voyage to Europe for the 1924 Games in Paris, his coach Tom Adrian, a First World War veteran suffering from shell shock, tried to commit suicide by throwing himself overboard. He was rescued, and Boy Charlton, determined to make him happy, beat Borg again with a world record time to win the 1500m Freestyle.

↑ *Ian Thorpe (centre) produced one of the greatest swims in Olympic Games history in the final of the 4 x 100m Freestyle Relay at Sydney 2000 to end the United States' hold on the title that stretched back to 1964.*

Relay trend-setters

The USA won the first seven 4 x 100m Freestyle gold medals before Australia ended their run in unusual circumstances at Sydney 2000. Ian Thorpe had won the 400m Freestyle only 55 minutes earlier and had barely had time to complete the Victory Ceremony before he swam the final two lengths. After one length he was 0.6 seconds down on Gary Hall Jnr, bronze medallist in the individual event. Not only did he catch him but he finished with a 0.19 second lead for a world record.

Olympic Games Records

100m Freestyle	21.30	Cesar Filho (Brazil)	16.8.2008
100m Freestyle	47.05	Eamonn Sullivan (Australia)	13.8.2008
200m Freestyle	1:42.96	Michael Phelps (US)	12.8.2008
400m Freestyle	3:40.59	Ian Thorpe (Australia)	16.9.2000
1500m Freestyle	14:38.92	Grant Hackett (Australia)	15.8.2008
100m Backstroke	52.54	Aaron Peirsol (US)	12.8.2008
200m Backstroke	1:53.94	Ryan Lochte (US)	15.8.2008
100m Breaststroke	58.91	Kosuke Kitajima (Japan)	11.8.2008
200m Breaststroke	2:07.64	Kosuke Kitajima (Japan)	14.8.2008
100m Butterfly	50.58	Michael Phelps (US)	16.8.2008
200m Butterfly	1:52.03	Michael Phelps (US)	13.8.2008
200m Individual Medley	1:54.23	Michael Phelps (US)	15.8.2008
400m Individual Medley	4:03.84	Michael Phelps (US)	14.8.2008

Relays

4 x 100m Freestyle	3:08.24	United States	11.8.2008
4 x 200m Freestyle	6:58.56	United States	13.8.2008
4 x 100m Medley	3:29.34	United States	17.8.2008

Hungarian fiddle

Hungarian swimming officials forgot to keep a record of their swimmers' times during 1996, so they 'invented' a fictional meeting in Budapest on 6–8 June, complete with results, to satisfy IOC regulations. Half of their eventual team at the Games qualified by this route, including Attila Czene, who took 200m Individual Medley gold and also broke the Olympic Games record.

Barrier breakers

100m Freestyle sub-60sec	58.6	Johnny Weissmuller (US)	9.7.1922
100m Freestyle sub-50sec	49.98	James Montgomery (US)	25.7.1976
100m Backstroke sub-60sec	59.6	Thompson Mann (US)	16.10.1964
100m Breaststroke sub-60sec	59.97	Roman Sloudnov (Russia)	29.6.2001
100m Butterfly sub-60 sec	59.0	Lance Larson (US)	26.6.1960
200m Individual Medley sub-2mins	1:59.36	Tamas Darnyi (Hungary)	13.1.1991
1,500m Freestyle sub-15 minutes	14:56.27	Vladimir Salnikov (Russia)	22.7.1980

Women's Swimming

Women's Swimming was staged for the first time at the 1912 Games in Stockholm with 27 competitors from eight nations contesting just two events: the 100m Freestyle and the 4 x 100m Freestyle Relay. By 2008 the number of events had grown to 17.

Women's 100m Freestyle winners

1912	1:22.2	Fanny Durack (Australia)
1920	1.13.6	Ethelda Bleibtrey (USA)
1924	1:12.4	Ethel Lackie (USA)
1928	1:11.0	Albina Osipowich (USA)
1932	1:06.8	Helene Madison (USA)
1936	1:05.9	Henrika Mastenbroek (Holland)
1948	1:06.3	Greta Andersen (Denmark)
1952	1:06.8	Katalin Szoke (Hungary)
1956	1:02.0	Dawn Fraser (Australia)
1960	1:01.2	Dawn Fraser (Australia)
1964	59.50	Dawn Fraser (Australia)
1968	1:00.0	Jan Henne (USA)
1972	58.59	Sandra Neilson (USA)
1976	55.65	Kornelia Ender (GDR)
1980	54.79	Barbara Krause (GDR)
1984	55.92	Nancy Hogshead (USA); Carrie Steinseifer (USA)
1988	54.93	Kristin Otto (GDR)
1992	54.64	Zhuang Yong (China)
1996	54.50	Le Jingyi (China)
2000	53.83	Inge de Bruijn (Holland)
2004	53.84	Jodie Henry (Australia)
2008	53.12	Britta Steffen (Germany)

Determined Durack

The honour of being the first Olympic Games women's Swimming champion went to Australia's Fanny Durack. She took the 100m Freestyle gold medal in 1912. The previous year, she had adopted the two-beat leg-kick for the Australian crawl and did not lose another race for eight years. However, the officials in charge of naming the Australian team believed it was wasteful to spend money on sending women to Sweden and refused to pay their fares. Eventually, Durack and her rival and close friend Mina Wylie were permitted to go if they raised the money themselves, and they did so by setting up a fund. In Stockholm, the pair finished first and second, after Durack had set a world record of 1 minute 19.8 seconds in the heat. Durack set 11 world records during her career from the distance of 100 yards to one mile.

↑ *Fanny Durack (left) holds the distinction of winning the first-ever women's Swimming gold medal at the Olympic Games. She eased to victory in the 100m Freestyle final at Stockholm 1912 with a 3.2-second winning margin.*

↙ *Gertrude Ederle put any disappointment she suffered at the 1924 Olympic Games behind her by becoming the first woman to swim the English Channel.*

Channel to stardom

Gertrude Ederle finished 'only' third in the 100m Freestyle at Paris 1924 and won gold in the 4 x 100m Relay. But two years later she earned international renown when she became the first woman to swim the English Channel. The American's time of 14 hours 31 minutes, helped by a wind-up gramophone playing popular songs on the accompanying boat, beat the men's record by almost two hours. An estimated two million people greeted her in New York, where she was welcomed by a ticker-tape parade. The city mayor described her achievement as being like 'Moses parting the Red Sea'. She recovered from a nervous breakdown in 1933 to live until she was 98, spending many years teaching deaf children to swim.

Holm over the limit

Eleanor Holm, winner of the 100m Backstroke in 1932, was favourite again in 1936. However, during the sea crossing to Europe, she outraged US officials by spending evenings carousing with other passengers and journalists and, despite a warning, drinking heavily. She was banned from competing in the Games by the US Olympic Committee led by its president, Avery Brundage, later the IOC president. Holm thus went to Berlin as a spectator and was lavishly entertained by the Nazis, despite being Jewish. Her highly publicised private life subsequently included two divorces, while her outspoken individuality was summed up in 1999, when, aged 85, she told Bill Clinton at a Washington reception: 'Mr President, you're a really good-looking dude.'

Fraser's historic hat-trick

Dawn Fraser became the first swimmer, male or female, to win three gold medals in the same event at the Games. Her victories in the 100m Freestyle from 1956 to 1964 led to her being voted in 1983 as Australia's greatest female Olympian. Her last victory, in Tokyo, was achieved despite her having been involved in a car crash in February 1964 which killed her mother and saw her spend more than a month in plaster because of a damaged vertebra. Fraser had frequent clashes with officials, climaxing at the 1964 Games in Tokyo when, together with two team-mates, she tried to steal the flag from the Emperor's Palace. Although she was arrested, the Emperor gave her the flag as a souvenir. However, the Australian authorities banned her for ten years.

↑ *Dawn Fraser dominated the 100m Freestyle event, winning gold in 1956, 1960 and 1964.*

Brilliant Bleibtrey

A pioneer of women's swimming, Ethelda Bleibtrey won every race she could enter at the 1920 Olympics – the 100m, 300m and Freestyle Relay – to become the United States' first-ever Olympic Swimming champion. Bleibtrey, who took up the sport after suffering polio, was imprisoned for indecency in 1919, because she took off her stockings before swimming at Manhattan Beach. A public outcry prompted her release. Three years later, she was again arrested when she swam in the reservoir in Central Park in New York in an attempt to force the authorities to build a public pool.

Andersen out on her own

Greta Andersen not only won the 100m title at London 1948 but was an outstanding long-distance performer, completing a 50-mile endurance feat. The Dane also swam the English Channel six times, setting records for the distance and regularly beating men in races across the straits. Her ability to drive herself to exhaustion was shown in the 1948 Olympic Games in London, when she was pulled out of the water unconscious in the 400m Freestyle. Four years later, in Helsinki, she reached the 400m Freestyle Final, despite being able to use only one leg because she had undergone surgery on the other.

⬇ *Shane Gould poses with her medals after her successes in Munich.*

'All that glitters is not Gould'

Those were the words with which the American women's team emblazoned their T-shirts in 1972, in defiance of the expected supremacy of the 15-year-old Australian Shane Gould – who would set 11 world records in a top-class two-year career. These included all Freestyle events from 100 to 1500m and also the 200m Individual Medley. Although American rivals won the 100m and 800m in Munich, Gould won three titles and two further medals to become the first female swimmer to take five medals at a single Games. She retired in 1973 after setting a world record in 1500m. As fellow Australian and Olympic champion Mike Wenden said: 'Shane was like a high-decibel concert which had such an impact it left your ears ringing.'

Donna DeVarona

Blonde Californian Donna DeVarona won two gold medals in 1964, including the first ever 400m Individual Medley. She also became the cover girl for magazines such as *Sports Illustrated, Life* and *Time*. Between 1960 and 1964, she was the best all-round female swimmer in the world. Subsequently, she travelled extensively as a sports commentator and a campaigner for women in sport, co-founding the Women's Sports Foundation.

Women's Swimming gold medallists at the Olympic Games

200m Breaststroke

1924	3:33.2	Lucy Morton (GB)
1928	3:12.6	Hildegard Schrader (Germany)
1932	3:06.3	Clare Dennis (Australia)
1936	3:03.6	Hideko Maehata (Japan)
1948	2:57.2	Petronella Van Vliet (Holland)
1952	2:51.7	Eva Skekely (Hungary)
1956	2:53.1	Ursula Happe (Germany)
1960	2:49.5	Anita Lonsbrough (GB)
1964	2:46.4	Galina Prozeumenschchikova (Soviet Union)
1968	2:44.4	Sharon Wichman (USA)
1972	2:41.71	Beverley Whitfield (Australia)
1976	2:33.35	Marina Kosheveya (Soviet Union)
1980	2:29.54	Lina Kachushite (Soviet Union)
1984	2:30.38	Anne Ottenbrite (Canada)
1988	2:26.71	Silke Horner (GDR)
1992	2:26.65	Kyoko Iwasaki (Japan)
1996	2:25.41	Penny Heyns (South Africa)
2000	2:24.35	Agnes Kovacs (Hungary)
2004	2:23.37	Amanda Beard (USA)
2008	2:20.22	Rebecca Soni (USA)

100m Butterfly

1956	1:11.0	Shelley Mann (USA)
1960	1:09.5	Carolyn Schuler (USA)
1964	1:04.7	Sharon Stouder (USA)
1968	1:05.5	Lynette McClements (Australia)
1972	1:03.34	Mayumi Aoki (Japan)
1976	1:00.13	Kornelia Ender (GDR)
1980	1:00.42	Caren Metschuck (GDR)
1984	59.26	Mary Meagher (USA)
1988	59.00	Kristin Otto (GDR)
1992	58.62	Qian Hong (China)
1996	59.13	Amy Van Dyken (USA)
2000	56.61	Inge de Bruijn (Holland)
2004	57.72	Petria Thomas (Australia)
2008	56.73	Lisbeth Trickett (Australia)

America's record breaker

Natalie Coughlan won an individual gold medal in the women's 100m Backstroke at the Athens 2004 Games, was part of the United States' world record-breaking, gold medal-winning quartet in the women's 4 x 200m Freestyle Relay. Four years later, at the Beijing 2008 Games, she was one of the stars of the show, winning gold in the women's 100m Backstroke (to become the first woman in history to defend her Backstroke title at the Games), silver medals as part of the US women's 4 x 100m Freestyle Relay and 4 x 100m Medley Relay quartets and bronze medals in the women's 100m Freestyle, the women's 200m Individual Medley and the women's 4x200m Freestyle Relay. In doing so, she became the first female American athlete in modern history to win six medals at one Games.

Miss all-rounder

Tracy Caulkins was perhaps the most versatile swimmer in history – yet she competed in only one Olympic Games, at Los Angeles 1984, because the United States boycotted the 1980 Games. In 1978, aged only 15, Caulkins won five gold medals, including both medleys, at the World Championships, but she never really overcame being unable to compete in Moscow. Still, in 1984, she was named her country's Sportswoman of the Year when she won both Individual Medleys and also swam the breaststroke leg for the victorious Medley Relay quartet.

⬆ *Tracey Caulkins finally got her hands on an Olympic Games gold medal (three of them) at Los Angeles 1984.*

100m Backstroke

Year	Time	Swimmer
1924	1:23.2	Sybii Bauer (USA)
1928	1:22.0	Maria Braun (Holland)
1932	1:19.4	Eleanor Holm (USA)
1936	1:18.9	Dina Senff (Holland)
1948	1:14.4	Karen-Margrete Harup (Denmark)
1952	1:14.3	Joan Harrison (South Africa)
1956	1:12.9	Judy Grinham (GB)
1960	1:09.3	Lynn Burke (USA)
1964	1:07.7	Cathy Ferguson (USA)
1968	1:06.2	Kaye Hall (USA)
1972	1:05.78	Melissa Belote (USA)
1976	1:01.83	Ulrike Richter (GDR)
1980	1:00.86	Rita Reinisch (GDR)
1984	1:02.55	Theresa Andrews (USA)
1988	1:00.89	Kristin Otto (GDR)
1992	1:00.68	Krisztina Egerszegi (Hungary)
1996	1:01.19	Beth Botsford (USA)
2000	1:00.21	Diana Mocanu (Romania)
2004	1:00.37	Natalie Coughlin (USA)
2008	58.96	Natalie Coughlin (USA)

Windmill in a hurricane

Janet Evans, despite a tiny frame of 1.66 metres and 46 kilograms weight, was years ahead of her time. Her 400m and 800m world records set in 1988 and 1989 lasted until 2006 and 2008 respectively, an astonishing achievement in a sport where records are broken frequently. She was swimming laps by the age of two and a year later could do both breaststroke and butterfly. She used an unusual straight-arm recovery in freestyle, saying: 'As I wanted to go down the pool the fastest, I figured the fastest way to get to the other end was to turn my arms over as fast as I could.' Evans won four gold medals over two Games and is still regarded as the premier female distance swimmer.

⬆ Janet Evans was always way ahead of her time and her 400m and 800m Freestyle world records lasted 18 and 19 years respectively.

The Mouse that roared

Krisztina Egerszegi was nicknamed the 'Mouse' by her Hungarian team-mates – Eger means 'mouse' in Hungarian – but there was nothing diminutive about her achievements. She won five Olympic titles, including three successive golds in the 200m Backstroke, emulating the feat of Australian Dawn Fraser. Yet she ranked her 200m Backstroke world record at the 1991 European Championships as probably her favourite moment. Her time of 2 minutes 06.62 seconds brought her a 10-minute standing ovation, and the mark lasted until 2008. She possessed a superbly smooth stroke, in which her long, purple-painted fingernails were also a trademark. In the later stages of her career, she opened a restaurant in Budapest, called The Mousehole.

⬇ Krisztina Egerszegi of Hungary powering her way to victory in the final of the 200m Backstroke at the 1992 Barcelona Games.

⬆ Susie O'Neill (left) slipped to a surprise second in the 200m Butterfly final in front of her home crowd at Sydney in the 2000 Games.

O'Neill, the unbeatable loser

Susie O'Neill was an Olympic champion at both 200m Butterfly (1996) and 200m Freestyle (2000), but she suffered one of the biggest upsets in Swimming history at the Games when she attempted to retain her 200m Butterfly title in Sydney. Not only was she competing before her home crowd, she had not lost at the distance for six years, had broken a 19-year-old world record and had just won the 200m Freestyle gold medal. The American Misty Hyman had been ill in the build-up to the Games, but won the final by 0.70 seconds.

Synchronised Swimming

A relatively new discipline to feature on the Summer Games Aquatics programme, Synchronised Swimming first appeared as an exhibition sport from 1948 to 1968, before gaining recognition as a fully-fledged discipline in Los Angeles in 1984. Known originally as 'water ballet', Synchronised Swimming, alongside Rhythmic Gymnastics, is the only exclusively female sport to feature at the Summer Games.

Making a splash in Hollywood

When the outbreak of the Second World War forced the cancellation of the 1940 Olympic Games in Tokyo, United States swimmer Esther Williams lost a chance to make a name for herself on the international sports stage. Instead her good looks and athletic ability saw her switch to performing alongside Olympian swimmer and screen star Johnny Weissmuller in Billy Rose's Aquacade – a music, dance and swimming show in New York. Williams went on to star in a number of Hollywood films in the 1940s and 1950s, performing elaborate swimming routines. *Bathing Beauty* was Hollywood's first swimming movie, and it created a new genre of 'aquamusicals' which helped popularise synchronised swimming. The best known was *Million Dollar Mermaid* (the nickname by which she would come to be known during her time at MGM) in which Williams portrayed the Australian swimmer Annette Kellerman.

A sport is born

The sport of synchronised swimming evolved from the ornamental swimming and theatrical water ballets of the late 19th and early 20th centuries. Australian swimmer Annette Kellerman, who performed water acrobatics in a glass tank at the New York Hippodrome in 1907, is often referred to as the first under-water ballerina.

⬆ *Australian Annette Kellermann is credited with inventing synchronised swimming after her 1907 performance of the first water ballet in New York.*

Changing times

Introduced to the Olympic Games in Los Angeles in 1984 with Solo and Duet events, the Synchronised Swimming programme has evolved still further. After featuring in Seoul in 1988 and in Barcelona in 1992, the Solo and Duet events were replaced in Atlanta in 1996 by an eight-person Team event. In 2000 the Duet event was reintroduced to the programme, alongside the Team event. London 2012 will be a landmark Games for Synchronised Swimming. This is where the sport made its Olympic debut in 1948 as an exhibition event.

First medals

In 1984, in front of a home crowd in Los Angeles, Tracie Ruiz and Candy Costie won the first-ever Olympic medals in the event, claiming gold in the Duet for the US. Ruiz went on to capture an additional gold medal a day later in the Solo event.

↖ *Candy Costie (left) and Tracie Ruiz perform their gold-medal Synchronised Swimming routine at the 1984 Games in Los Angeles.*

↑ *Canada's Sylvie Fréchette defied tragedy and controversy to share gold at Barcelona 1992.*

Barcelona tragedy

After exploding on to the world stage by winning the 1991 World Solo Championship, Canadian Sylvie Fréchette was an early favourite to capture Synchronised Swimming gold at Barcelona 1992. Days before her departure, however, Fréchette's fiancé and manager Sylvain Lake committed suicide. Despite her personal tragedy, she decided to compete, but there she was engulfed in sporting controversy. After a flawless performance by Fréchette, Brazilian judge Ana Maria da Silveira pressed the wrong button when scoring and awarded her an 8.7 instead of a 9.7. The error cost Fréchette the gold medal, which instead went to Kristen Babb-Sprague of the US. An appeal finally saw the gold medal shared.

Consistent Japan

Japan is the only country to have medalled in Synchronised Swimming at every single Olympic Games since the discipline was first introduced. However, despite the impressive record, the nation has never managed to win Synchronised Swimming gold at the Games and have to be satisfied instead with a haul of four silver and eight bronze medals.

⬇ *Spain's Synchronised Swimming team performs its routine at Beijing 2008 without their battery-powered swimsuits that were deemed to contravene competition rules.*

Costume controversy

The Spanish Synchronised Swimming team was caught up in a swimsuit controversy at Beijing 2008, when their specially designed costumes were banned from the competition. The Spaniards had planned to wear custom-made suits that were embedded with battery-powered sparkling lights, but Games officials deemed them an accessory and, as such, in breach of the rules of the event.

Russian dominance

Russia has won more gold medals than any other country in Synchronised Swimming, a record partly inspired by Anastasia Davydova. For a decade she has been one of the sport's best-known competitors and also the most successful – with four Olympic Games gold medals and ten World Championships titles. At the Games, Davydova's success was emulated by another Russian, Anastasia Ermakova, who shared her haul of four gold medals. The golden duet came to an end after the 2008 Games, when Ermakova decided on a career break. In 2009, reaffirming herself as the greatest athlete in the sport, Davydova, with new partner Svetlana Romashina, went on to win the Duet technical event at the FINA World Championships in Rome and also shared gold in the Team free event.

← *At Athens 2004, Anastasia Davydova (left) and Anastasia Ermakova added to Russia's impressive overall haul of six Synchronised Swimming gold medals.*

Water Polo

Water Polo was the first team sport to be contested in the Olympic Games, making its debut in Paris in 1900. Having evolved into two different forms, in the United States and Europe, it began as an inherently violent sport – largely because of the more brutal version preferred in the US, where outright violence, injuries and near-drownings were part of the game. Today, however, matches are played to European rules.

Clean sweep

The records show that, at the 1904 Games in St Louis, the United States won all the available medals in the Water Polo competition – gold, silver and bronze. That was because other nations refused to compete in the more violent version of the sport that was commonplace in the States and to which the event was due to be staged. In due course the International Olympic Committee adopted the more strategic, faster and less violent European style, which featured at the following 1908 Games in London, and which is practised universally today.

Hungarian domination

The Hungarians have been by far the greatest ambassadors of Water Polo at the Olympic Games. They won medals at every single one of the Games between 1928 and 1980, and between 1932 and 1976 won six of the ten gold medals available. In 2000 in Sydney, Hungary resurfaced as a powerhouse in the discipline, winning the seventh gold medal in their history. The country continued its dominance at Athens 2004 and Beijing 2008, when they claimed gold at both Games.

➜ *The Hungary team celebrates victory at the 1936 Olympic Games in Berlin. It was the second of an unprecedented nine Water Polo gold medals for the country, the latest of which was won at Beijing in 2008.*

Women's long wait

Women had to wait a full century before they contested Water Polo at the Games. In 2000 in Sydney, a full 100 years after the debut of the discipline, women's Water Polo made its first official appearance at the Olympic Games, with the Australian team claiming gold before an ecstatic home crowd.

⬅ *Australia became the first team to win women's Water Polo gold when they beat the United States 4–3 in the Final at Sydney in 2000.*

Blood in the water

Few sporting encounters have been more politically charged than when Hungary met the Soviet Union in the semi-final of the Water Polo competition at Melbourne 1956 – often referred to as 'the blood in the water match'. When the Hungarian team set off for Australia, the Soviet army had begun the invasion that would topple their country's reformist leaders. The match started with verbal taunts and soon became extraordinarily violent. With Hungary leading 4–0, blood staining the pool and the crowd on the verge of rioting, the match was brought to an early end, with Hungary declared the winners. They went on to claim gold.

← *Hungary's Ervin Zador suffers a gashed eye in the famous 1956 Final.*

Hungarian masters

Hungary's impressive record at the Games is evidence that they boast some of the most celebrated Water Polo players of all time. Among them was Oliver Halassy, who represented Hungary at three Games between 1928 and 1936, winning two gold medals and a silver. His athletic ability is made even more remarkable by the fact that he had his left leg amputated below the knee as a child, following a traffic accident. Another great Hungarian player was Dezs Gyarmati, often hailed as the greatest water polo player in history. His record of winning a medal at five different Games from 1948 to 1964 (three golds, one silver and one bronze) has never been matched.

Men's gold medal winners

City	Year	Gold
Paris	1900	Great Britain
St Louis	1904	United States
London	1908	Great Britain
Stockholm	1912	Great Britain
Antwerp	1920	Great Britain
Paris	1924	France
Amsterdam	1928	Germany
Los Angeles	1932	Hungary
Berlin	1936	Hungary
London	1948	Italy
Helsinki	1952	Hungary
Melbourne	1956	Hungary
Rome	1960	Italy
Tokyo	1964	Hungary
Mexico	1968	Yugoslavia
Munich	1972	USSR
Montreal	1976	Hungary
Moscow	1980	USSR
Los Angeles	1984	Yugoslavia
Seoul	1988	Yugoslavia
Barcelona	1992	Italy
Atlanta	1996	Spain
Sydney	2000	Hungary
Athens	2004	Hungary
Beijing	2008	Hungary

Women's gold medal winners

City	Year	Gold
Sydney	2000	Australia
Athens	2004	Italy
Beijing	2008	Netherlands

⬇ *Celebration time for the Netherlands after they beat the United States 9–8 to take women's Water Polo gold at the 2008 Games in Beijing.*

Chapter Three
Athletics

History relates that the most successful competitor in the Ancient Olympics was a runner – Leonidas of Rhodes, who won 12 running titles (both sprint and endurance) between 164 and 152 BC – and that track and field Athletics was at the centre of the modern Olympic Games as conceived of by Baron Pierre de Coubertin in 1892.

The first modern Games, four years later in Athens, featured 43 events, many now defunct such as the one-handed weightlifting contest. Greek shepherd Spiridon Louis ensured Athletics earned peak attention by winning the Marathon.

Men's Athletics at the Games includes ten individual competitions on the track (100m, 200m, 400m, 800m, 1500m, 5000m, 10,000m, 110m Hurdles, 400m Hurdles, 3000m Steeplechase) and eight field events (High Jump, Pole Vault, Long Jump, Triple Jump, Shot Put, Discus Throw, Hammer Throw and Javelin Throw).

There are also the 4 x 100 and 4 x 400m Relay events, and the Decathlon, which comprises ten different track and field disciplines. Three other events end and sometimes start in the stadium: the Marathon, the 20km Race Walk and the 50km Race Walk.

James Connolly of the United States was the first man to win an event at the Olympic Games, in the Triple Jump. He did not receive a gold medal, however. Winners at the first Modern Games in Athens received a silver medal, along with an olive branch and a certificate. The 1912 Games were the last at which the winners' medals were made entirely from gold. Since then they have been made of silver and then coated in gold.

Following his stunning success in the men's 100m Final in Beijing in 2008 (in a new world-record time of 9.69), Jamaica's Usain Bolt secured the sprint double when he streaked to victory in the men's 200m Final in another world record-breaking time of 19.30.

Men's 100m

The shortest outdoor sprint race, but often the most spectacular and always the most watched, the men's 100m is the Olympic Games' blue riband event with the winner awarded the moniker "The Fastest Man on Earth". The event has been staged at every Games since Athens in 1896.

How it all started

The first man to be credited with a 100m world record, albeit in the years before the IAAF, the sport's governing body, was formed in 1912, was Britain's William MacLaren. He was given a time of 11.00 seconds as part of a run over 110 yards at Haslingden, in Lancashire, on 27 July 1867. It was seven years short of a century before the 100m was run in 10 seconds – Armin Hary of West Germany did so in Zurich on 21 July 1960. American Jim Hines was the first man to go under, winning gold in 9.95 at Mexico City 1968.

← *Gold-medal winner at Barcelona 1992, Linford Christie's defence of the men's 100m crown came to an abrupt end when he was disqualified from the final at Atlanta 1996 following two false starts.*

Americans miss the bus

At Munich 1972 the men's 100m title was won by Valeriy Borzov, of the Soviet Union, whose time of 10.14 seconds saw him finish a tenth of a second clear of the field. Borzov had arrived at Munich as favourite – but who knows how he might have fared had Stan Wright, the US sprint coach in Munich, had the right bus timetable? Wright set off from the Olympic Village with his country's two top sprinters, Eddie Hart and Rey Robinson, accompanied by the third US 100m man Robert Taylor, in what he thought was good time for their second round of races on the evening of 31 August. But Wright was working to an out-of-date timetable, and rather than starting at 7pm, as he thought, the second round got underway at 4.15pm. While they waited for their bus, to their horror, the group saw a live TV transmission of the first race. Despite being rushed to the stadium in a TV car, Hart and Robinson, both of whom had clocked 9.9 seconds in the US Olympic trials, arrived too late. Taylor just made his heat, however, and went on to take silver behind the Russian.

↑ *The Soviet Union's Valeriy Borzov raises his arm in celebration as he wins the men's 100m Final at the 1972 Games in Munich.*

Starting over...

Nowadays, any athlete who false-starts in the 100m faces instant disqualification, but the rules have varied. Before the International Association of Athletics Federations voted in 2009 to bring in the current rule, one false start was allowed in any race without sanction, with anyone subsequently offending being disqualified. Before that the rule was that each athlete was entitled to one false start, but would be disqualified in the event of a second, a fate Britain's defending champion Linford Christie suffered before the men's 100m Final at Atlanta 1996. Different rules applied in the modern Games' early years. The men's 100m Final at Stockholm 1912, won by Ralph Craig of the United States in a time of 10.8 seconds, was marred by seven false starts, the first three of which came from the eventual gold medallist. Thirty-six years later Craig, then 59, reappeared at the Games as a member of the US Sailing team, and carried the US flag at the Opening Ceremony in Wembley Stadium. He only needed one attempt at this.

Brilliant Bolt

Usain Bolt improved his 100m world record to 9.58 seconds at the 2009 World Championships in Berlin. Bolt held the two previous marks too, having become the first man to break 9.70, at the Beijing 2008 Games, in a time of 9.69, which came less than three months after he had clocked 9.72 in what was only his fifth serious race at the distance.

⬇ *Usain Bolt celebrates with panache his decisive victory in the final of the men's 100m at the Beijing 2008 Games.*

Bailey's speed double

Canada's Donovan Bailey reached a speed of 27mph during a 10-metre stretch in winning the men's 100m title at Atlanta 1996 in a new world record of 9.84 seconds. Both those measures of speed were topped by Jamaica's Usain Bolt, who won the men's 100m and 200m titles at Beijing 2008 in world records of 9.69 and 19.30 respectively, before adding world titles the following year in times of 9.58 and 19.19. In the latter 100m race, Bolt was clocked at 27.45mph.

Super achiever

Robert Hayes, who won the men's 100m title at Tokyo 1964 in a world-record time of 10.00 seconds, went on to spend nine years playing American football for the Dallas Cowboys as a wide receiver and is the only athlete to have earned an Olympic gold medal and a Super Bowl victory ring.

Old gold...

The men's 100m final at Los Angeles 1932 was so close that if current rules had been applied the silver medallist, Ralph Metcalfe, would have won, rather than his fellow American Eddie Tolan. Both recorded a new Games record time of 10.3 seconds, but the verdict went to the first man to cross the line. Today Metcalfe would get the decision as the first man to reach the line.

Track student

Six months of extensive training, which placed an emphasis on his start, stride pattern and form, paid dividends for Great Britain's Harold Abrahams at the 1924 Games in Paris. Although only considered an outside bet for the men's 100m title, he clocked 10.6 seconds in the final to take gold. Sadly, a broken leg ended his athletics career in 1925.

The legend of Jesse Owens

Winning the men's 100m at Berlin 1936 was only a start for Jesse Owens, a sharecropper's son who defied the racist Nazi propaganda of the time, in which the Americans were taunted over their use of 'black auxiliaries'. The German spectators, by contrast, offered him warm support throughout the Games as he went on to add further golds in the 200m, the Long Jump and the 4 x 100m Relay – an achievement his fellow American Carl Lewis replicated at Los Angeles 1984. Owens had managed an even more astonishing athletic feat the year before, when he broke five world records and equalled a sixth in the space of 45 minutes while competing for his university in Michigan.

➡ *Jesse Owens explodes off the start-line en route to gold in a world record-breaking time of 20.7 seconds in the men's 200m Final at the 1936 Games in Berlin.*

Men's 200m and 400m

The men's 200m, contested at every Games since 1900, starts on the curve and finishes on the home straight. It attracts several competitors from the men's 100m and the 100m-200m double has been achieved on nine occasions at the Games – most recently by Usain Bolt. The men's 400m is contested over a single lap of the track and has been staged at every Games since Athens 1896.

The pride of Paris

The United States' John Tewkesbury won the first-ever men's 200m title, at Paris 1900, in a time of 22.2 seconds. It was his fifth medal of the Games (after taking gold in the 400m Hurdles, silver in the 60m and 100m Sprints and bronze in the 200m Hurdles).

Reynolds too late

In 1988, Butch Reynolds was the hot favourite to win the men's 400m title in Seoul, having recently beaten the 20-year-old world record of 43.86 seconds run by his fellow American Lee Evans when he took gold in the thin air of Mexico City in 1968. There was no altitude advantage for the big US runner as he recorded his mark of 43.29 in the Zurich meeting. But in Seoul a month later Reynolds misjudged the final, leaving himself with too much to do after lying fifth with 100 metres to go and just failing to catch the winner, 19-year-old team-mate Steve Lewis, at the line and had to be content with a silver medal.

⬇ *A clean sweep of medals in the men's 400m Final at Seoul 1988 for the US. From left to right: Butch Reynolds, Steve Lewis and Danny Everett.*

Black power protest

The men's 200m Final at Mexico City 1968 produced a world record run by Tommie Smith, who clocked 19.83 in the thin air. But the event is remembered more for what happened at the Victory Ceremony. As the American national anthem played, Smith and his US team-mate John Carlos, the bronze medallist, bowed their heads and raised black-gloved hands in a Black Power salute as a protest against racial inequality in the United States. Australia's silver medallist Peter Norman joined in their protest, wearing a civil rights badge they had given him. Both Americans were subsequently shunned by the US athletics establishment. Thirty-four years later, at Sydney 2000, Norman was conspicuous by his absence among past Australian medallists at the Opening Ceremony.

⬆ *Brothers in arms: Tommie Smith (centre) and John Carlos (right) make their infamous salute at the 1968 Games in Mexico City.*

Fact and fiction

Jackson Scholz, the US winner of the men's 200m title at Paris 1924, later made his living by writing sports fiction and published 31 novels. Another piece of fiction brought him to public attention at the age of 84. In the Oscar-winning film *Chariots of Fire*, which told the story of three British athletes at the 1924 Games, Scholz is shown handing a religious message to Britain's committed Christian Eric Liddell before the start of the men's 400m Final, which Liddell won. In answer to press enquiries, however, Scholz said the incident had never happened, adding: 'My religious background was rather casual.'

Johnson's handover to Bolt

The 1996 Games in Atlanta produced one of the most astonishing athletics performances in history in the men's 200m Final from home favourite Michael Johnson, whose hopes at the 1992 Games in Barcelona had been undermined by food poisoning. Just over one month before the Atlanta 1996 Games, and on the same track, Johnson had run 19.66 to better the world record of 19.72 set by Italy's Pietro Mennea in the thin air of Mexico City in 1979. Namibian rival Frankie Fredericks almost matched that in the 1996 Final, running 19.68, but Johnson had already crossed the line in the stunning time of 19.32 – a massive improvement and one which most observers of the sport expected to stand for at least as long as Mennea's mark (16 years ten months and 11 days). Twelve years later, however, at the 2008 Games in Beijing, Usain Bolt produced his own extraordinary mark of 19.30, before clocking a staggering 19.19 the following year at the IAAF World Championships in Berlin.

➔ *Texan Michael Johnson produced a stunning performance in the men's 200m Final at the 1996 Games in Atlanta, thrilling a partisan crowd by clocking a new world record of 19.32 seconds.*

Thornton's marker

The first man credited with a world 200m record was Percy Thornton (Britain), although his time of 24.00 seconds at the West London Ground on 24 February 1886 was set over 220 yards (201.17 metres). The IAAF first started differentiating world records over the 200m straight and the 200m made on a full turn in 1951, when Andrew Stansfield (US) set a world record of 20.6 over 220 yards on the turn. The first man officially credited with breaking 20 seconds was Tommie Smith (US), who clocked 19.83 to win gold in the men's 200m Final at Mexico City 1968.

The man who knew too much

Herb McKenley, of Jamaica, was widely expected to win the men's 400m at London 1948, although he insisted his 6ft 4½in team-mate Arthur Wint was the man to beat. McKenley was right: Wint took gold and he took silver. Four years later, in Helsinki, McKenley lost the gold medals in both the 100m and 400m on photo-finishes.

Frozen in history

Unlike his 200m record, Michael Johnson's men's 400m world record of 43.18, set at the 1999 World Championships in Seville, did survive Beijing 2008 and the 2009 World Championships. His 1999 time bettered the mark of 43.29 set 11 years earlier by fellow American Butch Reynolds.

Quick Cuban heels

Alberto Juantorena Danger of Cuba, winner of the men's 800m title at Montreal 1976 Games in Montreal in a world record time of 1:43.50, went on to win the men's 400m Final in a time of 44.26 seconds, passing US runner Fred Newhouse just before the line. In so doing he became the first man to win the 400m-800m double – apart from Paul Pilgrim at the 1906 'Intercalated' Games. The 6ft 2in Juantorena was known as 'El Caballo' – The Horse.

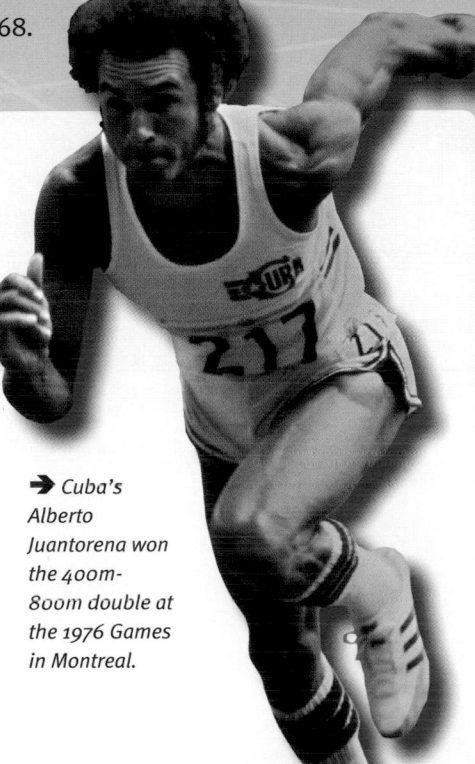

➔ *Cuba's Alberto Juantorena won the 400m-800m double at the 1976 Games in Montreal.*

Round the bend

John Nuttall, a British professional, was credited with a world record of 51 seconds on a curved track over 440 yards (402.34 metres) at Manchester on 19 December 1859. The first official IAAF mark was of 47.8 by Maxey Long of the United States on 29 September 1900. The first man to break the 46-second barrier was Jamaica's Herb McKenley on 2 July 1948. The first to break 45 seconds was Otis Davis, of the United States, who won gold at Rome 1960 with a time of 44.9, the same as that of silver medallist Carl Kaufman of West Germany. Both were credited with a world record, although Davis was 0.01 faster. The United States' Lee Evans was the first man to break the 44-second barrier with his 43.86 at the 1968 Games in Mexico City.

Men's 110m and 400m Hurdles

The men's 110m Hurdles is staged over ten 1.067-metre-high hurdles and has been contested at every Games since 1896. The men's 400m Hurdles is staged over one lap of the track (over ten evenly spaced 0.914m-high hurdles) and has been contested since 1900.

Moses leaves world in the wilderness

In securing gold at Los Angeles 1984, Ed Moses extended an astonishing winning streak over 400m Hurdles. Having lost to Harald Schmid on 26 August 1977, the American got his own back a week later by beating the West German by a 15-yard margin and from then on he remained unbeaten all the way through the 1984 Games and until 4 June 1987, when his long reign was ended by fellow countryman Danny Harris.

⬇ *The highlight of Ed Moses' domination of the men's 400m Hurdles came with a gold medal at Los Angeles 1984.*

That's what friends are for

Colin Jackson, the men's 110m Hurdles silver medallist at Seoul 1988, was favoured to go one better at Barcelona 1992, and he did finish the Games with a personal best time to his credit. Unfortunately for Jackson, his time of 13.10 seconds came in the opening round, and the gold went to Mark McKoy of Canada in 13.12 as Jackson, who had suffered a minor injury during the semi-final, faded to seventh in 13.46. Welshman Jackson's consolation after a stellar career was to have been crowned world champion twice, Commonwealth champion twice and European champion four times. The year before Barcelona 1992, Jackson had invited McKoy and his family to move in and they both trained under the guidance of Malcolm Arnold – who had guided John Akii-Bua to men's 400m Hurdles gold at Munich 1972. The year after the Games in Barcelona, McKoy beat Jackson to the world indoor title on home territory in Toronto after benefiting from a flying start. The two remain friends.

⬆ *Canada's Mark McKoy storms into the lead in the men's 110m Hurdles Final at the 1992 Games in Barcelona. He held on to his lead to take gold.*

Taking athletics to bed

Earl Thomson, the Canadian who won the men's 110m Hurdles title at Antwerp 1920 in a world record time of 14.8 seconds, took his sport very seriously. He used to tie his legs to the end of the bed so he wouldn't curl up and risk cramping.

Third referred

The first instance at the Games of a result in a final being altered following a video replay of the race was in 1932. Jack Keller of the United States was initially awarded the bronze medal for the men's 110m Hurdles after finishing in a time of 14.8 seconds in a race won by fellow US athlete George Saling. But after viewing the film the judges re-assigned bronze to Britain's Donald Finlay, also timed at 14.8. Keller sought out Finlay in the Olympic Village and passed the medal on.

Breaking the barriers

Britain's N. Paterson is the first athlete credited with a world record in the 400m Hurdles, clocking 67.00 seconds at Eltham on 27 April 1867. American Charles Bacon became the first world record holder of the IAAF era in winning the 1908 Olympic title in 55.00. The first man to break the 50-second barrier was Glenn Davis (United States), who ran 49.5 in 1956. Another American, Geoffrey Vanderstock, was the first to break 49 seconds, recording 48.8 in the US trials before Mexico City 1968.

➔ *The United States' Charles Bacon (right) edges into the lead against compatriot Harry Hillmand in the men's 400m Final at the 1908 Games.*

Curtis and the calculated gamble

US athlete Thomas Curtis won the inaugural men's 110m Hurdles Final at Athens 1896. Despite having qualified for the men's 100m Final, Curtis chose not to contest it in order to concentrate on the sprint hurdles. His decision paid off.

Ten years unbeaten and the nine fastest times for Moses

During almost a decade in which Ed Moses remained unbeaten over men's 400m Hurdles, he produced the nine fastest times ever run in the event. He brought the world record down to 47.02 seconds, a time which only one man, fellow American Kevin Young, has since bettered with his 46.78 in winning gold at Barcelona 1992. Moses set his first world record (47.13) on 3 July 1980, beating the eight-year-old mark of 47.82 set by Uganda's John Akii-Bua at Munich 1972: the first time an athlete had broken the 48-second barrier.

A drop of bad luck

As Boyd Gittens set off in the men's 400m Hurdles semi-final at the 1968 US Olympic trials, a pigeon dropping hit him in the eye and dislodged his contact lens before he reached the first hurdle. Happily he was able to take part in a run-off, where he secured his place in the United States squad for Mexico City. Sadly, a leg injury forced him to withdraw from his first-round heat.

➔ *World record holder Dayron Robles (of Cuba) heads to men's 110m Hurdles gold at Beijing 2008.*

Men's 110m Hurdles records tumble

The first official record holder in the sprint hurdles was Britain's Philip Norman, who was timed at Eton over the 120 yards (109.73 metres) hurdles at 18.00 seconds. The first world record holder in the IAAF era was Forrest Smithson of the United States, who won gold at 1908 Games in London in 15.00. Soon after taking the title at the 1936 Games in Berlin, another American Forrest – Forrest Towns – became the first man to break the 14-second barrier, winning at Oslo in 13.7. Another American broke the 13-second barrier: Ronaldo Nehemiah, who ran 12.93 in Zurich in 1981. The world record was lowered to 12.87 by Dayron Robles of Cuba in 2008.

Men's 800m and 1500m

The men's 800m is the shortest middle-distance track event (run over two laps) and requires both speed and endurance. The men's 1500m is considered the premier middle-distance race and has produced some legendary champions at the Games. Both events have been contested at every Games since Athens 1896.

Maximum returns

London accountants Price Waterhouse granted their 22-year-old Australian employee Edwin Flack a month's holiday in 1896 so that he could compete in the first modern Olympic Games. He made the most of it, winning gold in the 1500m and, two days later, in the 800m – on the morning of which he had played in the Tennis tournament. He also took part in the Marathon.

Perfect champion

Heading into the 1960 Games, Herb Elliott had won 44 consecutive races at either 1500m or one mile, but despite opening up a 15-metre lead with a lap remaining in the men's 1500m Final he did not allow himself to relax until he crossed the line in a world record time of 3:35.6. Time after time Elliott had practised for his biggest race by imagining an opponent on his shoulder who would be able to sense any weakness in him. 'I had practised a million times being challenged and winning that challenge,' said the Australian, who retired after his victory, unbeaten, and only 22.

⬇ *The 1960 men's 1500m medallists (from left to right): Michel Jazy (silver), Herb Elliott (gold) and Itsvan Rozsavolgi (bronze).*

British athletes Coe and Ovett get it wrong – and right

Even though the United States boycotted Moscow 1980, most observers were happy that the world's best two men's 800m and 1500m runners were present – the British pair of Sebastian Coe and Steve Ovett. Coe was widely expected to win the 800m (at which he held the world record), and Ovett the metric mile (in which he equalled Coe's world record of 3:32.1 on the eve of the Games and remained unbeaten in 42 races). Each left Moscow with a gold medal – but the 'wrong' gold. First Ovett took the 800m title with a characteristically bold flourish as Coe misjudged his tactics. But tactics favoured Coe in the longer final as East Germany's Jurgen Straub made a long run for home over the final 800 metres. Both Britons responded, but it was Coe who crossed the line in an agony of ecstasy. The ecstasy of redemption.

⬆ *The British trio of (from left to right) Steve Ovett, Steve Cram and Sebastian Coe hit the front during the men's 1500m Final at Moscow 1980.*

Third time lucky

Algeria's Noureddine Morceli dominated 1500m and mile events between 1991 and 1996, but suffered the agony of finishing seventh at Barcelona 1992 in a slow, tactical race won by home favourite Fermin Cacho. Four years later, at Atlanta 1996, Morceli took men's 1500m gold, but only after the next rising star in the event, Morocco's Hicham El Guerrouj, had fallen. By the time of Sydney 2000, El Guerrouj dominated his distance as Morceli had done, but the Moroccan finished stunned and tearful after he was beaten to the line by Kenya's Noah Ngeny. Four years later in Athens, it all came right for El Guerrouj just as it had done for Morceli. He completed the men's 1500m-5000m double.

Heads up

American Dave Wottle always wore a battered golf cap when he ran, and he did so in the 800m final at the 1972 Games, in which he passed Russia's Yevgheny Arzhanov just before the line to win gold by 0.03 seconds. The young runner was so shocked that he forgot to remove the cap during the Victory Ceremony and only did so when a reporter asked if he was staging a demonstration. Wottle then made a tearful, heartfelt apology to his fellow countrymen.

↑ *United States athlete Dave Wottle races to gold in the final stages of the men's 800m final at the 1972 Games in Munich.*

Not meant to be

American Jim Ryun was the men's 1500m world record holder by the time of the 1968 Games, but finished second behind Kenya's Kip Keino. Four years later in Munich, Ryun – still world record holder – was expected to win gold, but he tripped and fell in his qualifying heat.

World records

The men's 800m record stands at 1:41.01, set by David Rudisha in Rieti, in Italy, on 29 August 2010 – just a week after the Kenyan had bettered Wilson Kipketer's 13-year-old world mark with 1:41.09 in Berlin. Kipketer, a naturalised Dane born in Kenya, set his first outright world record of 1:41.24 in Zurich on 13 August 1997 before reducing it to 1:41.11 in Cologne 11 days later. Kipketer eclipsed an even longer standing world record – the mark of 1:41.73 set by Seb Coe in Florence in 1981, which Kipketer first equalled in July 1997. The first credited men's 800m world record was 2:05, which Britain's J. Blackwood ran over 880 yards (804.68 metres) at Addiscombe on 25 April 1857. In the professional ranks, however, Britain's John Leyland was timed at 2:01 at Peckham on 1 November 1847. Morocco's Hicham El Guerrouj set the current men's 1500m world record (3:26.00) at Rome on 14 July 1998, beating the mark of 3:27.37 set by Algeria's Noureddine Morceli three years earlier. British athlete Steve Cram produced the first sub-3:30 time when he won at Nice on 16 July 1985 in 3:29.67. France's J. Borel was the first credited world record holder with a time of 4:22.60 in 1892. The first athlete to break the four-minute barrier was Britain's Harold Wilson, who clocked 3:59.8 in 1908.

Heart of gold

American athlete Melvin Sheppard, who outsprinted Britain's world record holder Harold Wilson to win the men's 1500m title at London 1908, completed a middle-distance double when he won the men's 800m in a world record time of 1:52.8. Four years later when defending his title in Stockholm, Sheppard beat his own world record – but he was only one of four to do so and finished in the silver-medal position behind fellow American Ted Meredith. Sheppard, incidentally, had once applied to become a New York policeman, but his application had been rejected on the grounds that he had a 'weak heart'.

Paavo paves the way to a double

At the 1924 Games in Paris, Paavo Nurmi and Finnish team officials were upset to learn that there was only a half-hour gap in the schedule between the men's 1500m and the men's 5000m – which were the Flying Finn's two main distances. After a protest, the gap was widened, marginally, to two hours. Three weeks before the final, Nurmi simulated the challenge ahead of him by running the men's 1500m followed, an hour later, by a 5000m. He broke the world record in both races. So commanding was Nurmi's form in men's 1500m Final, during which he consulted his own stopwatch, that he would have bettered his world record of 3:52.6 if he had not slowed over the final lap to save his energy, settling instead for gold in a new Games record time of 3:53.6. Nurmi won the 5000m title later that day in another new Games record time.

↓ *Kenya's David Rudisha breaks the men's 800m world record in Berlin on 22 August 2010. He broke it again, in Rieti, Italy, seven days later.*

Men's 5000m and 10,000m

The track's longest distance races, the 5000m and 10,000m, challenge an athlete's speed and endurance. The two events were introduced at the 1912 Games in Stockholm and many athletes have competed in both over the years with the double achieved on seven occasions, most recently by Kenenisa Bekele at Beijing 2008.

Lasse brings it home

The enigmatic Finn Lasse Viren is the only man to retain the men's 5000m title at the Games and to achieve back-to-back 5000m-10,000m doubles (at the 1972 and 1976 Games). Even so, he is not as revered as other multiple gold medallists. A failure to produce performances of his medal-winning standard outside the Games, and a relative paucity of races internationally, created rumours and suspicion of his training techniques – although nothing was ever proven. What cannot be doubted, though, is his determination, as evidenced by his feat at Munich 1972, when he fell in the 10,000m Final, losing 30 metres in the process, but recovered to win the race.

➜ *Finland's Lasse Viren is the only man in history to have completed the 5000m-10,000m double at two Games (at Munich 1972 and Montreal 1976).*

Nurmi the 'Flying Finn'

Finland produced a string of world-beating long-distance runners in the first half of the 20th century, but the greatest of them all was Paavo Nurmi. This phenomenon from the Baltic port of Turku won a record nine gold medals across five distances at three Games in the 1920s (1920, 1924 and 1928) and set 35 world records from 1500m to 20km. No wonder his fellow countrymen decided to set up a statue in his honour outside the Olympic Stadium in Helsinki. The only thing he did not achieve was the 5000m-10,000m double at the same Olympic Games.

⬆ *Finland's Paavo Nurmi crosses the finishing line to take gold in the men's 5000m Final at the 1924 Games in Paris.*

Better late than never for Kuts

For a man who stumbled into the sport of athletics, Vladimir Kuts certainly made up for lost time. The Ukrainian, who ran under the Soviet banner in the 1950s, ran his first race at the age of 21. Just five years later he was the 5000m and 10,000m Soviet champion and within another 12 months he had broken the legendary Emil Zatopek's 5000m world record. Sporting immortality for the relentless Kuts was ensured at Melbourne 1956, when he became just the third man (after Zatopek and Hannes Kolehmainen) to claim the 5000m-10,000m double at a single Games.

Heroes from the horn of Africa

Ethiopians have won six of the eight gold medals awarded for these classic long-distance track races since 1996. It took a while for the successors to Miruts Yifter to come through, but in Haile Gebrselassie and Kenenisa Bekele the East African state has produced two of the all-time greats. Gebrselassie burst on to the scene in the 1990s and progressed to become the pre-eminent marathon runner. Bekele took over his crown as king of the men's 10,000m in 2004 and four years later laid claim to being the best ever at half the distance. Bekele is also arguably the finest cross-country performer the world has ever seen.

World records

Between the wars the men's 5000m world record was dominated by Finns, but the first great leaps were taken in the mid-1950s – the mark being reduced by 22 seconds in just three years. In 1987 Said Aouita ran the first sub-13-minute race. Vladimir Kuts, Ron Clarke and Haile Gebrselassie have each broken the record four times. The men's 10,000m has seen a more steady erosion of its record, although the current mark is over five minutes faster than the original standard set in 1912. The first landmark barrier, 30 minutes, was broken by Finn Taisto Maki in 1938, but the achievement of Emil Zatopek is unsurpassed. He lowered the record by more than 40 seconds over the course of five epic runs. No one has broken the men's 10,000m record on more occasions.

↑ *Ethiopia's Sileshi Sihine outsprints compatriot Haile Gebrselassie to take men's 10,000m gold at Athens 2004.*

↓ *Such was his domination of the race, Morocco's Said Aouita finds time to wave to the crowd en route to winning the men's 5000m Final at the 1984 Games in Los Angeles.*

Steeplechase & Decathlon

The men's 3000m Steeplechase is an obstacle race run over seven-and-a-half laps, with each circuit involving four 0.914-metre-high hurdles and a water jump. It has been contested at every Games since 1920. The Decathlon consists of ten track-and-field events and (with the exception of London 1908) has been part of the Olympic programme since 1904.

A Cold War hero

Horace Ashenfelter, the men's 3000m Steeplechase champion at Helsinki 1952, not only won a gold medal on the track but was viewed as a propaganda weapon by the Americans. In the early years of the Cold War, the sight of Ashenfelter (who was an FBI agent at the time) chasing down Soviet star Vladimir Kazantsev was like gold dust for the PR men.

Brasher backed by rivals

London Marathon founder Chris Brasher claimed the spoils in the men's 3000m Steeplechase at Melbourne 1956 thanks to backing from his rivals after he was initially disqualified. The Briton had eased his way through on the inside on the final lap, nudging Norwegian Ernst Larsen in the process. The judges took a dim view, but Larsen and others protested that Brasher would have won anyway and he was reinstated as the race winner.

↑ *Great Britain's Chris Brasher (226) leads the way in the men's 3000m Steeplechase Final at the 1956 Games in Melbourne.*

Steeplechase barriers broken

A world record for the men's 3,000m Steeplechase was not officially recognised by the athletics authorities until the mid-1950s, owing to inaccuracies with course distances and obstacles. Notable barriers broken through were 8:30, by Belgian legend Gaston Roelants in 1963, and 8:00 (the men's 3000m Steeplechase equivalent of the four-minute mile), by Kenya's Moses Kiptanui 32 years later.

Kenyans at a canter

Since 1968 the dominant force in the men's 3000m Steeplechase has been the East African state of Kenya. Other than the boycott years of 1976 and 1980, a Kenyan has won the title at every Olympic Games since Mexico City, often closely pursued by his team-mates. It was 1968 champion Amos Biwott who first showed the world at large the now-familiar leaping style of clearing the barriers, rather than the accepted one foot on, step off technique.

← *Amos Biwott's men's 3000m Steeplechase victory at the 1968 Games sparked a run of nine gold medals (out of 11) for Kenya in the event.*

Thorpe – giant of the Decathlon

The legend of Jim Thorpe dominates the history of the Decathlon. The man with a Native American-Irish family background utterly dominated the competition at the 1912 Games in Stockholm, his superiority so absolute that King Gustav of Sweden allegedly told Thorpe to his face that he was 'the greatest athlete in the world'. The phrase has stuck for the winner of the ten-discipline marathon event ever since, but rarely has it been as appropriate. A year later stories circulated that Thorpe had been paid to play baseball shortly before his Games triumph, contrary to the IOC rules of the time. He was disqualified and died in 1953 with his name still scratched from the record books. In 1982 he was reinstated posthumously as a gold medallist.

First to 8,000 points

Finn Paavo Yrjola was the first decathlete to achieve 8,000 points under the scoring tables used at the time; however, his performance in 1928 would earn him just over 6,500 nowadays. American Bob Mathias and Yang Chuan-Kwang of China notched equivalent historic scores in the 1950s and 1960s after revisions of the points structure but, although Yang accumulated 9,000, it was Roman Sebrle's effort in 2001 (9,026 points) that truly broke new ground.

⬇ *Great Britain's Daley Thompson was an imperious form at Los Angeles 1984 when he took Decathlon gold with a world record-breaking tally (8,798).*

Young master Mathias

Bob Mathias is the youngest gold medal winner in the history of Athletics at the Games. At London 1948 he claimed the Decathlon gold medal at the age of 17, and four years later in Helsinki he followed this up with another first by retaining the title. The only other athlete to have achieved the feat of winning consecutive Decathlon titles at the Games is Britain's Daley Thompson.

↖ *Bob Mathias in action during the discus stage of the Decathlon at the 1948 Games in London.*

Daley sees off teutonic titans to win gold

Arguably the most competitive Decathlon in history took place at Los Angeles 1984. It was billed as 'Daley versus the Germans', and with good cause as defending champion Daley Thompson was given a stern test by Jurgen Hingsen (the man who had taken the world record off him), Guido Kratschmer (another previous record holder), and Siggy Wentz. World-class performances from Thompson in the opening two events (the 100m and the Long Jump) laid down a marker, and Hingsen was unable to catch him; Wentz came third; and Kratschmer fourth. Thompson's tally (8,798) was recalculated as a world record a year later.

Men's 4 x 100m and 4 x 400m Relays

Relays are the climax of the Athletics programme at the Games. The aim is for a team of four athletes to carry a baton over a distance of either 400 metres (4 x 100m) or 1600m (4 x 400m), with the baton passed between competitors at the end of each 100m or 400m stint. Both events have been contested since Stockholm 1912.

Americans forced to wait

Wembley Stadium in 1948 was the scene of the most long-winded Victory Ceremony in history, and probably the first instance of a decision aided by video. The USA men's 4 x 100m team won their event, but were initially disqualified for a faulty exchange. On reviewing film of the race, officials decide to reverse the disqualification. However, the final decision did not become official for three days.

➡ *Avery Brundage (centre), President of the US Olympic Committee, talks to the disqualified US quartet at the 1948 Games. They were later awarded the gold medal.*

Blazing batons in Paris

The men's 4 x 100m Relay competition at the 1924 Games in Paris was about far more than just the final. This meet was the biggest step forward for the discipline. A bewildering set of races saw the old world record shattered four times inside two days. Harold Abrahams inspired Great Britain to clock 42 seconds dead in the first heat, and this was equalled by the Netherlands in the third. In the sixth race USA improved their old best time by a whole second – an astonishing margin for this event – and in the semis the Americans took it down to 41.0. Spare a thought for the Swiss... They equalled the old record in each of their first two races and were disqualified in the final.

⬇ *Harold Abrahams (number 419) was part of Britain's silver medal-winning quartet at Paris 1924.*

Best for the test

Relay running is a team game, but talented individuals are required to make up a quartet good enough to claim gold. In 1924, Great Britain's men's 4 x 400m team was denied the services of the men's 400m champion, Eric Liddell, a religious man, because the final fell on a Sunday. Britain came third. In 1936, the United States curiously chose to leave out both the men's 400m gold and bronze medallists, Archie Williams and Jimmy LuValle, and were beaten by Great Britain. In 1948, Jamaica were favoured to win with newly crowned men's 400m champion Arthur Wint in their ranks. On the third leg Wint set out in pursuit of the Americans, but pulled a muscle and Jamaican hopes were dashed.

Gone in a Hayes...

At the 1964 Olympic Games in Tokyo anchor runner Bob Hayes ran arguably the fastest men's 4 x 100m Relay leg ever seen to come from fifth place to first and claim gold for the United States in a world record-breaking time of 39.0 seconds. Estimates of Hayes' run vary from between 8.5 and 8.9 ... but even for a rolling start that is a lightning pace.

← *Bob Hayes ran a stunning final leg to take the United States quartet to a memorable gold in the men's 4 x 100m Relay at Tokyo 1964.*

Much ado about nothing

The men's 4 x 400m Relay at Antwerp 1920 was one of the most bizarre events held in the Games' history. Only six nations bothered to enter teams. Simple? A straight final? No. The organisers decided to run two semi-finals with three teams each in order to ascertain ... six finalists. The teams went through the motions to 'qualify' in pedestrian times – in what was an utterly pointless exercise.

Right Roman battle

The men's 4 x 100m Relay Final was one of the most dramatic races of the Games at Rome 1960. The USA and Germany quartets had an epic duel, with the lead changing hands four times owing to a combination of the Americans' superior foot speed and the Germans' more efficient baton exchanges. In the end technique won against raw talent as race winners USA were eliminated for an illegal hand-over.

→ *Jamaica's quartet of (from left to right) Asafa Powell, Nesta Carter, Usain Bolt and Michael Frater ended the USA's dominance of the men's 4 x 100m Relay with a world record-breaking victory at Beijing 2008.*

World records

The Usain Bolt-inspired Jamaica team in 2008 are just the second squad from outside the United States to hold the men's 4 x 100m Relay world record since 1968. When Nesta Carter, Michael Frater, Bolt and Asafa Powell scorched around the Bird's Nest Stadium in Beijing in 37.10 seconds, they claimed one of the longest-standing marks in the book; erasing the 37.40 set by the USA's Olympic Games- and World Championship-winning quartets in 1992 and 1993. There have been a few twists and turns of the world record for the men's 4 x 400m Relay, but the one constant since 1960 is that a United States team has held it. In fact, a team from Jamaica in 1952 are the only non-American side ever to hold the mark. It took an amazing 24 years for the altitude-enhanced first sub-three-minute time in the men's 4 x 400m, set in Mexico City in 1968, to be bettered.

Men's Race Walks

Men's Race Walks are road races that are staged over two distances: 20km (since 1956) and 50km (since 1932). Contestants are obliged to keep in contact with the ground at all times and must also keep their supporting leg straight until the body has passed directly over it. Failure to do so results in disqualification.

Korzeniowski the walking legend

Robert Korzeniowski has to be regarded as the greatest race walker of all time. He recovered from the bitter disappointment of disqualification close to the finish of the men's 50km Race Walk in his first Olympic Games in 1992, when battling for the silver medal, to become the only man to win both the men's 20km and 50km titles when he achieved the double at the 2000 Games in Sydney. The Pole claimed an unprecedented fourth Race Walk gold medal when he claimed his third consecutive men's 50km Race Walk gold at the 2004 Games in Athens.

↖ *Poland's Robert Korzeniowski reigned supreme in the men's 50km Race Walk, winning three successive gold medals between Atlanta 1996 and Athens 2004.*

Demise of the 'Hitler Oak'

Harold Whitlock, the men's 50km Race Walk champion at Berlin 1936, returned to Britain after the Games and ensured his name would not be forgotten by planting a tree at his old school in London. Whitlock, along with the other gold medallists, had been presented by Adolf Hitler with an oak sapling about 50 centimetres in height. The tree stood at Hendon School for 70 years and was nicknamed the 'Hitler Oak'. However, in 2007, by then 16 metres tall, it was chopped down after contracting a fungal disease.

↑ *Britain's Harold Whitlock took men's 50km Race Walk gold in 1936.*

The hero no one wanted

At Melbourne 1956 Norman Read won men's 50km Race Walk gold for New Zealand, having fought a battle to be recognised by the 'land of the long white cloud'. Born in Portsmouth, Read emigrated to New Zealand in 1954, but still tried to compete in a British vest at the 1956 Games. The AAA rejected his request, and so did their New Zealand counterparts – until he won the Australian Championship over the Olympic Games course in Melbourne, after which he was hurriedly accepted by the Kiwis

Soviets on top of the world

The first man to break through the one-and-a-half-hour barrier for the men's 20km Race Walk was the Soviet Union's Vladimir Guk in 1957. There has been a steady eroding of the mark since, with Sergey Morozov wiping 33 seconds off the previous record in June 2008 to take it below 1:17. Gennady Agapov was responsible for the greatest landmark performance in walking when the Soviet smashed the world record for the 50km Race Walk by over five minutes in 1965 to become the first man to go under four hours for the endurance test. Denis Nizhegorodov regained the record for Russia in 2008 at the expense of Australian Nathan Deakes.

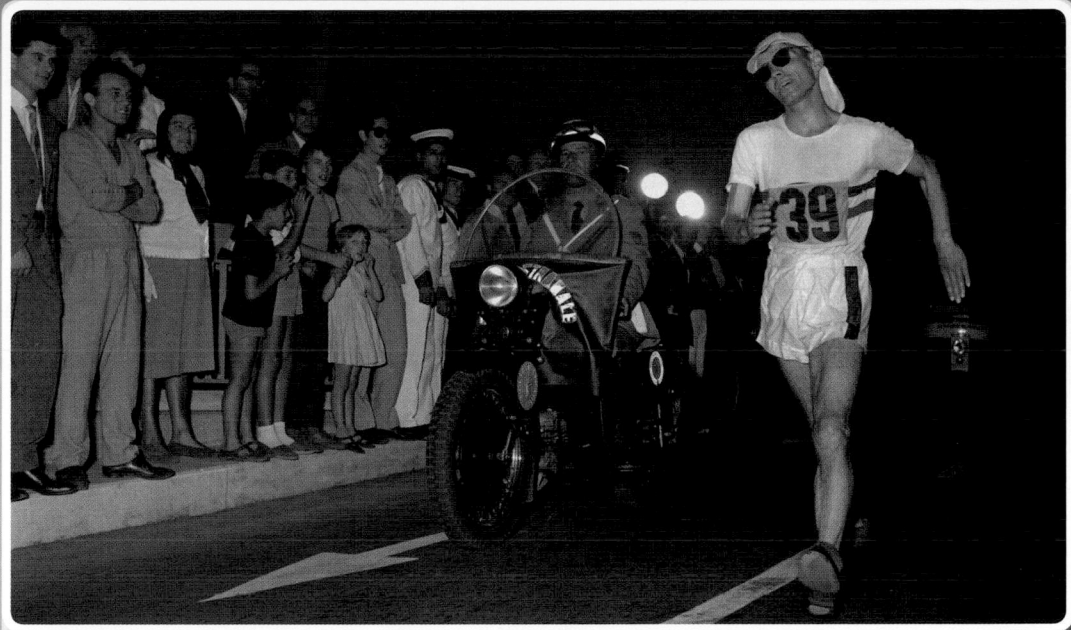

Steam room Don sweats to victory

Don Thompson claimed Britain's only Athletics gold medal at the Rome 1960 Games in the 50km Race Walk after going to extreme lengths to prepare himself for the fierce Roman summer. The diminutive insurance clerk, who was dubbed 'Il Topolino' (The Mouse) by the Italians, trained in temperatures of up to 38° Celsius in the bathroom of his home by using a heater, kettles of boiled water and even a stove to turn it into a steam room.

⬆ *Detailed preparation paid dividends for Great Britain's Don Thompson at the 1960 Games in Rome. He took 50km Race Walk gold in a new Games record time of 4:25.30.*

Walking 'sprint' finish classic

Soviet Union walker Vladimir Golubnichy regained the men's 20km Race Walk title in 1968 after the most dramatic finish in race-walking history at the Games. Golubnichy held off José Pedraza, who was roared on by 80,000 of his compatriots in the stadium in Mexico City, by a mere handful of metres after over 90 minutes of walking, with the Soviet Union's Nikolay Smaga only three seconds behind.

⬅ *Vladimir Golubnichy wins 20km Race Walk gold in 1968.*

Men's Marathon

Named after the legend of Pheidippides, who, according to legend, ran non-stop from the battlefield at Marathon to Athens to announce victory over the Persians, only to drop dead having delivered the news, the Marathon is a road race run over 42.195 kilometres that has been contested at every Games since 1896.

➔ *Czech Emil Zatopek clinched a unique treble at the 1952 Games in Helsinki.*

↑ *Ethiopia's Abebe Bikila, running barefoot, won the men's Marathon at Rome 1960 to become the first black African gold medallist in history.*

Bikila breaks the mould

When runners lined up for the men's Marathon at Rome 1960, no one outside his own country had heard of 28-year-old Ethiopian Abebe Bikila. He had been drafted into his country's team at the last moment only after Wami Biratu broke his ankle playing football. By the end of the race, he had claimed the first gold medal won by a black African in the Games' history – in bare feet, and in a world record time of 2:15.16. Four years later, he contracted appendicitis just six weeks before the Tokyo Games but jogged around the hospital to maintain his fitness. This was his first marathon in shoes, and he won in another record time (2:12.11), over four minutes clear of Britain's silver medallist Basil Heatley. In 1968, Bikila went to Mexico City attempting to clinch a hat-trick of gold medals. He kept a foot injury secret, but the pain was too much and he dropped out just short of half-way. In 1969, Bikila was involved in a car accident in Addis Ababa, which left him paralysed and he died four years later from a brain haemorrhage. His funeral was attended by 75,000 people and Emperor Haile Selassie proclaimed a national day of mourning. A stadium in the city is named in his honour.

Zatopek the Czech locomotive

When Czechoslovakia's Emil Zatopek claimed the men's Marathon title at Helsinki 1952 he set a record that surely will never be equalled: he had won gold in each of the classic distance races (5000m, 10,000m and Marathon) at the same Games. At London 1948, Zatopek had won the men's 10,000m and come second in the men's 5000m, but he went one better in Helsinki to achieve the double. Not content with that, the Czechoslovak followed up by running his first marathon – in the ultimate arena of the Games. World record-holder Jim Peters tried to burn off the track star by setting a scorching pace, but Zatopek stuck tenaciously to the Briton before going clear soon after the 15-kilometre mark and winning easily – and breaking the Games record in the process. Zatopek attempted to defend the men's Marathon title at Melbourne 1956, but a groin injury badly disrupted his training and he trailed in sixth.

Marathon that never was?

Hannes Kolehmainen, the first in a succession of great Finnish distance runners, surged to victory in the men's Marathon at Antwerp 1920 – but was it a 'marathon'? The official report from the Games states that the course was 42.75 kilometres, approximately 400 metres further than the classic distance. However, the Association of Road Racing Statisticians have estimated that the route was only 40km long, which casts doubt on whether Kolehmainen actually smashed the 'world best' by more than three-and-a-half minutes, as is claimed in many record books.

In the footsteps of Pheidippides

The first Marathon of the modern Olympic Games, held in Athens in 1896, saw 17 runners (13 from the Host Country and four from elsewhere) trace the route of the original endurance athlete, Pheidippides, the ancient Greek who in 490 BC, it is claimed, ran from the battle of Marathon to Athens (a distance of roughly 40 kilometres) as a messenger to proclaim the victory of the Athenians over the Persians. Legend has it that he delivered the news and then collapsed and died. In 1896, only nine runners finished the 40km race, which Spyridon Louis won, despite, allegedly, stopping en route to have a glass of wine!

↑ Italy's Dorando Pietri crosses the line to win men's Marathon gold at London 1908 ... or so he thought: he was later disqualified for having been helped to his feet by his manager while in a state of collapse.

Pietri's place in history

It was the London 1908 Olympic Games which provided the event, previously run over 26 miles, with its idiosyncratic extra 385 yards. A lap of the track at the Olympic Stadium was included in addition to the 26-mile course, so that the finish could be in front of the royal box. If it wasn't for this, Italian Dorando Pietri would surely have won; as it is, he gained greater fame as the most gallant of losers. Pietri initially went the wrong way round the track and then proceeded to stagger to the finish line, falling to the ground with exhaustion several times. Officials helped him to his feet each time, but their actions cost Pietri the gold – American Johnny Hayes (who finished second) was later deemed to be the winner after the Italian was disqualified for accepting assistance.

Americans set the world pace

The first Marathon race over the now-accepted distance of 42.195 kilometres (26 miles 385 yards) was staged at London 1908. American gold medallist Johnny Hayes set the standard, but it was only six months before his effort was chalked off by compatriot Robert Fowler. The first sub 2:30 Marathon was recorded by yet another American, Albert Michelsen in 1925, but Halle Gebrselassie's epic in Berlin in 2008 (2:03.59) has lowered the mark by almost 20 per cent since Michelsen's performance to the brink of the magical two hours – a barrier generally considered unbreakable. No athlete has broken the world record as many times as Britain's Jim Peters (four).

← Great Britain's Jim Peters broke the men's Marathon world record four times in the 1950s and, in 1953, became the first athlete in history to cover the distance in under 2 hours 20 minutes.

Men's High Jump and Pole Vault

The men's High Jump and Pole Vault are two of 12 track and field events to have formed a part of the Athletics programme at every Games since Athens 1896. Both disciplines have benefitted enormously from advances in technique and technology over the years.

Osborn's double special

American Harold Osborn is the only athlete to have won an individual event in the Olympic Games as well as the men's Decathlon, having achieved the feat in the 1924 Games in Paris. A doctor of osteopathy, he was a leading high jumper from 1920 to 1936. He mastered the trick of pressing the bar back towards the uprights as he passed over them, a practice that was subsequently not permitted.

⬆ *Harold Osborne (United States) took men's High Jump gold at the 1924 Games in Paris – ahead of compatriot Leroy Browne – with a leap of 1m98.*

Talking the talk, walking the walk

Canadian Duncan McNaughton was a student at the University of Southern California (USC) in Los Angeles, the venue for the 1932 Games. Despite his evident ability, however, the Canadians refused to include him in the team and it was only when he pestered officials on their arrival in California that they finally succumbed. It was just as well. In the final jump-off, McNaughton faced his university team-mate Robert Van Osdel, who like McNaughton had been advised by the famous USC coach Dean Cromwell. In the end, McNaughton cleared the crucial height to take the gold, while Van Osdel secured silver.

Beau Brumel...

Ukrainian Valery Brumel and American John Thomas were friends, despite the political differences betwen their countries. However, both missed out on the men's High Jump title at Rome 1960 when another Soviet jumper, Robert Shavlakadze from Georgia, finished ahead of them. Then began a series of duels between the pair, in which Brumel was usually victorious. So it proved at Tokyo 1964, with Brumel winning on countback. However, a year later Brumel was severely injured in a motorcycle accident, breaking his right leg, and subsequently underwent about 20 operations. He cherished a well-wishing telegram from Thomas, who had hoped that the Ukrainian would jump again. He did, even managing to clear 2.12 metres, but he never competed at an elite level again.

Anything but a flop...

The 'Fosbury Flop' transformed the technique of the high jump. Developed by American Dick Fosbury, it involved clearing the bar backwards and landing head first on the inflated cushion. Disappointed by his results with the conventional straddle, Fosbury gradually evolved the 'Flop', and it was revealed to an international audience for the first time in Mexico City at the 1968 Games, when he cleared 2.24 metres on his final attempt to defeat his compatriot Edward Caruthers and take the gold medal. Subsequently Fosbury suffered a series of injuries, but he still won the US national collegiate title the following year. Within three years most leading jumpers had adopted his style.

⬇ *The revolutionary technique that took Dick Fosbury (United States) to High Jump gold in 1968 was soon adopted by most leading high jumpers.*

Hooker leaps to gold

Born on 16 July 1982 to parents of athletic stock (his mother, Erica, was a 1972 Olympian and a silver medallist in the women's Long Jump at the 1978 Commonwealth Games and his father, Bill, represented Australia at the 1974 Commonwealth Games), pole-vaulter Steve Hooker first came to prominence at the 2006 Commonwealth Games in his hometown Melbourne when he set a new Games record (5.80 metres) to take gold. He went even better at Beijing 2008, leaping 5.96m to break Tim Mack's Olympic Games record (5.95m set in 2004) to become the first Australian male in 40 years to secure an Athletics gold medal since Ralph Doubell won the 800m at Mexico City 1968.

⬆ *Steve Hooker celebrates winning Pole Vault gold at Beijing 2008.*

Poles apart

The Pole Vault competition at Munich 1972 was marred by controversy over the use of a new type of pole, the Cata-pole. The IAAF had first prohibited its use and then lifted the ban, before finally reimposing it. East Germany's Wolfgang Nordwig took gold ahead of American world record holder Robert Seagren. It was the first time a non-US athlete won the event.

Record-breaker Bubka

Sergey Bubka, who initially represented the Soviet Union and later the Ukraine, is the greatest name in pole-vaulting history, winning six world titles and setting 17 ratified world outdoor records, including the current one of 6.14 metres. However, he collected only one gold medal at the Games, at Seoul 1988, and then he had to take three attempts at 5.90m to ensure he got a medal – the gold as it turned out. In 1992 he failed to register a height, and in 1996 he withdrew because of an injury sustained in the warm-up.

➡ *The greatest pole-vaulter in history, the finest moment of Sergey Bubka's career came when he took gold at the 1998 Games in Seoul.*

Heavenly twins

One of the most entrancing sequences in Leni Riefenstahl's film of the 1936 Olympic Games was the Pole Vault Final when Americans Earle Meadows and Bill Sefton, nicknamed 'The Heavenly Twins', from the University of Southern California, faced the Japanese duo Shuhei Nishida and Sueo Oe. Meadows won, and the Japanese declined to jump off against each other, choosing to settle the places by lot, which left Nishida second and Oe third. When they returned to Japan, they had their medals cut in two and soldered together, so they both had medals which were half silver and half bronze.

Pole and a prayer...

The only man to have won two Pole Vault titles at the Games was the American, the Rev. Bob Richards, who took gold medals in Helsinki 1952 and Melbourne 1956. He was also an outstanding decathlete (as many pole vaulters have proved to be, because the individual event requires such a combination of physical abilities). Richards once apologised for an indifferent performance by his standards, which he explained by revealing that he had delivered five sermons in the previous five days in five different cities. Maxwell Stiles of the Los Angeles *Daily News* wrote: 'Not every vicar has the advantage of propelling himself high enough to speak to the angels face to face.'

Men's Long Jump and Triple Jump

The men's Long Jump and Triple Jump are leaping events that rely on strength and speed. The former, the only known jumping event at the ancient Games, consists of a run-up followed by a single leap; the latter, a run-up followed by a 'hop, skip and jump leap'. Both events have been contested at each of the modern Games.

Hubbard's breakthrough

William DeHart Hubbard was the first black athlete to win an individual gold medal at the Games, when he captured the Long Jump title in Paris in 1924. Remarkably, his winning distance of 7.44m was less than that of another American, Robert LeGendre, who had reached 7.76m when coming third in the Pentathlon the previous day.

⬇ *Bob Beamon leaps to the gold medal and immortality with his world record-breaking jump at the 1968 Games in Mexico City.*

Immortal Jesse Owens

Jesse Owens, one of the most celebrated names in international athletics, set a world long jump record of 8.13 metres, a mark which lasted for more than 25 years. It was one of a total of six world records (both metric and imperial) that he set within an hour on his 'day of days', 25 May 1935, at Ann Arbor, Michigan. Owens was clear favourite for the gold medal at the 1936 Games in Berlin the following year. However, the American's first two attempts were no jumps. Then Germany's Luz Long suggested he take off well behind the board to ensure qualification. Owens followed his advice ... and qualified by one centimetre. That afternoon, Long equalled Owens's best effort with a leap of 7.87m in the fifth round. However, Owens responded with two longer jumps, winning the title with 8.06m, and was congratulated by the German. The pair became friends, and although Long was killed in the war, Owens continued to maintain contact with his family until his own death in 1980.

⬆ *Germany's Luz Long (left) and Jesse Owens pose for the camera at the 1936 Games in Berlin. Owens beat the German to take Long Jump gold.*

Beamon the destroyer

The most publicised moment in long jump history occurred on 18 October 1968, when Bob Beamon, an unheralded American, leapt 8.90m to improve the world record by 55 centimetres, a performance that still resonates nearly half a century later. Although he was aided by the fact that those Olympic Games were held at altitude, thus reducing the air resistance, and the fact that the wind advantage was a maximum 2m per second, it was still an extraordinary feat and a record that stood for 23 years. Beamon's first-round effort completely demoralised the rest of the field, with Britain's Lynn Davies, the defending champion, saying: 'You have destroyed this event.' Beamon was so overcome by the experience that he had a cataplectic fit and did not jump again in Mexico, and in subsequent competitions never jumped further than 8.21m. Still, his athletic immortality was assured. His autobiography was entitled *The Man Who Could Fly*.

Brazilian double

Every athlete aims to peak at the Olympic Games, but few have been as expert at this as Adhemar Ferriera da Silva, the Brazilian triple jumper. In Helsinki in 1952 he broke his own world record four times in six efforts to win the title by 24 centimetres with a best of 16.22m. Then four years later, he set a new Games record in retaining his title with 16.35m. Although only a moderately fast sprinter, da Silva had an impressive technique, honed by his German coach Dietrich Gerner.

Victor Viktor...

Of all triple jumpers, none was more consistently impressive in major events than the Soviet Union's Viktor Saneyev. He set a world record of 17.39 metres in winning gold at Mexico City 1968, retained his crown in 1972 with the third best mark of all time (17.35m), and then won his third gold medal in the event by coming through on the fifth round to snatch victory in 1976. Only in Moscow in 1980, with the Soviet crowd jeering the foreign competitors, did Saneyev lose a final at the Games, although he did win the silver medal with his last attempt, falling 11 centimetres short of his compatriot Jaak Uudmae.

Edwards's long wait

Britain's Jonathan Edwards was favourite to win men's Triple Jump gold at Atlanta 1996. The previous year, he had broken the world record three times, finally reaching 18.29 metres to become world champion in Gothenburg. In Atlanta, however, he came up against American Kenny Harrison, who had only been permitted to compete because the International Association of Athletic Federations allowed a distance recorded indoors rather than outdoors (as was the usual practice) to serve as a qualifying mark. Harrison beat Edwards to gold by 21cm with a leap of 18.09m – a lifetime best. Four years later, at Sydney 2000, Edwards, again the favourite, finally fulfilled his dream, finishing well clear of the field. Edwards's successor was Swede Christian Olsson, who had won the world outdoor and indoor titles before taking gold at Athens 2004 with a jump of 17.79m. Olsson's career was later beset by a series of injuries.

↗ Carl Lewis secured Long Jump gold in 1984 with a single leap of 8.54m.

↓ Britain's Jonathan Edwards was the class act of the Triple Jump field at Sydney 2000.

How Lewis emulated Owens

American Carl Lewis always saw himself as the successor to Jesse Owens, and in Los Angeles at the 1984 Games he won the same four gold medals as Owens did in 1936 – the men's 100m, 200m, 4 x 100m Relay and Long Jump. However, Lewis went on to do what Owens was never able to do – win gold in the same event at four successive Olympic Games. The closest he came to defeat in the Long Jump at the Games was in 1992, when fellow countryman Mike Powell – who had upset Lewis in winning the 1991 World Championships and breaking Beamon's world record with a leap of 8.96 metres – came within 3 centimetres of Lewis. However, Lewis held on and was victorious again in Atlanta four years later, after which he scooped some sand from the long jump pit to mark his departure from the sport.

Men's Discus and Hammer Throw

The object of both the Men's Discus Throw (one of the events of the Ancient Pentathlon and contested at every Games since 1896) and Hammer Throw (part of the Olympic programme since 1900) is to throw the object further than the rest of the competitors in the field. The former is a 2-kilogram metal disc; the latter is a 7.257kg ball attached to a 1.215-metre chain.

Champagne goes flat

The 1932 Games were held in Los Angeles at the height of Prohibition, so the French team brought its own supply of wine. During the men's Discus Throw event, Jules Noël used to leave the field after each of his efforts to have some champagne with fellow Frenchmen in the changing rooms. This seemed to inspire Noël and his fourth throw landed beyond the mark of the eventual gold medallist John Anderson. However, the attention of the officials was centred on the men's Pole Vault competition and they missed where the discus had landed. Noël was therefore awarded a further attempt, but he was unable to duplicate the effort and eventually finished fourth.

Oerter the expert

In all of the four throwing events the greatest competitor in the history of the Games is Al Oerter, who won four successive gold medals and on each occasion defeated the world record holder at the time. He said: 'I beat inexperience in 1956, public expectancy in 1960, injury in 1964 and old age in 1968.' Probably his greatest feat was at Tokyo 1964, when he was suffering from disc problems in his back that forced him to wear a surgical collar, and then damaged his ribcage while practising. However, he was determined to compete, was given pain-killing injections and, although trailing, reached the fifth round, at which point he took off the collar, uttering the words: 'These are the Olympics, you die for them.' He then set a new Games record of 61.00 metres. In 1980, aged 43, he even took part in the US Trials – after the boycott of the Games had been announced – and finished fourth. If following the Trials the leading three Americans had gone to the Games, then at least one of them might have buckled under pressure and Oerter would have been on the team yet again.

Sheridan's beat

Like several pioneers in the hammer, Martin Sheridan was born in Ireland but emigrated to the United States and became a New York policeman. He won his first men's Discus title at St Louis 1904, defeating Ralph Rose, the Shot Put champion, after both athletes had extra attempts. He then took men's Discus Throw gold at the 1906 Intercalated Games in Athens, as well as the Shot Put gold and three silver medals in other events, before winning a third men's Discus Throw title in London in 1908. Sadly, he died of pneumonia in 1918.

⬆ *An Irish-born New York policeman, Martin Sheridan won men's Discus Throw gold for the United States at St Louis 1904 and London 1908.*

⬅ *The greatest discus thrower of all time, Al Oerter defied to injury to produce a Games record-breaking throw to claim gold at Rome 1960.*

Schmidt's border break

Wolfgang Schmidt was unusual as an East German athlete because he rebelled against the State's control. He was second in the 1976 Games in Montreal and then, two years later, set a world discus record of 71.16 metres. However, following a fourth-place finish at the 1980 Games at Moscow and his failure to qualify for the East German squad for the 1981 World Championships, in 1982, he made plans to pursue his Athletics career in the West. The State Police discovered these plans and he was sentenced to one-and-a-half year's imprisonment. After his release from jail, he was eventually allowed to cross the 'Iron Curtain' in 1988 and, three years later, after the Berlin Wall had come down, achieved a fourth-place finish for a combined German team in the men's Discus Throw competition at the World Championships in Tokyo.

➜ *Wolfgang Schmidt won silver for East Germany in the men's Discus Throw at the 1976 Games with a throw of 66.22 metres – 1.28m behind gold medal winner Mac Wilkins (US).*

Whale of a games

The early years of hammer throwing at the Olympic Games were dominated by a group of Americans of Irish extraction, who came to be known as the 'Irish Whales'. The first was John Flanagan, winner of three successive gold medals at the Games from 1900 to 1908. Flanagan's technique inspired both his contemporaries and successors, such as Pat 'Chicken' Ryan, born in County Limerick, winner of men's Hammer Throw gold in 1920, and Matt McGrath, born in Tipperary, who picked up a silver medal in 1908, a gold medal in 1912, a fifth-place finish in 1920, when injured, and a second silver in 1924. The trio were pioneers of the event and were well ahead of other international competitors, frequently setting world records.

⬇ *The first of the great Irish-born hammer throwers, John Flanagan won the men's Hammer Throw at the 1900, 1904 and 1908 Games.*

Doctor of Olympism

Patrick O'Callaghan, one of the most remarkable sportsmen Ireland has ever produced, was unlike many predecessors in not emigrating to the United States. Instead, he stayed in Ireland, studying in Dublin, where, in 1926, he qualified as a doctor at the age of 20. He was not allowed to practise immediately because he was too young, so he served in the Royal Air Force Medical Corps for three years. In 1928, he won the gold medal in the Hammer Throw at the Amsterdam Games and four years later he retained his title in Los Angeles, after spending the time between rounds filing down the spikes on his shoes – he had not been informed that the event was being held on a concrete circle rather than one of clay or cinders. He was unable to compete at the 1936 Olympic Games in Berlin because the Irish Association was not affiliated to the world governing body. In his final competition the following year, he broke the world record with a throw of 59.55m, although in reality it was worth much more because the hammer was overweight and the distance was measured from the middle and not the edge of the circle.

Hal the hammer

American hammer thrower Hal Connolly, who competed at four Olympic Games and won gold in 1956, was the centre of international attention through his romance with Olga Fikitova, the Czech women's Discus champion. Their relationship began at Melbourne 1956, when the Cold War was at its most intense. At the end of the Games, the pair had to return to their own countries. The following year, Connolly went to Prague to plead, successfully, to be allowed to marry Fikitova and take her back to the United States. However, their marriage was dissolved in the 1970s.

Men's Shot Put and Javelin Throw

Men's Shot Put competitions have been held at the Olympic Games since their inception in 1896 and use a 7.26-kilogram shot. Men's Javelin Throw events (which have been staged at every Games since 1908) are used with spears measuring 2.6–2.7 metres in length and weighing 800 grams.

One-way traffic

At 1.98 metres in height and weighing more than 120 kilograms, American Ralph Rose was physically a forerunner of modern competitors, although he had a rudimentary technique and lacked the explosive speed of modern-day competitors. He took the men's Shot Put title in front of his home crowd at the 1904 Games in St Louis – with a world record of 14.81 metres – and retained his title in London four years later, when he was handed the honour of carrying the US flag at the Opening Ceremony. In the London final he defeated Irishman Denis Horgan, who in 1907 had nearly been killed in a brawl while working as a New York policeman. At Stockholm 1912, Rose lost his title to another New York policeman, Patrick McDonald, who was a point duty traffic officer in Times Square.

➔ *Bill Nieder headed an American one-two-three in the men's Shot Put Final at Rome 1960 with a new Games record throw of 19.68 metres – compatriots Parry O'Brien and Dallas Long finished second and third respectively.*

⬇ *East Germany's Ulf Timmermann won the men's Shot Put Final at Seoul 1988 with his final throw of the competition – a new Games record mark of 22.47 metres (a mere 8 centimetres ahead of United States' Randy Barnes).*

United States revolutionary

American Parry O'Brien always remembered the words of his coach Jesse Mortensen: 'The orthodox is another word for the obsolete.' Whereas previously the accepted shot put technique was a sideways glide across the circle, O'Brien's method was to crouch, facing backwards to begin the movement, allowing him to push the weight for longer and propel the shot farther. He took gold at the 1952 and 1956 Games and won 116 successive competitions during that period. His world record of 19.33 metres in 1960 was finally overhauled by compatriot Bill Nieder, who went on to beat O'Brien into second place at the 1960 Games, and at Tokyo 1964, his fourth successive Games, O'Brien could only finish fourth. However, his revolutionary technique was adopted by most shot-putters, until the arrival of the spiral style, in which athletes turn as they cross the circle, before releasing the weight.

Timmermann's title

East German shot putter Ulf Timmermann was a supreme exponent of the glide technique. He broke the world record for the first time in 1985 (with a throw of 22.62 metres) and, in the build-up to Seoul 1988, became the first shot putter in history to break the 23m barrier (with a throw of 23.06m). And as the men's Shot Put final in Seoul progressed, it soon became clear that Timmermann was the man to beat: he hit the front of the 12-man field as early as the third round (with a throw of 22.16m), extended his lead in the fourth round (21.09m) and, after increasing it yet again in the fifth round (with a Olympic record-breaking throw of 22.29m) seemed set for gold. But the USA's Randy Barnes had other ideas, producing a throw of 22.39m to take the lead. It was now or never for the East German ... and he duly lived up to the sense of occasion, producing a throw of 22.47m to take gold.

Towering success

The Finns have always had a profound affection for the Javelin Throw, and their most revered figure was the bespectacled Matti Jarvinen, who won gold at the 1932 Games in Los Angeles with a throw of 72.71 metres, a distance that his countrymen honoured by making it the height of the tower in the Olympic Stadium when the Games were staged in Helsinki in 1952. He set ten world records during his career, with a best of 77.23m.

← *Finland has a rich history in men's Javelin Throw at the Games, producing a total of six gold medallists in the event, but none was revered more than Matti Jarvinen, champion at the 1932 Games in Los Angeles.*

Friendly rivals

When Janis Lusis was a small boy, he saw his father being shot by Nazi soldiers as the German army overran Latvia. At the 1972 Olympic Games in Munich, he was the defending champion and world record holder with a distance of 90.48 metres. In the final, Germany's Klaus Wolfermann took the lead with a throw of 90.48m, only for Lusis to launch another enormous throw on his last attempt. It fell a tantalising 2 centimetres short and Wolfermann was crowned the champion. However, Lusis and the German showed the redemptive power of sport by becoming close friends.

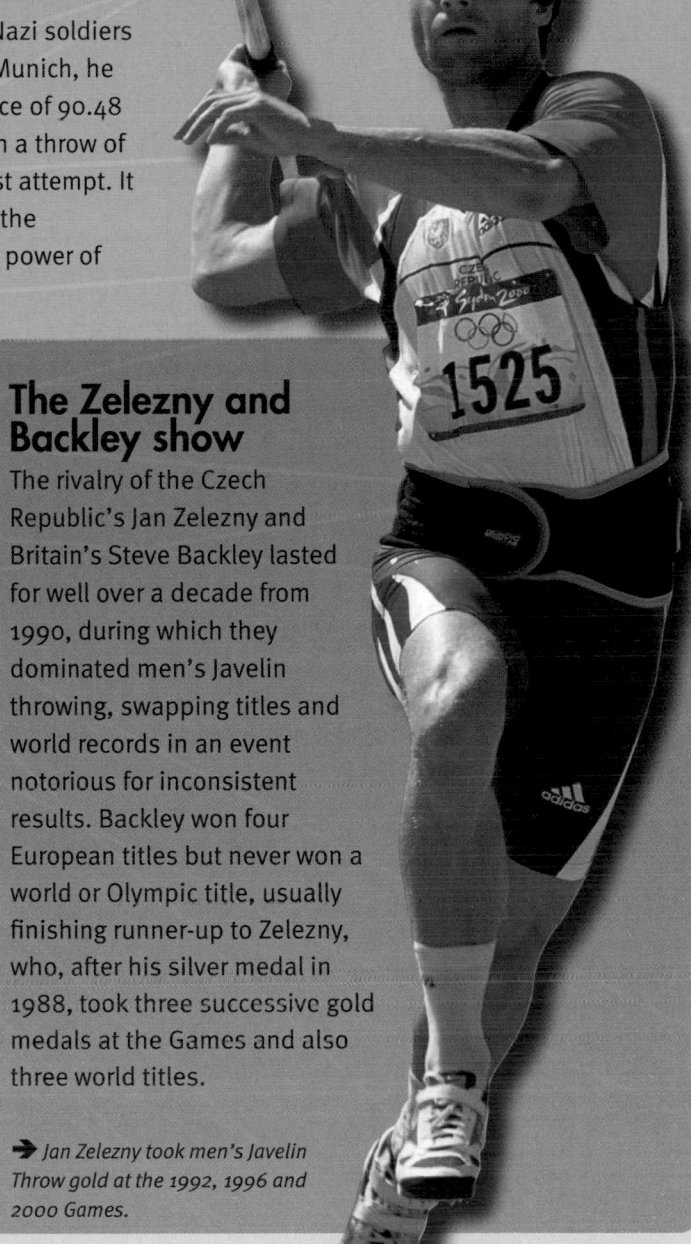

Loan winner

Norwegian Egil Danielsen took the men's Javelin Throw title at Melbourne 1956 with a world record throw thanks to help from two of his rivals. Poland's Janusz Sidlo, the world record holder and twice European champion, lent Danielsen his steel javelin – other competitors, including the Norwegian, had been using wooden spears. Frenchman Michel Macquet also gave him a cup of coffee. Danielsen never usually drank coffee and the stimulating effect gave him a sudden lift. He was only in sixth place with a best of 72.60 metres, but then produced the throw of his lifetime, 85.71m, to take the title, and the generous Sidlo immediately congratulated him.

Family stuff

Hungarians Imre and Miklos Nemeth occupy a unique position in the pantheon of Athletics at the Olympic Games. They are the only father and son both to have won gold medals. Imre took the men's Hammer Throw title in 1948, and Niklos the men's Javelin Throw crown in 1976. Niklos set a world record in taking the title in Montreal after years of failing to produce his best in major competitions.

The Zelezny and Backley show

The rivalry of the Czech Republic's Jan Zelezny and Britain's Steve Backley lasted for well over a decade from 1990, during which they dominated men's Javelin throwing, swapping titles and world records in an event notorious for inconsistent results. Backley won four European titles but never won a world or Olympic title, usually finishing runner-up to Zelezny, who, after his silver medal in 1988, took three successive gold medals at the Games and also three world titles.

→ *Jan Zelezny took men's Javelin Throw gold at the 1992, 1996 and 2000 Games.*

Women's 100m

As is the case in the men's competition, the women's 100m is considered the blue riband event of the women's Athletics programme. It was one of only five Athletics events that women contested at the 1928 Games in Amsterdam, the first time women's events were included at the Games.

← *Jamaica's Shelly-Ann Fraser took women's 100m gold at Beijing 2008.*

Queen Merlene

Jamaican-born sprinter Merlene Ottey has earned the title 'Queen of the Track' for a remarkable career which, by the age of 50, had included competition at seven different Olympic Games. Inspired to take up running by a radio commentary on the Montreal 1976 Games, she won a bronze medal in the women's 100m four years later in Moscow. Further medals in the women's blue riband event would elude Ottey for 16 years before she took silver at the Atlanta 1996 Games and a second bronze medal followed at Sydney in 2000, when she competed at the age of 40. In 2008, aged 48, having become a Slovenian national in order to qualify again, Ottey failed by just 0.28 seconds to reach her eighth Olympic Games.

↑ *Merlene Ottey picked up her third Olympic Games medal in the women's 100m (bronze) at Sydney 2000 at the tender age of 40.*

Zero to heroes

Jamaica's rise to the top of sprinting at the Olympic Games was nothing short of meteoric. Prior to Beijing 2008, the nation had never won a gold medal. However, one day on from the sensational track exploits of compatriot Usain Bolt, Shelly-Ann Fraser led home a clean sweep of the medals for the Reggae Nation in the women's 100m Final. Fraser, who clocked a personal best time of 10.78 seconds, was followed home by team-mates Sherone Simpson and Kerron Stewart, who both finished in a time of 10.98 and were awarded silver medals – completing the first sweep of medals in the women's 100m by any nation at any Olympic Games or World Championships.

Golden debut

Elizabeth ('Betty') Robinson of the United States was the inaugural winner of the women's 100m at the 1928 Games in Amsterdam. She proved that inexperience was no barrier to success, claiming the gold medal in only her fourth competition, at the tender age of 16. In just her second race she had equalled the world record and she emulated that feat in the final in Amsterdam. Three years later she came 'back from the dead' following a plane crash. A man found her unconscious in the wreckage and wrongly thought she was dead. He put her in his car boot and drove her to an undertaker's, where she was diagnosed as very much alive, albeit in a coma that would last for seven months. She was unable to walk properly for over two years but, remarkably, would perform again at the Games – in the women's 4 x 100m Relay at Berlin 1936.

Fabulous Flo-Jo

The women's 100m world record has stood for more than 20 years now. The time of 10.49 seconds was set by the late Florence Griffith-Joyner, during the US Olympic trials in July 1988. In the mid-1980s she became popularly known as Flo-Jo and was instantly recognisable for her extremely long and colourful finger nails. The record-breaking performance aroused controversy as witnesses questioned whether it was wind-assisted. What was never in doubt was Flo-Jo's speed, and she duly won the gold medal at Seoul 1988 in a time of 10.54. The inspirational effect of the Games competition may be judged by the fact that her best time, before that 1988 season, had been 10.96. Griffith-Joyner retired after her Seoul triumphs – she won two golds and a silver – and died 10 years later at the tragically young age of 38.

➡ *Florence Griffith-Joyner was the class act of the women's 100m Final field at Seoul 1988: her margin of victory was 0.29 seconds.*

Clock watching

Fully automatic timing (to a hundredth of a second) only became the IAAF's accepted method in January 1977. At the Olympic Games, the gold medal-winning performances by American Wyomia Tyus in 1968 and East German Renate Stecher in 1972, both in 11.07 seconds, were the fastest recorded fully electronic 100m races to that time and were declared world records.

Ashford's breakthrough

The 11-second barrier remained impenetrable in women's 100m competition at the Olympic Games until Evelyn Ashford finally broke the hoodoo in a gold medal-winning time of 10.97 in Los Angeles in 1984. In all, Ashford broke the barrier on no fewer than 30 occasions in the course of a glittering career.

Best of times...

At the 1976 Games the women's 100m event felt like a tale of two cities: the Host City Montreal and the home city of the main protagonists – Dortmund in West Germany. The eyes of the world were already firmly fixed on Dortmund's Ingeborg Helten, who set a world record of 11.04 seconds just before the Games. In Montreal, however, her effort petered out as her compatriot Annegret Richter, also from Dortmund, set a world record of 11.01 in the semi-finals before beating defending champion and former world record holder Renate Stecher of East Germany in the final. Richter's performance remains the most recent case of the world women's 100m record being broken during the Games.

Flying Dutchwoman

The 1948 Olympic Games in London heralded the arrival of an unlikely superstar who would be dubbed 'The Flying Housewife'. Dutch athlete Francina Blankers-Koen, better known as Fanny, was the winner of four gold medals at those Games – and a mother of two at a time when women's competition was largely disregarded. She was the first woman to win four gold medals at the Games, which remains a track and field record to date. In 1999, in recognition of her performance, she was voted 'Female Athlete of the Century' by the International Association of Athletics Federations (IAAF).

⬅ *Evelyn Ashford (centre) took women's 100m gold after recording a new Games record time of 10.97 seconds at Los Angeles 1984.*

Women's 200m and 400m

Part of the Games programme since 1948 and 1964 respectively, the women's 200m and 400m have spawned some legendary champions, including Fanny Blankers-Koen and Florence Griffith-Joyner, but only one woman in history has claimed the 200m-400m double: France's Marie-José Pérec at the 1996 Games in Atlanta.

Two by two

The event has been staged on 16 occasions, but only two women have successfully retained their women's 200m crowns at the Games. The first to do so was East German sprinter Bärbel Wöckel (née Eckert), who struck gold at the 1976 Games in Montreal and again four years later in Moscow. Her achievement was emulated in 2008 by Jamaican athlete Veronica Campbell-Brown, who had previously won the event at the 2004 Games in Athens.

⬆ *Veronica Campbell-Brown (right) held off the challenge of Allyson Felix to retain her women's 200m crown at the 2008 Games in Beijing.*

Marjorie's the governor

Marjorie Jackson-Nelson, AC, CVO, MBE, sits high in the annals of Australian track and field achievement at the Olympic Games. She finished her sporting career with an impressive haul of nine Olympic Games and Commonwealth Games gold medals, having broken ten world records and held every Australian State and National title she contested for a four-year period. Her zenith came at the 1952 Games in Helsinki, when she completed the women's 100m-200m double, to become her nation's first Athletics gold medallist since 1896. At the Opening Ceremony of the 2000 Games in Sydney, Jackson-Nelson was one of eight flag-bearers given the honour of carrying the Olympic Flag. She later became Governor of South Australia, a position she held until 31 July 2007.

⬆ *Australia's Marjorie Jackson surged to women's 200m gold at the 1952 Games in Helsinki some 0.5 seconds ahead of her nearest competitor.*

From podium to studio

Valerie Brisco-Hooks was the leading women's track and field athlete at Los Angeles 1984. Not content with capturing gold in the women's 200m, she accomplished what no other man or woman had ever done by completing a double in the 400m at the same Games, before winning a third gold medal as part of the United States' winning 4 x 400m Relay team. Two years later she achieved another kind of stardom, appearing on television with Bill Cosby as a guest in an episode of *The Cosby Show*, entitled 'Off to the Races'.

Anything he can do

Michael Johnson, who dominated the men's 200m and 400m at Olympic Games in the 1990s, had a female equivalent in the French athlete Marie-José Pérec. Her breakthrough title at the Games came at Barcelona 1992, when she captured the women's 400m. Four years later in Atlanta, Pérec doubled up by winning the women's 200m as well as retaining her women's 400m crown in a new Games record time of 48.25 seconds. Her Olympic Games journey ended on a sour note when she quit ahead of Sydney 2000, allegedly the victim of harassment from the Australian press.

→ *After taking women's 400m gold at Barcelona 1992, Marie-José Pérec went one better at Atlanta 1996 when she claimed the 200m-400m double.*

Flo-Jo the fastest ever

At Seoul 1988 the women's track and field events were dominated by Florence Griffith-Joyner, known universally as Flo-Jo. She had already won the women's 100m gold medal and ruled supreme in the 200m, progressing to the final with faster qualifying times in each round. Flo-Jo first broke the world record (which had stood for nine years) in the quarter-finals before setting a new standard of 21.56 seconds in her semi-final heat. In the final she was imperious, creating a new mark of 21.34 that has never been challenged. In the space of one day Flo-Jo bettered her world best by 0.4 seconds, earning the accolade 'the fastest woman that ever lived'.

Against all odds

Following the disqualification of Marion Jones from the women's 200m at Sydney 2000, Sri Lanka's Susanthika Jayasinghe was promoted to the silver medal position. It was one of her country's finest moments at the Olympic Games – but it almost never happened. Jayasinghe, who was raised in poverty in a tiny village 60 kilometres from Colombo, had been unable to afford running spikes and did not have access to either proper equipment or coaches. Yet, in the face of political pressure, she pursued her belief, going heavily into debt to fund her bid to compete at the Games. Having retired from the sport to have a baby boy, Jayasinghe announced her impending return to competition in November 2010.

The face of the games

In September 2000, the world focused on the women's 400m Final in Sydney to watch Cathy Freeman, an Australian Aborigine, who had become the face of the Games, after lighting the Olympic Flame at the Opening Ceremony. Freeman duly won gold, becoming the first Australian Aboriginal track and field Olympic champion. On her victory lap she carried both the Aboriginal and Australian flags, and throughout the competition she had the words 'Cos I'm Free' tattooed mid-way between her shoulder and elbow. Freeman later represented Oceania, carrying the Olympic Flag at the Opening Ceremony of the next Winter Games, in Salt Lake City, alongside world dignitaries including Archbishop Desmond Tutu, John Glenn, Lech Walesa and Steven Spielberg.

← *Cathy Freeman wore an all-in-one body suit to reduce air resistance on her way to 400m gold at Sydney 2000.*

Golden Betty

Australia's original 'Golden Girl', Elizabeth 'Betty' Cuthbert won four gold medals at the Games, the highest number by any Australian track and field athlete. In a glittering career the golden-haired sprinter set individual world records at 60m, 100yd, 200m, 220yd and 440yd, and at Melbourne 1956 she won gold in the women's 100m and 200m, as well as contributing to her team's 4 x 100m Relay victory. Injury prevented her from performing at her best in 1960, but at Tokyo 1964 she claimed her fourth title when she took the inaugural women's 400m title.

Women's 100m and 400m Hurdles

Women's Hurdles events are contested over two distances – 100m (10m shorter than the men's equivalent) and 400m – and have been part of the Games programme since 1972 and 1984 respectively. Remarkably, no woman in history, in either event, has been able to defend her crown.

Changing times

The East German athlete Annelie Ehrhardt competed at a time of transition for the women's sprint Hurdles contest. The event had been a part of the Games programme since Los Angeles 1932, but had been raced over 80 metres until Ehrhardt's inaugural success over 100m at the 1972 Games. Her new electronic world record performance of 12.59 seconds in the final also came during the transition between hand and electronic timing, and a year later she set the last recognised hand-timed world record for the 100m hurdles of 12.3 in the East German national championships at Dresden.

Records, records

The women's world 100m Hurdles record of 12.21 seconds was set during what proved a glorious 1988 for Bulgarian sprinter Yordanka Donkova. She had come to prominence during 1986, when she broke four world records and became European champion, but in 1988 she set the world record just one month before the 1988 Games in Seoul. Although she failed to better that time, she set a new Games record time of 12.38 in winning the gold medal.

Devers disaster

The Athletics track at Barcelona 1992 was the setting for one of the biggest shocks in the history of track and field at the Olympic Games. The final of the women's 100m Hurdles was expected to be the defining moment in American superstar Gail Devers' career. However, she had not reckoned on the surprise element in Greek competitor Paraskevi ('Voula') Patoulidou, the first woman to represent her nation in a track final at the Games. Devers, the red-hot favourite for gold, tripped on the last hurdle, allowing Patoulidou to join her on the finishing line in a time of 12.64 seconds. Voula immediately celebrated her silver-medal achievement – and then learned that she had in fact won gold, making her the first Greek woman in history to do so. Her victory inspired a nation, and subsequent Greek athletes have referred to Patoulidou's triumph as the catalyst for their ambitions.

⬆ *Gail Devers crashes to the track after hitting the final hurdle in the women's 100m Hurdles Final at the 1992 Games in Barcelona.*

⬋ *Joanna Hayes edged to women's 100m Hurdles gold by 0.08 seconds (ahead of the Ukraine's Olena Krasovska) at the 2004 Games in Athens.*

Olympic ideal in action

While an Olympic Games gold medal is regarded by many as a form of heroism, Athens 2004 women's 100m Hurdles champion Joanna Hayes has targeted a different level of success at grass-roots level. Hayes is the daughter of Los Angeles homeless advocate Ted Hayes but was primarily raised by her mother. Following her crowning moment on the track, during which she set a new Games record time of 12.38 seconds, she has established the Joanna Hayes Foundation, whose aim is: 'To open the eyes and broaden the horizons of children living in the most challenging situations and help them see new options and prepare for new futures.'

Golden track into IOC

Nawal El Moutawakel, the first-ever women's 400m Hurdles champion at the Games at Los Angeles 1984, was also the first African-born female Muslim to win a gold medal. Her victory was seen as a breakthrough for Muslim and Arabic woman athletes, and the King of Morocco telephoned El Moutawakel afterwards to offer his congratulations – he also declared that all girls born on the day of her victory were to be named in her honour. In 1995 she became a council member for the IAAF and three years later was appointed to the International Olympic Committee, attaining the position of President of Evaluation Commissions for the selection process for the Host City in 2012 and 2016. In 2007, El Moutawakel was also named the Minister of Sports in Morocco.

➜ *Nawal El Moutawakel's comfortable victory in the women's 400m Hurdles Final at Los Angeles 1984 – she won by 0.59 seconds – was a first for an African-born female Muslim.*

Long wait

Although for men's 400m Hurdles has been contested at every Games since Paris 1900, women did not compete in this discipline until the 1984 Games in Los Angeles. The first documented women's 400m hurdles race took place in 1971, and the IAAF introduced the event officially as a discipline in 1974, but a further ten years passed before Los Angeles witnessed the crowning of Moroccan athlete Nawal El Moutawakel, as the first-ever winner of the women's 400m Hurdles in Olympic Games history.

Newcomers' glory

Jamaica's domination of sprinting events at the Games is a relatively recent track and field phenomenon. Only at Atlanta 1996 did Deon Hemmings become the first Jamaican woman to win a gold medal when she won the women's 400m Hurdles. Her Games record time of 52.82 seconds lasted eight years. No champion has successfully defended her title in this event at the Games, but Hemmings came closest when she won the silver medal behind Russian Irina Privalova at Sydney in 2000.

Missing medal

The 2005 women's 400m hurdles world champion, Russia's Yuliya Pechonkina, appeared to have the world at her feet. Her world record time of 52.34 seconds, set in 2003, remains the fastest time in history. Yet her Olympic Games career was limited to Athens, in 2004, where she finished last in the final.

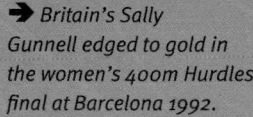

➜ *Britain's Sally Gunnell edged to gold in the women's 400m Hurdles final at Barcelona 1992.*

Super Sally

Several athletes have made the transition from the 100m Hurdles to 400m or vice versa, but Britain's Sally Gunnell stands as the most successful convert, having started her career as a long jumper and pentathlete. After winning gold in the Commonwealth Games 100m Hurdles in 1986, she decided to move up in distance and remains the only woman to have held the European, World, Commonwealth and Olympic 400m Hurdles titles at the same time. Her gold medal at the Games was achieved at Barcelona 1992, where she narrowly edged out her great rival American Sandra Farmer-Patrick. The following year she beat Farmer-Patrick again, this time in a world record time of 52.74 seconds, to become world champion.

Women's 800m and 1500m

Women's 800m was first contested at Amsterdam 1928 and, after a 32-year break, at every Games since Rome 1960; the women's 1500m has been staged since 1972. Three women – Tatyana Kazankina (1976), Svetlana Masterkova (1996) and Kelly Holmes (2004) – have achieved the 800m-1500m double.

Long-distance champion

For many years it seemed Karoline ('Lina') Radke-Batschauer would stand alone as the only ever winner of the women's 800m at the Olympic Games. With assistance from her husband and coach Georg Radke, she trained hard for the 1928 Games in Amsterdam and set a world record of 2:16.8 en route to the final. She went on to win the gold medal, but the race was overshadowed by concerns for several of her competitors, who finished it completely exhausted, and the IOC banished the event from its programme, fearing that women did not have the constitution to compete over such a distance. The women's 800m did not return to the programme until the 1960 Games in Rome.

↗ *Mozambique's Maria Mutola, women's 800m champion at Sydney 2000, made the last of her six appearances at the Beijing 2008.*

Magic Mutola

Over the last two decades no women's 800m event was complete without Maria Mutola. Mozambique's superstar athlete competed in her sixth Olympic Games in Beijng, making her only the fourth athlete to accomplish this feat. After previous near misses, the 'Maputo Express' had her moment of glory when she won gold in Sydney in 2000. She was appointed an honorary United Nations youth ambassador in 2003, and now her Lurdes Mutola Foundation aims to bring more young Mozambicans to sport and help them achieve their sporting and educational potential.

Kelly Holmes at the double

Kelly Holmes came to full-time athletics at the late age of 22. Having been an outstanding junior athlete, she joined the British Army where she continued to compete, even running against the men over 800 metres. Sebastian Coe's exploits at the Games had inspired the young Holmes, and in 1992, after watching the Games in Barcelona, she returned to the sport full-time. Her career was continually beset by injuries, but she arrived at Athens in 2004 injury free and duly won gold in both the women's 800m and 1500m, becoming Britain's first double gold medallist at the same Games since 1920. A year later she became a Dame Commander of the Order of the British Empire.

← *Double delight for Kelly Holmes as she completes the women's 800m-1500m double at Athens 2004.*

Soviet superstar

Tatyana Kazankina competed for the old Soviet Union over middle distances, setting seven world records and winning three Olympic Games gold medals along the way. Having become the first woman to break the four-minute barrier over 1500m a month before the 1976 Games, she struck gold in both the women's 800m and 1500m (to become the first woman in history to win the double), breaking the world record in the former with a new mark of 1:54.94. Four years later she retained her women's 1500m title in Moscow and shattered that event's world record in a time of 3:52.47, which remained unbeaten for 13 years. In 1976, Kazankina was also awarded the Order of the Red Banner of Labour and the title Honoured Master of Sports of the USSR.

Packer's pride

Britain's middle-distance women – unlike the men with their pedigree in the 800m at the Games – had failed to make an impression before 1964. Ann Packer was the unlikely heroine who would change things. Packer began her career as a sprinter and at Tokyo 1964 had high hopes of winning gold – in the women's 400m. In the event she took the silver medal behind Australian Betty Cuthbert, but sought to improve on it in the women's 800m, an event she had only ever raced on five occasions. She qualified for the final as the slowest of the eight competitors, but used her old sprinting style in the final to win gold in a world record time of 2:02.8 – before retiring from the sport.

Golden girl

The Soviet Union's Nadezhda Fyodorovna Olizarenko became a national heroine when she won gold in the 1980 Olympic Games in Moscow. The Soviet athlete won the women's 800m ahead of compatriots Olga Mineyeva and Tatyana Providokhina and broke the world record that same year with a time of 1:53.43. That time has only once been bettered, by Jarmila Kratochvílová, in a time of 1:53.28 in 1983.

↑ *Tatyana Kazankina (left) wins women's 800m gold at the 1976 Games in Montreal; she later won the 1500m to become the first woman in history to complete the double.*

➜ *Kenya's Pamela Jelimo was the class act of the women's 800m Final at Beijing 2008: her winning margin over compatriot Janeth Jepkosgei was a crushing 1.2 seconds.*

Brilliant Bragina

The women's 1500m is a relatively new event at the Olympic Games. Although the men have competed over this distance since 1896, women have only had the opportunity since the 1972 Games in Munich, when Soviet athlete Lyudmila Bragina dominated the event, shattering the world record three times en route to taking the inaugural gold medal.

Kenya catch-up

The 2008 Games in Beijing were a watershed for Kenya's women track and field athletes. While the men had long been admired as leading middle-distance competitors, it was only in 2008 that the women began to match that success. Pamela Jelimo became the first Kenyan woman to win a gold medal at the Games when she won the women's 800m aged 18, having partly funded her venture by working as a police constable. A few days later her compatriot Nancy Langat won the women's 1500m, making it a double celebration for Kenya.

Women's 5000m and 10,000m

Women's long-distance track events are relatively new to the Games programme: it wasn't until 1996 that a women's 5000m event was introduced and the women's 10,000m did not make its debut until the 1988 Games in Seoul. Only one woman, Ethiopia's Tirunesh Dibaba at the Beijing Games in 2008, has achieved the accolade of claiming the 5000m-10,000m double.

Wang Junxia's Chinese revolution

China's Wang Junxia dominated the world of women's long-distance running for a short but memorable period in the mid-1990s. Having won the women's 10,000m world junior championship in 1992, she claimed the world senior title for the 25-lap distance a year later in Stuttgart. In 1993, at the Chinese National Games, Junxia set her iconic women's 10,000m world record of 29:31.78 which was also the first ever sub-30-minute performance by a woman. Although she never improved on her peak form of 1993, Junxia went on to win the inaugural women's 5000m gold medal at the 1996 Games in Atlanta (ahead of Kenya's Pauline Konga) and also claimed the silver medal in the women's 10,000m event (behind Portugal's Fernanda Ribiero).

➔ *China's Wang Junxia surged to a comfortable victory in the first-ever women's 5000m Final at the 1996 Games in Atlanta.*

Hand in hand

Following her dramatic victory in the women's 10,000m Final at Barcelona 1992, Ethiopia's Derartu Tulu waited at the finish line for her opponent Elana Meyer, a white South African, and the two set off hand in hand for a victory lap that came to symbolise new hope for Africa. At Sydney 2000, having regained her form of eight years earlier, Tulu again won gold in the women's 10,000m event, becoming the first woman to win two gold medals in long-distance races at the Games and the only woman to win 10,000m gold twice.

⬆ *Ethiopia's Derartu Tulu (left) and South Africa's Elana Meyer (right) celebrate after the women's 10,000m Final at the 1992 Games in Barcelona.*

Barefoot and controversial

Zola Budd – born, brought up and awarded star status in South Africa – attracted headlines of controversy in 1984 when she was then awarded British citizenship on the strength of a British grandfather. Her subsequent decision to run for Britain at Los Angeles 1984 caused uproar among those who deemed the move as a convenient way to bypass the ban that had been imposed on South African athletes as a result of apartheid. The controversy pursued her all the way into the Games, in which, in the women's 3000m, she collided with the American favourite Mary Decker, who fell and failed to finish the race. The following year, Budd smashed the women's 5000m world record, running the race barefoot in 14:48.07 – 10 seconds faster than the previous record. In fact, the race was really her second women's 5000m world record, but the first could not be recognised because it was set during a race in South Africa.

Family business

For the Dibaba family of Ethiopia, long-distance running is a family trade. Tirunesh Dibaba won the women's 10,000m in a new Games record (29:54.66) in Beijing in 2008; her elder sister Ejegayehu won silver in the women's 10,000m at Athens 2004; her younger sister Genzebe was the 2010 world junior women's 5000m champion, and Tirunesh is also a cousin of the Games' two-time women's 10,000m gold medallist Derartu Tulu. Nicknamed the 'Baby-Faced Destroyer', Tirunesh also won the women's 5000m in Beijing, becoming the first, and to date only, female runner in history to win the 5000m-10,000m double. Adding more Olympic Games medals to the family mantelpiece, Tirunesh Dibaba is married to double Olympic Games men's 10,000m silver medallist Sileshi Sihine.

➜ *At the 2008 Games in Beijing, Ethiopia's Tirunesh Dibaba became the first woman in history to complete the 5000m-10,000m double.*

Ethiopian dominance

The Oromo ethnic group found in Ethiopia must be one of the most athletically blessed on earth. The list of long-distance running champions it has produced includes Haile Gebrselassie, Abebe Bikila, and Sileshi Sihine, as well as the Dibaba sisters and Derartu Tulu.

Step too far for 'Queen' Kristiansen

Ingrid Kristiansen boasts a unique achievement in, simultaneously, having held world records at women's 5000m, 10,000m, 15 kilometres, half marathon and marathon. The Norwegian's fabulous career also brought an IAAF World Championship women's 10,000m victory plus multiple triumphs in the marathons of London (four), Stockholm (three), Boston and Houston (two each) plus Chicago and New York City. But the Olympic Games were a step too far. She was fourth in the women's Marathon at the 1984 Games in Los Angeles, was halted in the women's 10,000m in Seoul in 1988 by a foot injury and had retired by the time the women's 5000m was added to the Games schedule in 1996.

Szabo finds her métier

After flirting with gymnastics and swimming in her younger years, Romania's Gabriela Szabo switched to track and field events when it became apparent that she would not be good enough to make it professionally in the other disciplines. In 1996, after failing to qualify for the women's 5000m Final, Szabo won silver in the women's 1500m competition. Then, four years later at Sydney 2000, Szabo ran a world record of 14:40.79 in the women's 5000m Final to win the gold medal.

← *Romania's Gabriela Szabo raced to women's 5000m gold in a new Games record time of 14:40.79 at the 2000 Games in Sydney. She also took bronze in the women's 1500m Final.*

Women's Heptathlon and Steeplechase

The women's Heptathlon consists of seven events – 100m Hurdles, High Jump, Shot Put, 200m, Long Jump, Javelin Throw and 800m – and has been contested at every Games since Los Angeles 1984. The women's 3,000m Steeplechase was staged for the first time at Beijing 2008.

Heptathlon breakthrough

The image of women athletes in the Olympic Movement has undergone a startling evolution. Whereas in the early days they were considered to be delicate creatures, who needed to be restricted from competing in endurance events, they are now regarded as hardened athletes. The former impression prevailed until 1964, when the women's Pentathlon was first admitted to the programme in Tokyo. The five-event formula was replaced by the current Heptathlon in 1984, comprising seven events over two days: on the first day the 100m hurdles, the high jump, the shot put and the 200m run; on the second day the long jump, the javelin throw and finally the gruelling 800m.

J-K a class apart

In the pantheon of Olympic Games Heptathlon greats, Jackie Joyner-Kersee stands alone as the greatest competitor. Having won the silver medal in Los Angeles, she became the first woman to score over 7,000 points at the Goodwill Games in 1986 and bettered that with her gold medal-winning and world record score of 7,291 points at the 1988 Games in Seoul. Joyner-Kersee remains the only woman to retain her title, capturing a second gold at Barcelona 1992. Not content with Heptathlon competition, the gifted American set a new Games record of 7.40 metres in the women's Long Jump in Seoul and later played professional basketball for the Richmond Rage. Joyner-Kersee was voted the Greatest Female Athlete of the 20th Century by *Sports Illustrated for Women* magazine.

↗ *Women's Heptathlon gold medallist at the 1988 Games in Seoul, Jackie Joyner-Kersee made a successful defence of her title at the 1992 Games in Barcelona.*

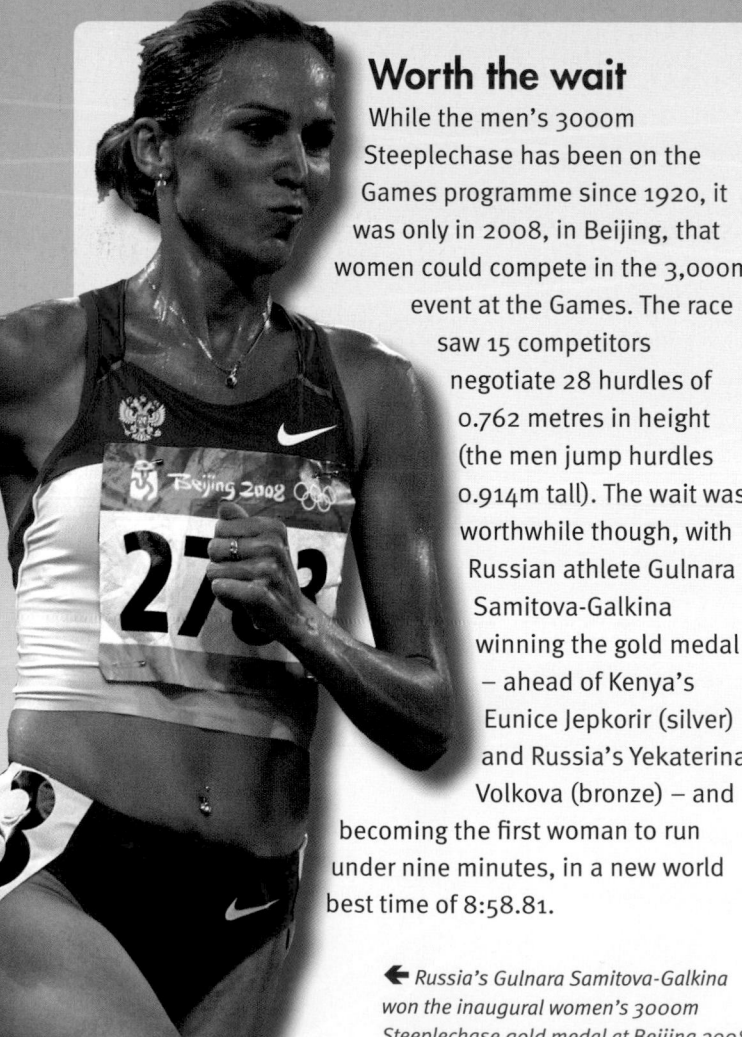

Worth the wait

While the men's 3000m Steeplechase has been on the Games programme since 1920, it was only in 2008, in Beijing, that women could compete in the 3,000m event at the Games. The race saw 15 competitors negotiate 28 hurdles of 0.762 metres in height (the men jump hurdles 0.914m tall). The wait was worthwhile though, with Russian athlete Gulnara Samitova-Galkina winning the gold medal – ahead of Kenya's Eunice Jepkorir (silver) and Russia's Yekaterina Volkova (bronze) – and becoming the first woman to run under nine minutes, in a new world best time of 8:58.81.

← *Russia's Gulnara Samitova-Galkina won the inaugural women's 3000m Steeplechase gold medal at Beijing 2008 in a world record-breaking time.*

Unique Australian

The inaugural Heptathlon event at Los Angeles 1984 was eventually won by Glynis Nunn, the only Australian to have won a multi-discipline Athletics event at the Games. Her triumph came at a price: a year earlier the former physical education teacher had quit her job and gone on the dole in order to concentrate on preparing for the Games. Los Angeles witnessed a desperately close competition, which was sealed by the long jump. This was traditionally a strong event for Nunn's great rival Jackie Joyner-Kersee, but she only recorded one clean jump and her points tally gave her a vulnerable lead going into the final event, the 800m. Nunn recorded a time 2.46 seconds faster than Joyner-Kersee and amid much confusion (due to the close points tallies), was announced the gold medallist with a final score of 6,390 points.

Braun's German double

Although her haul of Olympic Games medals consists of a single bronze in the Heptathlon, Germany's Sabine Braun has a high rank in the history of the sport as a double world champion, having captured gold at the 1991 and 1997 World Championships as well as a silver in 1993. The year before, Braun had won the bronze medal at the 1992 Games in Barcelona. With a score of 6,985 points, she remains the German record holder.

Evolving event

The women's Heptathlon replaced the Pentathlon, but may in time be replaced by a women's Decathlon (over ten events) at the Olympic Games. In recent years a number of Decathlon competitions have taken place and the IAAF has started to keep records for the sport. In the meantime Heptathlon remains the standard.

Klüft coronation

Carolina Klüft dominated the women's Heptathlon since the turn of the century. The Swede remained unbeaten in 22 heptathlon and pentathlon competitions from March 2002, winning nine consecutive gold medals in major championships, including three World Championships and the Olympic Games gold medal at Athens 2004, where she won by a new Games record margin of 517 points. Her personal best score of 7,032 points, achieved at the 2007 World Championships in Osaka, Japan, sits second on the all-time list behind Jackie Joyner-Kersee.

↑ Carolina Klüft's domination of the Heptathlon climaxed with a gold medal at Athens 2004.

Dancing queen

Denise Lewis made her Games debut at Atlanta 1996, winning bronze. By the time of the 2000 Games, the Briton was already European champion. In Sydney, the world champion Eunice Barber and defending Olympic Games champion Ghada Shouaa both had to abandon the competition through injury, clearing the path for Lewis's gold-medal assault. The turning point came in the javelin, where her throw of 50.19 metres took her into first place with just one event remaining, the 800m. Although her nearest rival, the Belarusian Natallia Sazanovich, finished ahead, Lewis completed in a time of 2:16.83 – just enough to hold on to the gold medal. Injury hampered Lewis's hopes of defending her title, but she later appeared in the finals of television show *Strictly Come Dancing*.

↓ Britain's Jessica Ennis will start the Heptathlon at London 2012 among the favourites for gold.

Enter Jessica Ennis...

In 2008, Carolina Klüft announced that she would no longer compete in the Heptathlon, preferring to concentrate on the Long Jump and Triple Jump. Her decision, announced in an Olympic Games year, paved the way for a new era in Heptathlon. Ukrainian Nataliya Dobrynska was the benefactor, winning the gold medal in Beijing. With Denise Lewis retired and Kelly Sotherton injured, a new British contender emerged in the Heptathlon in the shape of Jessica Ennis. A career-threatening injury in 2008 merely served to motivate the Sheffield athlete, who became European and World Champion in the following two years. Her duel with Dobrynska at the European Championships saw the Briton prevail by just 45 points, setting up a thrilling prospect for the 2012 Games in London.

Women's 4 x 100m and 4 x 400m Relays

The first women's 4 x 100m Relay at the Games was held in 1928, 16 years after the first men's event in 1912. Women had to wait even longer to compete in the 4 x 400m Relay, which was introduced in 1972, a massive 60 years after the men's event. But it was worth the wait, as the women's Relay races brought some of the world's greatest sprinters together in formidable teams, such as the 1988 USA team, which featured the mighty Evelyn Ashford and the fastest woman in history, Florence Griffith-Joyner.

⬇ *Florence Griffith-Joyner won her third gold at Seoul 1988 in the women's 4 x 100m final.*

Quick wrap-up

The sprint events at Seoul 1988 belonged to one American, Florence Griffith-Joyner, known to her fans as 'Flo-Jo'. Hailed as the fastest woman of all time (as long-term holder of records for the women's 100m and 200m), Flo-Jo capped off a remarkable Games by helping the US team to victory in the women's 4 x 100m Relay. In the Final, Griffith-Joyner came into the passing area first in her leg of the race, and anchor Evelyn Ashford, in spite of their poor handover, completed the win for the American team in 41.98 seconds, giving Griffith-Joyner her third gold medal of the Games. Her bid for a fourth gold fell short as the United States took silver in the women's 4 x 400m Relay. Griffith-Joyner, born in Los Angeles, was the wife of triple jumper Al Joyner and the sister-in-law of heptathlete and long jumper Jackie Joyner-Kersee. She first came to prominence when finishing fourth in the 200m at the inaugural World Championship in 1983.

The Flying Housewife

As the Relay Races are among the final track running events at the Olympic Games, many of the best sprinters have used these events to cap off individual solo successes. At 30 and a mother of two, Dutch athlete Fanny Blankers-Koen was dismissed by many as being too old in the run-up to the 1948 Games in London, before the 'Flying Housewife' went on to win four gold medals in the women's sprint events. Blankers-Koen began her haul with the women's 100m, which she won in 11.9 seconds, and continued with wins in the 80m Hurdles – in a new Games record time of 11.2 – and the women's 200m. She then completed her sweep in the women's 4 x 100m Relay, running the anchor leg. The Netherlands took the gold medal in a time of 47.5.

⬆*Fanny Blankers-Koen anchors the Netherlands to victory in the women's 4 x 100m Final at London 1948.*

US dominance

The United States women's teams have dominated the relay events at the Olympic Games. The American women have won nine women's 4 x 100m titles out of the 19 contested between 1928 and 2008. Meanwhile in the women's 4 x 400m event, they have also continued to claim more honours than any other team, winning five of the ten titles on offer between 1972 and 2008, including four consecutive victories between 1996 and 2008.

Showdown in Seoul

The 1988 Games in Seoul was the stage for a thrilling women's 4 x 400m Final showdown between the Soviet Union and the United States. Having bagged the gold in the women's 4 x 100m event, the USA was on track for a clean sweep in the sprint events. The US team – again including Florence Griffith-Joyner – took a narrow lead after the first leg with Denean Howard taking the early advantage in 49.82 seconds. The Soviets fought back on leg two with Olga Nazarova before the advantage swung back in favour of the USA on leg three with Valerie Brisco. However, the Soviets prevailed after a heart-stopping battle in the decisive anchor leg between women's 400m gold medallist Olga Bryzgina and Griffith-Joyner. The Soviet quartet posted a world record of 3:15.17 that still stands today.

⬇ *The Soviet Union's Olga Bryzgina (left) and the United States' Florence Griffith-Joyner prior to the women's 4 x 100m Final at Seoul 1988.*

Evelyn Ashford

Evelyn Ashford of the United States claimed three of her four career Olympic Games gold medals in the women's 4 x 100m Relay, winning three consecutive titles between 1984 and 1992. In the 1984 Final in Los Angeles, Ashford ran an anchor leg of 9.77 seconds, the fastest ever, to win her second gold medal of the Games following her success in the women's 100m Final. During the final of the 1988 Games, Ashford recovered from a sloppy handover with Florence Griffith-Joyner to overcome her long-time rival Marlies Göhr of East Germany in the anchor leg.

⬆ *The United States women's 4 x 100m gold medal-winning quartet at the 1992 Games in Barcelona. From left to right: Carlette Guidry-White, Evelyn Ashford, Esther Jones and Gwen Torrence.*

Dropped out...

Jamaica, who had swept the medals in the women's 100m Final, were overwhelming favourites to win the women's 4 x 100m Relay Final at Beijing 2008, but lost out to Russia following a sloppy baton exchange. Newly crowned 100m champion Shelly-Ann Fraser ran a perfect first leg and passed the baton on to Sherone Simpson, who put Jamaica in front going into the first bend. However, Jamaica's hopes fell to pieces as Sherone Simpson did not pass on to Kerron Stewart, meaning women's 200m champion Veronica Campbell-Brown did not get a chance to run the anchor leg. The Russians moved into the lead coming off the final turn and Yuliya Chemoshanskaya crossed the line in 42.31 seconds.

➡ *Veronica Campbell-Brown (left) and Kerron Stewart make a mess of the baton exchange in the women's 4 x 100m Relay Final at Beijing 2008.*

🏃 Women's Road Events

Although the Marathon has been contested by men at every Games since Athens 1896, the first women's Marathon did not take place until Los Angeles 1984. The women's 20km Race Walk has been part of the Games programme since Sydney 2000.

Oldest Marathon champion

At 38 years of age, Romania's Constantina Tomescu won the 2008 women's Marathon in Beijing in 2:26:44, beating her nearest rival by 22 seconds. Her gold medal triumph not only made her the oldest Marathon champion ever, male or female, but also the oldest Marathon medallist in the history of the Games.

Women make their point

In 1966, after not being granted an official entry into the Boston Marathon, Roberta Gibb joined the race from behind a bush – and finished in an unofficial time of 3:21:25. The following year, K.V. Switzer entered the Boston Marathon and it wasn't until two miles into the race that officials realised the runner was a woman, Kathrine Switzer. Despite the officials' best efforts, 20-year-old Switzer finished the race, and the following day the national papers propelled the issue of women's long-distance running into the public eye. Switzer went on to lobby for the inclusion of a women's Marathon at the Olympic Games and was instrumental in the IOC's decision in 1981 to introduce the event.

First for Japan

Naoko Takahashi created history at the 2000 Olympic Games in Sydney, becoming the first Japanese woman to collect a track and field gold medal when she won the women's Marathon. She joined the record books in style, setting a new Olympic record time of 2:23:14. Afterwards she went on to become the first woman to break the magical 2:20 barrier, running 2:19:46, the world's fastest time, at the 2001 Berlin Marathon.

Debut drama

Perhaps the most dramatic scenes at the inaugural women's Marathon at Los Angeles 1984 – and indeed of the entire Games – came after the medals had been decided. Entering the stadium around 20 minutes after winner Joan Benoit, Swiss competitor Gabriele Andersen-Scheiss had spectators gasping in horror when she staggered on to the track, painfully exhausted. Cheered on by the crowd, she stumbled and limped towards the finish line in clear distress, before collapsing into the arms of waiting medics. Her courageous effort placed her 37th of 44 finishers, with a time of 2:48:42, and immortalised Andersen-Scheiss in Games folklore as a symbol of courage and determination.

← *Romania's Constantina Tomescu heads the women's Marathon field at Beijing 2008.*

→ *Japan's Naoko Takahashi takes women's Marathon gold at Sydney 2000.*

↑*A moment of quiet despair for Paula Radcliffe after she pulled out of the Marathon at Athens 2004.*

Remarkable Radcliffe

Paula Radcliffe is synonymous with female Marathon running. The British runner enjoyed massive success on the big-city marathon circuit, with multiple wins in London, New York and Chicago. Following an impressive track career, Radcliffe's Marathon debut in London in 2002 set a best time (2:18:56) for a women's-only race, a European record and the fastest ever debut over the 26-mile distance. After she had smashed the world record by 1:29 in Chicago later that year with a time of 2:17:18, it was on home soil that Radcliffe set her incredible world record of 2:15:25 at the 2003 London Marathon – a time not bettered by any British male in that year. Radcliffe's dream of Olympic Games gold was shattered at Athens 2004. Having gone into the race a firm favourite, she pulled out at the 23-mile mark. Her disappointment at the Games continued at Beijing 2008, when she struggled to a 23rd-place finish.

Time out...

Paula Radcliffe confirmed her place in marathon folklore in 2005 with a 15-second toilet stop on the side of the road five miles from the finish of the London Marathon. She duly powered to her third London title in 2:17:42.

World record

Vera Sokolova broke the world record in the women's 20km walk at the 2011 Russian national championships, shaving 33 seconds off the previous record set by fellow Russian Olimpiada Ivanova in 2005.

Walking in

The women's Race Walk has only recently been welcomed into the Olympic Games programme. After being introduced as a 10-kilometre event in 1992, it was then replaced by a 20km walk in 2000. At the 2008 Olympic Games in Beijing, Olga Kaniskina won the gold medal and set a new Games record for the fastest women's 20km Race Walk in a time of 1:26:31, smashing the previous record of 1:29.05 set by Wang Liping in 2000 in Sydney.

↓*Russia's Olga Kaniskina beat the rain to take women's 20km Race Walk gold at Beijing 2008.*

History girl

The women's Marathon was finally introduced to the Olympic Games programme at Los Angeles 1984, marking the day that women runners had long been campaigning for. American runner Joan Benoit was one of 50 competitors from 28 nations who started the first women's Marathon, and she went on to be the first champion, winning on home soil in 2:24:52. Norwegian Grete Waitz finished second and Portugal's Rosa Mota third.

↑ *Joan Benoit made history in 1984 when she won the Games' first-ever women's Marathon.*

Women's High Jump and Pole Vault

The High Jump is one of five events – along with 100m, 800m, 4 x 100m and Discus Throw – to have been contested by women at every Games since Amsterdam 1928. In contrast, the women's Pole Vault is a relative newcomer to the Olympic Games programme: it was staged for the first time at Sydney 2000.

Rolling and diving

High jumping has long been regarded as an event open to experimental technique, the most prominent example being the introduction of the Fosbury Flop by US athlete Dick Fosbury at Mexico City 1968. However, in 1932, when Babe Didrikson leaped to a new world record of 1.67 metres, tying with her US compatriot Jean Shiley in Los Angeles, it was Shiley that was awarded the gold medal. Didrikson had used the Western Roll technique, which at the time was regarded as 'diving', so was awarded silver.

Test of time

In 1987, Bulgaria's Stefka Kostadinova set a women's high jump world record of 2.09 metres. It remained one of the longest-standing world records in modern athletics and was one of seven world records (both indoor and outdoor) that Kostadinova set in a glittering career. Having won a silver medal at the 1988 Games in Seoul, Kostadinova went one better at Atlanta 1996, winning the gold medal with a new Games record of 2.05m. Later she became President of the Bulgarian Olympic Committee.

⬇ *Bulgaria's Stefka Kostadinova leaps to gold in the women's High Jump at Atlanta 1996. She had won a silver medal in the event at Seoul 1988.*

Saskatoon Lily

The women's High Jump competition at the Games began with a touch of glamour at Amsterdam 1928. The winner, Ethel Catherwood, broke the world record with a height of 1.59 metres, becoming the first (and still the only) Canadian female athlete to have won individual gold in track and field at the Games. Her natural good looks did not go unnoticed and a *New York Times* correspondent labelled her the 'prettiest girl athlete', while she earned the nickname 'Saskatoon Lily'. After her success Catherwood became embroiled in scandal, with two failed marriages conducted in the media spotlight. She later moved to California and admitted she was really an American, having been born in Hannah, North Dakota.

← *Ethel Catherwood became the first Olympic Games' women's High Jump champion at Amsterdam 1928.*

Csak's special celebration in Berlin

Hungarian high jumper Ibolya Csák won one of the closest women's High Jump competitions ever seen at the Games, at Berlin 1936. Three competitors cleared 1.60 metres, but all failed to clear 1.62m, until Csák succeeded at the fourth attempt. As a Jew, her victory had extra poignancy, coming at a time of increasing anti-Semitism in Germany. Two years later she became European champion in bizarre circumstances, after the winner, Dora Ratjen, was disqualified for being a man; his participation was a ploy by the Nazis.

Meyfarth the mighty

Ulrike Meyfarth went into the record books as the youngest and then the oldest women's High Jump champion at the Games. The German's first gold medal came in 1972 at her home Games in Munich. The 16-year-old was among athletes who had already and eagerly adopted Dick Fosbury's technique and her enterprise saw her win the gold medal with a world record-equalling height of 1.92 metres. After that her career went into decline, but in 1982 she returned to set a new world record (2.02m), becoming European champion for good measure. The absence of Soviet bloc competitors at Los Angeles 1984 enabled Meyfarth to reclaim her title 12 years on, this time as the oldest woman ever to win the High Jump.

Women on pole

The men's Pole Vault competition has been a part of the modern Games programme since Athens 1896. However, women's competitive pole vaulting is a relatively new phenomenon and the first world record was only recognised by the IAAF as recently as 1992. The first-ever women's Pole Vault competition at the Games was contested at Sydney 2000 (and was won by the USA's Stacy Dragila). Russia's Yelena Isinbayeva, the only woman to exceed 5 metres, dominated the event at both the 2004 and 2008 Games.

Dragila leads the way

American Stacy Dragila was the first star of women's pole vaulting. Her accomplishments include being a two-time world champion (1999, 2001) and the 1997 world indoor champion, while she broke the world record no fewer than ten times. Fittingly, at Sydney 2000, the Californian became the first Olympic Games women's Pole Vault champion with a winning vault of 4.60 metres.

← *Stacy Dragila cleared 4.60 metres to become the Games' first-ever women's Pole Vault champion.*

Isinbayeva: gold after gold

Yelena Isinbayeva is regarded as the golden girl of athletics in the modern era. She is a two-time gold medallist in the women's Pole Vault at the Games, has been world champion on five occasions and has broken the world record (indoors and outdoors) on 27 occasions, with her current mark set at 5.06 metres. Unsurprisingly, she is considered the greatest female pole vaulter of all time and is often compared to the great Sergey Bubka, who dominated the men's event.

↓ *Yelena Isinbayeva: the queen of women's Pole Vault.*

Russian titans

Svetlana Feofanova and Yelena Isinbayeva – compatriots and great rivals – repeatedly broke the world outdoor record in 2004. This set up a titanic clash at the Olympic Games in Athens that year, where, having finally broken her rival's resistance at 4.90 metres, Isinbayeva set a world record of 4.91m in winning the gold medal. She was subsequently named Female Athlete of the Year by the IAAF and won the same accolade in 2005 and 2008. By the time of the 2008 Games in Beijing, Isinbayeva had established herself as one of the main superstar attractions in the track and field events. She accordingly defended her title with consummate ease, requiring just two vaults to win a second gold medal and then going on to break the world record with a new height of 5.05m. Svetlana Feofanova had represented Russia as a gymnast at the 1996 Games in Atlanta before switching sports and becoming world champion in 2003 and world record holder with a jump of 4.88m in July 2004. That same year, in Athens, she won the silver medal behind Isinbayeva.

↓ *Russia's Svetlana Feofanova had to settle for a silver medal in 2004 and bronze in 2008.*

Women's Long Jump and Triple Jump

The women's Long Jump has been part of the Games programme since London 1948. Remarkably, no woman has retained her title, although Germany's Heike Drechsler took gold in 1992 and 2000. The women's Triple Jump was staged for the first time at Sydney 2000.

Lebedeva's long wait

At Athens 2004, Russian athlete Tatyana Lebedeva went into the women's Long Jump Final with a frustrating succession of Olympic Games silver and bronze medals behind her. She had already twice been a triple jump world champion, but now she had been thwarted three times in her bid for Olympic Games gold after being hot favourite for that event. In Greece, fortunately, compensation was at hand in the women's Long Jump. Her leap of 7.07 metres took her to the gold medal by just two centimetres, ahead of her Russian team-mates Irina Simagina and Tatyana Kotova. It is the only time the event has seen a clean sweep of the medals by one nation.

Dominant Drechsler

Across three decades East Germany's Heike Drechsler was a name to fear in women's Long Jump or sprint races. During 1986, she twice equalled the women's 200m world record, but is perhaps best remembered for her Long Jump exploits. Drechsler is the only athlete to have won two women's Long Jump gold medals at the Games and, in 1983, she became the inaugural world champion. Her first gold medal came at Barcelona 1992; that same year Drechsler jumped 7.63 metres at altitude in Sestriere, a distance 11 centimetres further than the current world record. She won a second gold medal at Sydney 2000, at which point it was claimed she had won more than 400 Long Jump competitions with jumps over 7 metres.

The gifted Mary Rand

Great Britain's women have a long and successful history in track and field events at the Games. It all started with Mary Rand, who took the gold medal in the women's Long Jump competition at Tokyo 1964. A successful pentathlon competitor, Rand had disappointed in the women's Long Jump at Rome 1960, but four years later in Tokyo, she jumped 6.52 metres in the qualifying round, to set a new Games record. In the final, Rand broke the world record with a leap of 6.76m and followed up with a silver medal in the Pentathlon and a bronze in the women's 4 x 100m Relay. Her room-mate Ann Packer, who won the women's 800m gold medal in Tokyo, later paid tribute to Rand : 'Mary was the most gifted athlete I ever saw. She was as good as athletes get; there has never been anything like her since. And I don't believe there ever will.'

↑ Mary Rand won the women's Long Jump at the 1964 Games in Tokyo to become Britain's first female track and field gold medallist.

← Heike Drechsler leaps to women's Long Jump gold at the 2000 Games in Sydney. Following her win in 1992, she is the event's only two-time winner.

Golden Kiwi Yvette

Yvette Williams became a national heroine in New Zealand when she became the first woman from her nation to win a gold medal at the Games. Williams's triumph came in the women's Long Jump at Helsinki 1952. She had already won a Commonwealth Games gold medal two years earlier in the same event and would repeat that feat in 1954. A gifted athlete, Williams also won gold medals in the discus and javelin competitions at the 1954 Commonwealth Games in Vancouver and was inducted into the New Zealand Hall of Fame in 1990.

New jump on the block

While the women's long jump has a long history, the women's triple jump is a relatively recent innovation. The first world record was only recognised by the IAAF in 1991. The first major star of the sport was Ukrainian Inessa Kravets, the current world record holder and inaugural Olympic Games champion. Kravets leapt to prominence at the 1995 World Championships, during which Jonathan Edwards, the men's world champion, offered inspiration. 'After two jumps [in which she had fouled] I thought about Edwards,' said Kravets later. 'I had been carrying around a picture of him, I thought to myself, "I should do the same as him"' – and she promptly won the championship, setting a world record of 15.50 metres. The following year, Kravets won the gold medal at Atlanta 1996, with a leap of 15.33m, which remains a Games record.

Expanding the Empire

Sydney 2000 women's Long Jump champion Tereza Marinova comes from good sporting stock. Her father Moncho was a leading 800m runner who at one time set the Bulgarian record for the event, while her brother Tsvetomir competed in the 400m. Marinova's expertise, however, lay in jumping events, and although she took part in the long jump at the European Championships, it was the triple jump that secured her fame. She remains the world junior record holder and crowned her career with the Triple Jump gold medal at Sydney, her leap of 15.20 metres a career best.

Kick-start for Niger

Chioma Ajunwa set the standard for female athletes across Africa in 1996, when she became the first African woman to win an Olympic gold medal in a field event. Ajunwa had already represented Nigeria at football, but it was her success in the women's Long Jump at Atlanta 1996 that ultimately led to the police officer being made a Member of the Order of Niger. In the final, she jumped 7.12 metres to secure gold – as well as a chieftaincy title from her home state Imo.

↑ *Chioma Ajunwa beat off the challenge of Italy's Fiona May to take women's Long Jump gold in 1996.*

Solidarity pays off

Françoise Mbango Etone's glittering triple jump career was significantly boosted by the Olympic Solidarity Fund, which provided her with support from November 2002. The Fund aimed to help athletes from poorer countries to benefit from the training and assistance needed to bring them up to international athletic standards. Mbango Etone's scholarship to attend St John's University, New York, was richly rewarded and she became the first athlete from the Cameroon to win gold at the World Championships and at the Olympic and Commonwealth Games. She switched her allegiance to France in September 2010.

→ *Cameroon's Françoise Mbango Etone made a successful defence of her women's Triple Jump crown at the 2008 Games in Beijing.*

Women's Discus Throw and Hammer Throw

The women's Discus Throw is one of five events to have been contested by women at every Olympic Games since Amsterdam 1928. The women's Hammer Throw, on the other hand, is a relatively new event: it has only been part of the Games programme since the Sydney 2000.

Renaissance girl

The lineage of French athlete Micheline Ostermeyer suggested that she might be artistically inclined. The great-niece of author Victor Hugo was also the niece of composer Lucien Paroche so, unsurprisingly, Ostermeyer's formative years were spent playing the piano. The outbreak of the Second World War saw Ostermeyer return to her family home in Tunisia, where she began to participate in sports. On returning to France, she became a formidable athlete, and at London 1948 won the women's Shot Put and the Discus Throw – having only picked up a discus for the first time a few weeks before. Afterwards, at the French base, she provided her team-mates with an impromptu performance of piano music by Beethoven.

← *Micheline Ostermeyer won women's Discus Throw gold at London 1948.*

⬆ *Nina Ponomaryova won women's Discus Throw gold at the 1952 Games in Helsinki.*

Soviet starter

Nina Ponomaryova's story is a remarkable tale of glory in an era of heightened world tension. Ponomaryova competed at four Olympic Games, twice winning the gold medal in the women's Discus Throw. However, her gold medal at Helsinki 1952, where she set a new Games record of 51.42 metres, has the distinction of being the first gold medal for any Soviet athlete. It was the first time her country had competed at the Games since 1912. Her huge strength and fitness earned her the nickname the 'Iron Lady'. She followed up with a second gold medal at Rome 1960. Ponomaryova's rise to prominence was remarkable given that she lived in one of Stalin's gulags until the age of six, when her parents moved to a Cossack village in Southern Russia.

Lost century

The men's Hammer Throw contest has been contested since the 1900 Games, but it took another 100 years before a women's competition was established. The IAAF started to ratify women's marks only from 1995, and the first major event was the 1999 World Championships, with Sydney playing host to the first Olympic Games competition a year later.

Prize pole

Halina Konopacka's success in the first women's Discus Throw event at the Games, at Amsterdam 1928, made her Poland's first Olympic Games champion. This was the first women's gold-winning track and field event in the Olympic Games and Konopacka broke her own world record with a throw of 39.62 metres. After she retired from sport, Konopacka became a renowned poet and painter, releasing a collection of poems in 1929 called *Someday*. She later moved to the United States, became a member of the Board of the International Women's Sports Federation and played a role in the Polish Olympic Movement.

Discus delight

Evelin Jahl holds the distinction of being the only woman to retain her women's Discus Throw title at the Games. The East German won the gold medal at Montreal 1976, defeating the world record holder Faina Melnyk. Two years later she broke the record with a throw of 70.72 metres, before defending her women's Discus Throw title at Moscow 1980.

↑ *A hammer throw silver medallist at the European Under 23 Championships in 2003, Belarus' Askana Miankova struck gold at Beijing 2008 with a Games record-breaking throw of 76.34 metres.*

Russian's revival

Although she had set no fewer than nine world records prior to the 2004 Games in Athens, Russia's Olga Kuzenkova was in danger of becoming a nearly woman in the hammer competition, having collected silver medals at three World Championships and filling the same position at Sydney 2000. Seven years before, she had become the first woman to throw over 70 metres, but her best form had deserted her since 1999. The 2004 Games saw Kuzenkova return to prominence with a vengeance: leading the competition throughout, she won the gold medal with a distance of 75.02m – a new Games record.

Prescription for success

Aksana Miankova's hopes of competing at the Olympic Games could have been dashed in her formative years. The 2008 gold medallist came from a family of doctors in Belarus, and such was her mother's disapproval of her daughter's athletic aspirations that Miankova had to attend training while her mother was at work. She was introduced to the hammer aged 15 and began to win regional titles before stepping into international competition. Her crowning moments came in 2008, when first she achieved her personal best throw of 77.32 metres and then, in Beijing, won the gold medal with a new Games record throw of 76.34m.

Out of reach

Cuban hammer thrower Yipsi González was twice world champion, but glory at the Olympic Games escaped her. Gonzalez won her first world title in 2001 and successfully defended it two years later, which led to her being named Cuban Sportswoman of the Year for 2003. The following year, in the run-up to Athens 2004, she threw the longest throw recorded that year, making her the favourite to win the gold medal. In the event, however, she disappointed with four fouls and her best throw of 73.36 metres was only good enough for silver. In Beijing in 2008 González again came close, winning a second silver medal behind Aksana Miankova – who set a new Games record.

↓ *Poland's Kamila Skolimowska won women's Hammer Throw gold at Sydney 2000. Nine years later, she was dead.*

Sad Skolimowska

At the 2000 Olympic Games in Sydney the first-ever women's Hammer Throw competition was won by Kamila Skolimowska of Poland, who was the tender age of 17 years 331 days old at the time. Skolimowska won the gold medal after the favourite Mihaela Melinte (of Romania) had failed a drug test, and she was awarded the Polish Golden Cross of Merit for her success. It appeared that she would dominate the sport for years to come, but tragedy struck at her training camp in February 2009 when Skolimowska, training with the Polish national team in Portugal, died suddenly of a pulmonary embolism at the age of 26.

Women's Javelin Throw and Shot Put

Two of the more established events on the women's Athletics programme, women's Javelin Throw and Shot Put have been staged since Los Angeles 1932 and London 1948 respectively. Both disciplines have been dominated by Eastern European athletes over the years.

Talented Babe

The women's Javelin Throw was contested at the Games for the first time at Los Angeles 1932. The first winner was fittingly an American, Mildred 'Babe' Didrikson, who threw 43.69 metres to claim gold and then went on to achieve a second success in the women's 80m Hurdles. This, however, represents only a fraction of her achievements: Didrikson reached All-American status at basketball, played organised baseball and softball, was an expert diver, roller skater and bowler and even recorded records as a singer and harmonica player. Outside the Olympic Games, however, Didrikson's main exploits were in golf. Having been denied amateur status, she competed against the men in the Los Angeles Open – a PGA event – in 1938. No woman would repeat this for another 60 years. 'The Babe' was named the tenth Greatest North American Athlete of the 20th Century by ESPN, and the ninth Greatest Athlete of the 20th Century by the Associated Press.

↖ *A woman of many talents, Babe Didrikson won women's Javelin Throw gold at the 1932 Games in Los Angeles.*

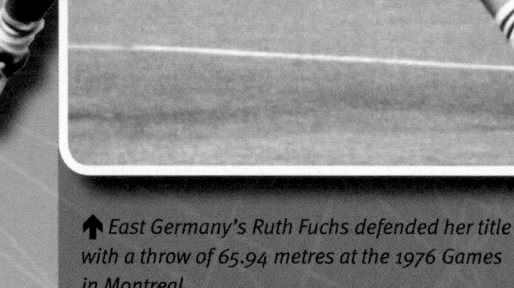
↑ *East Germany's Ruth Fuchs defended her title with a throw of 65.94 metres at the 1976 Games in Montreal.*

Gale force Fuchs

Only two women have made a successful defence of their titles in women's Javelin Throw at the Games, the first being East German Ruth Fuchs. During the 1970s Fuchs broke the world record six times, but her defining moments came at the 1972 and 1976 Games. She later became a Member of Parliament in the unified Germany.

Winning words

Czechoslovak javelin thrower Dana Zátopková was as formidable a character in her press conferences as she was a competitor at the 1952 Olympic Games in Helsinki. Remarkably, her husband Emil Zátopek won men's 5000m gold barely an hour before she won the women's Javelin Throw competition with a throw of 50.47m. At the press conference that ensued, Emil suggested his victory had inspired his wife, to which she replied, 'Really? OK, go inspire some other girl and see if she throws a javelin 50 metres!' She became the oldest woman (at 35) to set a world record, with a throw of 55.73m in 1958, and two years later won a silver medal at the Olympic Games in Rome.

Kiwi crowning

When Valerie Vili threw a personal best of 20.56m in the women's Shot Put Final at Beijing 2008, she won New Zealand's first track and field gold medal since John Walker's victory in the 1976 men's 1500m Final. Of Tongan descent, Vili received the accolade of the 2008 New Zealand Sports Award for her success and was crowned world champion the following year.

Eastern effort

For over two decades Soviet bloc countries dominated the women's Shot Put event at the Olympic Games. Nadezhda Chizhova of the Soviet Union won three consecutive titles from 1968, including the gold medal at the 1972 Games in Munich. In a glittering career, Chizhova also set seven world records and became the first woman to break both the 20-metre and 21-metre barriers.

East German enigma

For many years women's shot-putting was dogged by controversy. Margitta Gummel competed for the unified German team at Tokyo 1964 and for East Germany at the next two Games. She won the women's Shot Put gold medal at Mexico City 1968, becoming the first woman to throw further than 19 metres. Four years later she won the silver medal behind her rival Nadhezhda Chizhova. However, it was later revealed that Gummel had been one of the first East German athlete to undergo steroid treatment and an analysis of her results indicated that her performances had improved by 2m in the space of three months prior to her Mexico City success.

Sanderson v Whitbread...

Tessa Sanderson reached the pinnacle of her long Javelin career with a gold-medal performance at the 1984 Games in Los Angeles. The Jamaican-born British athlete unexpectedly beat her compatriot Fatima Whitbread to become the first black British woman to win gold at the Games. Her success came at the half-way point of her career and she went on to become only the second track and field athlete in history to compete at six Games, from Montreal 1976 to Atlanta 1996. Sanderson was vice-chairman of Sport England for six years and is a current Board member of the Olympic Park Legacy Company, overseeing the long-term benefits of the 2012 Games.

↑ *Tessa Sanderson (right) took gold and Fatima Whitbread (left) took bronze in the women's Javelin Throw at the 1984 Games in Los Angeles.*

Petra's unbeatable javelin throw

Petra Felke ensured East German continuity in the javelin, in the wake of Ruth Fuchs. Her career saw her break the world record on four occasions, most notably with a throw of 80.00 metres in 1988. Her throw remains in the record books, as the design of the javelin was changed in 1999 for safety reasons to ensure it could not be thrown as far again, putting other athletes or the crowd at risk. A few weeks after setting her world record, Felke won the gold medal at the 1988 Games in Seoul, defeating the luckless Fatima Whitbread.

↑ *World record holder Petra Felke struck gold in the women's Javelin Throw at Seoul 1988.*

Six of the best

Soviet athlete Natalya Lisovskaya is almost certainly the greatest shot-putter in the history of the sport. She set the first of her world records in 1984, aged 21, with a throw of 22.53 metres. Her mark of 22.63m in 1987 remains the world record, but perhaps the clearest demonstration of her dominance came at Seoul 1988. Lisovskaya not only won the gold medal, but also every one of her six throws was good enough to win the competition.

Press gang

Two Soviets dominated track and field events in the early 1960s. The Press sisters, Irina and Tamara, each won two gold medals at both the 1960 and 1964 Games. Tamara specialised in the throwing events, winning gold in the women's Shot Put and silver in the women's Discus at Rome 1960; she won both four years later – becoming the the first woman to defend her Shot Put title. But rumours about the sisters began to circulate and when gender tests were introduced in 1966, they both disappeared from their sports.

↑ *Tamara Press in women's Shot Put action at the 1964 Games in Tokyo.*

Chapter Four
Ball sports

Six ball sports feature in the Olympic Games summer schedule for London 2012 compared with eight in Beijing after which Baseball and Softball fell by the wayside.

Football was the first to come aboard, at the second of the modern Games in Paris in 1900. It has been present ever since, with the exception of Los Angeles in 1932. Up until 1928 in Amsterdam, the Olympic Games tournament was considered the unofficial world championship, but then the sport launched its own World Cup and that tournament quickly established pre-eminence.

London 1908 saw Hockey accepted to the Games programme, with Basketball and Handball 'arriving' in Berlin in 1936. Volleyball had to wait until Tokyo 1964,

with the most recent addition being Beach Volleyball. This was a demonstration event at Barcelona 1992 and confirmed as a medal sport in 1996 in Atlanta.

The women's versions of the first four sports endured long waits for equality with Football needing the prospect – fulfilled – of a United States victory to join the Games in Atlanta in 1996.

Hockey produced the most bizarre twist in the equality tale. Its first women's tournament coincided with the boycott-hit Moscow Games of 1980. A makeshift Zimbabwe team – selected only the weekend before the Opening Ceremony – carried off the gold medal.

Brazil's Giba, in the world-famous yellow and green, spikes the ball despite the vain attempts of the United States' David Lee and William Priddy during the men's Volleyball showdown at the 2008 Olympic Games in Beijing. Brazil won the match 3–1.

Basketball

Men's basketball was contested for the first time at Berlin 1936, with the United States beating Canada (19–8) in the final. It was a sign of things to come: the United States have been the event's dominant team, winning gold on 13 (out of 16) occasions. It has been a similar story in women's Basketball, with the United States winning five of the seven tournaments contested since 1976.

Men's Basketball Finals

1936	United States 19, Canada 8 (Bronze: Mexico)
1948	United States 65, France 21 (Bronze: Brazil)
1952	United States 36, USSR 25 (Bronze: Uruguay)
1956	United States 89, USSR 55 (Bronze: Uruguay)
1960	Gold: United States; Silver: USSR; Bronze: Brazil *
1964	United States 73, USSR 59 (Bronze: Brazil)
1968	United States 65, Yugoslavia 50 (Bronze: USSR)
1972	USSR 51, United States 50 (Bronze: Cuba)
1976	United States 95, Yugoslavia 74 (Bronze: USSR)
1980	Yugoslavia 86, Italy 77 (Bronze: Soviet Union)
1984	United States 96, Spain 65 (Bronze: Yugoslavia)
1988	USSR 76, Yugoslavia 63 (Bronze: United States)
1992	United States 117, Croatia 85 (Bronze: Lithuania)
1996	United States 95, Serbia 69 (Bronze: Lithuania)
2000	United States 85, France 75 (Bronze: Lithuania)
2004	Argentina 84, Italy 69 (Bronze: United States)
2008	United States 118, Spain 107 (Bronze: Argentina)

* No play-offs – medals awarded for league standings

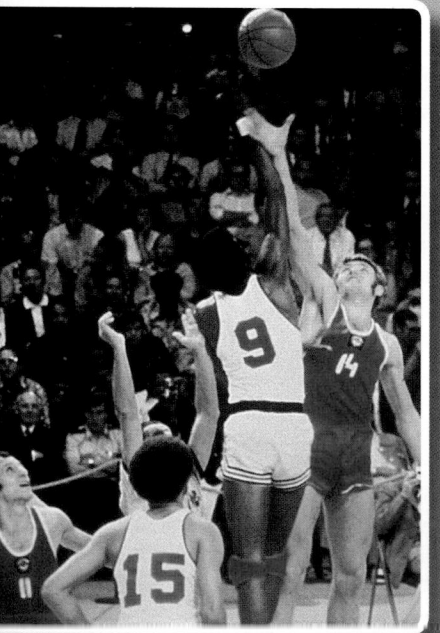

Undying hurt

After seven consecutive gold medals, the first United States Basketball team to be denied the top prize at an Olympic Games felt so upset by their 51–50 defeat to the USSR, that they refused to accept the silver medals they were due. Four decades on from the dramatic 1972 Final, the silver medals still remain in the possession of the International Olympic Committee.

🏀 *The tip-off at the 1972 Olympic Games Basketball Final that saw the United States lose for the first time.*

Schmidt, Gaze and Cruz

Only three men have played Basketball at five different Games – and two of them lead the overall rankings for points scored. Brazil's Oscar Schmidt scored 1,093 points in the 1980, 1984, 1988, 1992 and 1996 tournaments, and his average of 28.8 per match is also a record. Second is Australia's Andrew Gaze, with 789 points spread across the 1984, 1988, 1992, 1996 and 2000 events – he also had the honour of carrying the host nation's flag at Sydney 2000's Opening Ceremony. His father Lindsey Gaze had played Basketball for Australia at the 1960, 1964 and 1968 Games and coached the team in 1972, 1976, 1980 and 1984. Puerto Rico's Teofilo Cruz was not only the first Basketball player, but also the first athlete in any team sport, to compete at five Olympic Games (1960, 1964, 1968, 1972 and 1976).

⬆ *Australia's Andrew Gaze in action against Russia at his record-equalling fifth and final Games at Sydney in 2000.*

Men's medals by country

United States	16 (13 gold, 1 silver, 2 bronze)
USSR	9 (2 gold, 4 silver, 3 bronze)
Yugoslavia	5 (1 gold, 3 silver, 1 bronze)
Brazil	3 (3 bronze)
Lithuania	3 (3 bronze)
Argentina	2 (1 gold, 1 bronze)
France	2 (2 silver)
Italy	2 (2 silver)
Spain	2 (2 silver)
Uruguay	2 (2 bronze)
Canada	1 (1 silver)
Croatia	1 (1 silver)
Serbia	1 (1 silver)
Cuba	1 (1 bronze)
Mexico	1 (1 bronze)

Women's overall medals

United States	8 (6 gold, 1 silver, 1 bronze)
Australia	4 (3 silver, 1 bronze)
USSR	3 (2 gold, 1 bronze)
Brazil	2 (1 silver, 1 bronze)
Bulgaria	2 (1 silver, 1 bronze)
China	2 (1 silver, 1 bronze)
Yugoslavia	2 (1 silver, 1 bronze)
Russia	2 (2 bronze)
Unified Team	1 (1 gold)
South Korea	1 (1 silver)

American dream

'Like Elvis and the Beatles put together' was how US Basketball coach Chuck Daly described the excitement and impact of his country's so-called 'Dream Team' at the 1992 Olympics in Barcelona. A change in the rules made three years earlier meant that this was the first Games at which professional players were allowed to compete. Household names such as Earvin 'Magic' Johnson, Michael Jordan and Larry Byrd starred in a scintillating side whose average winning margin was as high as 43.8 points. The final against Croatia was their tightest game of the tournament – and yet they still cruised to a 117–85 win ... a margin of 32 points.

Five games, four golds

Teresa Edwards became the first – and, to date, only – female basketball player to compete at five different Games, when she won a gold medal with the United States team at Sydney 2000. She also won golds in 1984, 1988 and 1996, and a solitary bronze in 1992. The triumph in 1984, when aged 20, made her the youngest woman to win a Basketball gold medal at the Games – and the 2000 success made her the oldest, at 36.

↖ *Teresa Edwards is the only woman to play at five different Games.*

Dome from home

The Basketball Finals at the 2012 Summer Games will be played at London's O2 Arena, which will be called the North Greenwich Arena for the duration of the Games. The other Basketball matches will be played at a temporary arena located in the Olympic Park. The 12 qualifying places will be shared between the hosts Great Britain, the reigning world champions, two teams from the Americas, two from Europe, one apiece from Africa, Asia and Oceania, and three late 'wild card' entries.

➜ *Former NBA star John Amoechi was part of the team that brought the Games to London in 2012.*

Women's Basketball Finals

1976	Gold: USSR; Silver: United States; Bronze: Bulgaria*
1980	USSR 104, Bulgaria 73 (Bronze: Yugoslavia)
1984	United States 85, South Korea 55 (Bronze: China)
1988	United States 77, Yugoslavia 70 (Bronze: USSR)
1992	Unified Team 76, China 66 (Bronze: United States)
1996	United States 111, Brazil 87 (Bronze: Australia)
2000	United States 76, Australia 54 (Bronze: Brazil)
2004	United States 74, Australia 63 (Bronze: Russia)
2008	United States 92, Australia 65 (Bronze: Russia)

* No play-offs – medals awarded for league standings

Football

The FIFA World Cup is the only rival the Olympic Games has for the title of the world's pre-eminent sporting event. While most footballers regard the World Cup as their sport's top prize, the Olympic Games Football tournament has achieved its own niche after introducing a new rule in 1992, limiting the tournament to under-23s except for three over-age players per squad.

Pioneering champions

Before the first FIFA World Cup was held in 1930, the four-yearly Olympic Games Football tournament was considered an equivalent world championship. Uruguay, who would both host and win the 1930 World Cup, went into the tournament having clinched Football gold in both 1924 and 1928 Games. José Nasazzi, José Andrade, Hector Scarone and Pedro Petrone played in all three winning teams.

⬆ Uruguay's 1928 gold medal-winning team line up before the Final.

Africa calling

An injury-time winner by Emmanuel Amuneke not only gave Nigeria victory over Argentina in their 1996 Final showdown, but also secured Africa's first Football gold at the Games. Four years earlier, Ghana had finished third to become the continent's first Football medallists.

⬇ Celebration time for Nigeria after they beat Argentina 3–2 in the 1996 final.

Men's Football Finals

1896 Not played

1900 (Paris, France) Gold: Upton Park FC (GB); Silver: USFSA XI (France); Bronze: Université Libre de Bruxelles (Belgium) Two exhibition matches played only

1904 (St Louis, US) Gold: Galt FC (Canada); Silver: Christian Brothers College (US); Bronze: St Rose Parish (US) Five exhibition matches played only

1908 (London, England) Great Britain 2, Denmark 0 (Bronze: Netherlands)

1912 (Stockholm, Sweden) Great Britain 4, Denmark 2 (Bronze: Netherlands)

1916 Not played

1920 (Antwerp, Belgium) Belgium 2, Czechoslovakia 0 (Silver: Spain; Bronze: Netherlands)

1924 (Paris, France) Uruguay 3, Switzerland 0 (Bronze: Sweden)

1928 (Amsterdam, Netherlands) Uruguay 1, Argentina 1; Uruguay 2, Argentina 1 (Bronze: Italy)

1932 Not played

1936 (Berlin, Germany) Italy 2, Austria 1 (aet) (Bronze: Norway)

1940 Not played

1944 Not played

1948 (London, England) Sweden 3, Yugoslavia 1 (Bronze: Denmark)

1952 (Helsinki, Finland) Hungary 2, Yugoslavia 0 (Bronze: Sweden)

1956 (Melbourne, Australia) USSR 1, Yugoslavia 0 (Bronze: Bulgaria)

1960 (Rome, Italy) Yugoslavia 3, Denmark 1 (Bronze: Hungary)

1964 (Tokyo, Japan) Hungary 2, Czechoslovakia 1 (Bronze: Germany)

1968 (Mexico City, Mexico) Hungary 4, Bulgaria 1 (Bronze: Japan)

1972 (Munich, West Germany) Poland 2, Hungary 1 (Bronze: USSR / East Germany)

1976 (Montreal, Canada) East Germany 3, Poland 1 (Bronze: USSR)

1980 (Moscow, USSR) Czechoslovakia 1, East Germany 0 (Bronze: USSR)

1984 (Los Angeles, USA) France 2, Brazil 0 (Bronze: Yugoslavia)

1988 (Seoul, South Korea) USSR 2, Brazil 1 (Bronze: West Germany)

1992 (Barcelona, Spain) Spain 3, Poland 2 (Bronze: Ghana)

1996 (Atlanta, USA) Nigeria 3, Argentina 2 (Bronze: Brazil)

2000 (Sydney, Australia) Cameroon 2, Spain 2 (Cameroon won 5–3 on penalties) (Bronze: Chile)

2004 (Athens, Greece) Argentina 1, Paraguay 0 (Bronze: Italy)

2008 (Beijing, China) Argentina 1, Nigeria 0 (Bronze: Brazil)

Women's Football Finals

1996 (Atlanta, USA) USA 2, China 1 (Bronze: Norway)

2000 (Sydney, Australia) Norway 3, USA 2 (golden goal) (Bronze: Germany)

2004 (Athens, Greece) USA 2, Brazil 1 (aet) (Bronze: Germany)

2008 (Beijing, China) USA 1, Brazil 0 (aet) (Bronze: Germany)

Prolific women

Women's Football was introduced at the 1996 Games in Atlanta – and the USA have won three of the four tournaments held, finishing runners-up only in 2000. But Germany's Birgit Prinz is the only female footballer to have scored in all four tournaments. She and Brazil's Cristiane have ten goals at the Games apiece, an all-time competition record.

⬆ Joy Fawcett (left) and Carin Gabarra celebrate victory in 1996.

Women's tournament top scorers

Year	Scorer
1996	Ann Kristin Aarones (Norway); Linda Medalen (Norway); Pretinha (Brazil) – 4
2000	Sun Wen (China) – 4
2004	Cristiane (Brazil); Birgit Prinz (Germany) – 5
2008	Cristiane (Brazil) – 5

Far, far away...

Los Angeles may have been the official Host City for the 1984 Games, but the Football tournament was played in two venues situated more than 3,200 kilometres away: the Navy-Marine Corps Memorial Stadium in Annapolis, Maryland; and the Harvard Stadium in Boston, Massachusetts.

Men's Football tournament top scorers

Year	Scorer
1896	n/a
1900	Unknown
1904	Alexander Hall (Canada); Tom Taylor (Canada) – 3
1908	Sophus Nielsen (Denmark) – 11
1912	Gottfried Fuchs (Germany) – 10
1916	n/a
1920	Herbert Karlsson (Sweden) – 7
1924	Pedro Petrone (Uruguay) – 8
1928	Domingo Tarasconi (Argentina) – 9
1932	n/a
1936	Annibale Frossi (Italy) – 7
1948	John Hansen (Denmark); Gunnar Nordahl (Sweden) – 7
1952	Rajko Mitic (Yugoslavia); Branko Zebec (Yugoslavia) – 7
1956	Neville D'Souza (India); Dimitar Milanov (Bulgaria); Todor Veselinovic (Yugoslavia) – 4
1960	Hans Nielsen (Denmark) – 8
1964	Ferenc Bene (Hungary) – 12
1968	Kunishige Kamamoto (Japan) – 7
1972	Kazimierz Deyna (Poland) – 9
1976	Andrzej Szarmach (Poland) – 6
1980	Sergei Andreev (USSR) – 5
1984	Daniel Xuereb (France); Borislav Cvetkovi (Yugoslavia); Stjepan Deveri (Yugoslavia) – 5
1988	Romário (Brazil) – 7
1992	Andrzej Juskowiak (Poland) – 7
1996	Hernán Crespo (Argentina); Bebeto (Brazil) – 6
2000	Ivan Zamorano (Chile) – 6
2004	Carlos Tévez (Argentina) – 8
2008	Giuseppe Rossi (Italy) – 4

Future generations

Many players who have appeared in the Football tournament at the Olympic Games have gone on to become FIFA World Cup winners, including: Brazil's Dunga, Taffarel, Bebeto, Romario, Ronaldo and Roberto Carlos; Italy's Fabio Cannavaro, Andrea Pirlo, Daniele De Rossi and Gianluigi Buffon; France's Patrick Vieira, West Germany's Andreas Brehme and Jürgen Klinsmann, and Spain's Xavi Hernandez and Carles Puyol.

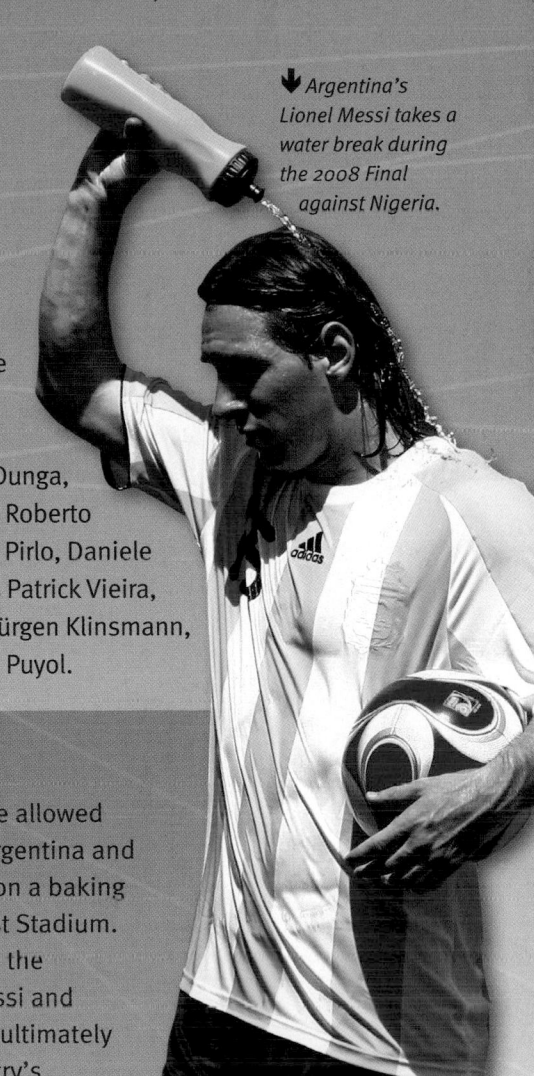

⬇ Argentina's Lionel Messi takes a water break during the 2008 Final against Nigeria.

Water works

Unusually, two breaks for water were allowed during the Football Final between Argentina and Nigeria at the 2008 Games, played on a baking hot afternoon in Beijing's Bird's Nest Stadium. With the temperature at 42° Celsius, the Argentina side, including Lionel Messi and winning goal-scorer Angel Di Maria, ultimately prevailed, winning 1–0 for the country's second successive Football gold medal.

Handball

Men's Handball made its debut as at the Games at Berlin 1936 but did not feature again until the 1972 Games in Munich. Russia (in its various guises) have been the most successful team, claiming gold on four occasions. Women's Handball has been a regular feature of the Games since Montreal 1976 and Denmark lead the way with three victories.

There and back again

Like Basketball, Handball was introduced as a competitive sport at the 1936 Games in Berlin – but, unlike Basketball, which was back 12 years later, it had to wait another 36 years before returning. Romania went into the 1972 Olympic Games in Munich as favourites for Handball gold – and as reigning world champions – but were surprised in the final by the ultimate winners Yugoslavia. Women had to endure another four-year wait before making their Handball debut at the 1976 Games in Montreal. The game is played by 31 million people across 183 different countries, according to the International Handball Federation, but nothing gives it more exposure than its four-yearly place in the Olympic Games.

Men's Handball Finals

1936: Germany (Silver: Austria; Bronze: Switzerland)
(No play-offs – medals awarded for rankings/league standings)
1972: Yugoslavia 21, Czechoslovakia 16 (Bronze: Romania)
1976: USSR 19, Romania 15 (Bronze: Poland)
1980: East Germany 23, USSR 22 (Bronze: Romania)
1984: Yugoslavia 18, West Germany 17 (Bronze: Romania)
1988: USSR 32, South Korea 25 (Bronze: Yugoslavia)
1992: CIS 22, Sweden 20 (Bronze: France)
1996: Croatia 27, Sweden 26 (Bronze: Spain)
2000: Russia 28, Sweden 26 (Bronze: Spain)
2004: Croatia 26, Germany 24 (Bronze: Russia)
2008: France 28, Iceland 23 (Bronze: Spain)

Women's Handball Finals

1976: USSR (Silver: East Germany; Bronze: Hungary)
1980: USSR (Silver: Yugoslavia; Bronze: East Germany)
1984: Yugoslavia (Silver: South Korea; Bronze: China)
1988: South Korea (Silver: Norway; Bronze: USSR)
(No play-offs – medals awarded for rankings)
1992: South Korea 28, Norway 21 (Bronze: CIS)
1996: Denmark 37, South Korea 33 (Bronze: Hungary)
2000: Denmark 31, Hungary 27 (Bronze: Norway)
2004: Denmark 38, South Korea 36 (Bronze: Ukraine)
2008: Norway 34, Russia 27 (Bronze: South Korea)

Great Danes

The gold medal in the women's Handball events at the Games has been a Scandinavian monopoly since 1996, when Denmark won the first of three consecutive titles. Their triumphant run only came to an end at the 2008 Games in Beijing, when they were knocked out in the quarter-finals and neighbours Norway took the top prize instead. Recent Scandinavian dominance should come as no surprise – Denmark and Sweden were among the countries where the game was pioneered in the late 19th century, though the first official rules were published in 1917 by Germans Max Heiser, Karl Schelenz and Erich Konigh.

The International Amateur Handball Federation was founded 11 years later, to coincide with the 1928 Olympic Games in Amsterdam – although it would be another eight years before Handball was contested at the Games for the first time.

Celluloid heroines

South Korea's women's Handball team just missed out on gold, in agonising circumstances, at Athens 2004. Their final against Denmark went to extra time twice, before a penalty shoot-out finally separated the teams and gave Denmark a third championship in a row. But the epic efforts of the South Korean team, after coming into the tournament with little fanfare or expectation, inspired a film called *The Best Moment of Our Lives*, which went on to become a hit with the country's cinema-goers.

Opening gold

Croatia's 27–26 victory over Sweden in the men's Handball Final at the 1996 Olympic Games in Atlanta gave the newly independent Balkan state their first ever Games gold medal. They went on to win gold again in 2004 – having failed to even qualify for the Handball tournament at the 2000 Games.

← *Tears all round for South Korea after their agonising final defeat to Denmark in 2004.*

⬆ *Sweden's Magnus Wislander shoots during the Sydney 2000 Handball final against Russia.*

So near and yet so far

Sweden could claim to be the near-invincibles, with their men's Handball team winning every match at three consecutive Games – except, on each occasion, the final. Their last-ditch conquerors were the post-Soviet Confederation of Independent States (CIS) in 1992, Croatia in 1996 and Russia in 2000. Each of these Swedish sides featured the 'World Handball Player of the Century', as Magnus Wislander was dubbed in 1999 by the International Handball Federation. Wislander represented his country for 19 years, following his debut in January 1985, and played not only at the 1992, 1996 and 2000 Games, but also in 1988, when Sweden finished fifth. Although the gold medal eluded him, Wislander did help Sweden become world champions in 1990 and 1999 and European champions in 1994, 1998, 2000 and 2002.

Handball appeal

Britain has never entered a Handball team at the Olympic Games, either in the men's or women's events – but as hosts will enter both tournaments in 2012. During the Beijing 2008 Games, the British Handball Association issued an appeal for recruits interested in taking part in 2012, promising to send them for specialist training in Denmark – but specifying that men should be at least 6ft 3in and women above 6ft.

Doubling up

Both East Germany and the USSR came close to a male-female Handball double at Moscow 1980, when East Germany took gold and the Soviets silver in the men's Final – and the medal positions were reversed in the women's event. Roswitha Krause was the first woman to win medals at two different Summer Games, when she was part of East Germany's Handball teams that claimed silver in 1976 and bronze four years later. She had previously won a silver medal as a swimmer, in the women's 4 x 100m Freestyle Relay in 1968. Her feat was bettered by Britain's Rebecca Romero, who won silver in the women's Quadruple Sculls in 2004, then struck gold on the cycling track four years later.

Talented talant

Talant Duyshebaev has won men's Handball medals at the Games for two different nations. The Kyrgyzstan-born player represented the CIS at the 1992 Games, helping his side take gold while finishing as tournament top scorer with 47 goals. After moving to Spain and taking Spanish citizenship, he represented his new nation at the 1996 and 2000 Games – winning bronze each time.

On thin ice

Handball gave the world its final sight of Olympic Games sporting action in 2008 when France's 28–23 victory over Iceland in the men's Final was the last of the 302 events to be completed in Beijing. The French victory meant Iceland are still waiting for their first-ever gold – either at the Summer or Winter Games. In the build-up to the Final, Iceland's President Olafur Ragnar Grímsson described 24 August 2008 as the biggest day in the country's sporting history. Although they just fell short of gold, clinching silver was Iceland's best achievement at any Olympic Games for 52 years.

⬇ *France celebrate their 28–23 victory over Iceland at Beijing 2008. It was the last of the 302 events to be completed at the Games.*

⬆ *Spain's Talant Duyshebaev in action at Athens 2004; 12 years earlier he had won bronze with Kyrgyzstan.*

Hockey

One of the oldest team sports on the Games roster, men's Hockey has been played at every Olympiad since London 1908 (bar 1912 and 1924). India were the event's early powerhouses, winning six consecutive gold medals between 1928 and 1956, although their dominance waned with the advent of astroturf pitches at Montreal 1976. Women's Hockey has been contested since Moscow 1980 and Australia have been the event's most successful team, with three victories.

← *England on the attack during their 8–1 victory over Ireland in the first-ever men's Hockey Final in 1908.*

India and Pakistan

The roots of hockey stretch back 4,000 years to 'stick-and-ball' games in Egypt. The sport first appeared at the Olympic Games with a men's competition at London 1908, since when it has featured at every Games except for those of 1912 and 1924. Hockey was dominated by India and Pakistan, where the sport is followed most fanatically, until the 1970s. India won all six gold medals at the Games from 1928 to 1956 and either they or Pakistan continued to be the teams to beat until 1972, when hosts West Germany took gold. Even since then India and Pakistan have never failed to qualify for a men's Hockey competition at the Games, although Pakistan boycotted Moscow 1980. The two countries' relative demise may be connected, as some believe, with the switch to artificial turf at the 1976 Games in Montreal, but India still managed to take gold again four years later and Pakistan four years after that. Women's Hockey first appeared on the Olympic Games programme at Moscow 1980, where Zimbabwe snatched a surprise gold.

Out ... and in

Men's Hockey was removed from the Games schedule at Paris 1924 owing to the lack of an international sporting structure. This led to the formation of the International Hockey Federation, and the sport became a permanent feature from 1928 onwards.

Women under way

Women's Hockey became full-medal sport at the Moscow 1980 Olympic Games (some 72 years after the men's Hockey competition had made its first appearance at the Games), but the outcome was one that few could have predicted as Zimbabwe (who had not trained together as a team in the build-up the event) snatched a surprise gold, pipping Czechoslakia at the top of the Championship Pool by a single point. Their victory chant was 'Forward with the rooster' – Robert Mugabe's party slogan. Their minister of sports promised each squad member a gift of an ox when they arrived home.

Men's Hockey Finals

Year	Result
1908	England 8, Ireland 1
1912	Not held
1920	Great Britain-Denmark (round robin)
1924	Not held
1928	India 3, Netherlands 0
1932	India-Japan (round robin)
1936	India 8, West Germany 1
1948	India 4, Great Britain 0
1952	India 6, Netherlands 1
1956	India 1, Pakistan 0
1960	Pakistan 1, India 0
1964	India 1, Pakistan 0
1968	Pakistan 2, Australia 1
1972	West Germany 1, Pakistan 0
1976	New Zealand 1, Australia 0
1980	India 4, Spain 3
1984	Pakistan 2, West Germany 1
1988	Great Britain 3, West Germany 1
1992	Germany 2, Australia 1
1996	Netherlands 3, Spain 1
2000	Netherlands 3, South Korea 3 (5–4 on pens)
2004	Australia 2, Netherlands 1
2008	Germany 3, Spain 0

Hat-trick hero

Dhyan Chand is arguably the greatest player the game of hockey has ever known. He won three gold medals as a centre-forward for India at the Games of 1928, 1932 and 1936. His birthday, on 29 August, is India's national sports day.

↑ *Dhyan Chand (standing on the back row, second left) led India to men's Hockey gold at the 1928, 1932 and 1936 Olympic Games.*

Flag switch

In 1936, India, then still a British colony, had to march behind the Union Flag at the Opening Ceremony in Berlin, but the country's defiant men's Hockey players saluted the flag of the Indian National Congress before their 8–1 gold-medal victory over Germany. A barefoot Dhyan Chand scored six goals. Reports of Adolf Hitler's reaction are mixed: one claims that he left the match at half-time; another that he offered Chand German citizenship and a commission in the army.

Record success

The widest winning margin in a men's Hockey Final at an Olympic Games was seven goals. In 1908, England beat Ireland 8–1 in London, and in 1936 India beat Germany in Berlin by the same score. The highest margin of victory in any men's Hockey match at the Games was achieved by India at the 1932 Olympic Games in Los Angeles when they beat the United States 24–1.

Independent success

In 1948, a year after gaining independence, India came to the post-war Games in London as reigning men's Hockey champions. The team had lost some players of English descent and a number of Muslims, who had moved to the new nation of Pakistan. These included Ali Dara, who in 1936 had played for India but in 1948 was Pakistan's captain. Nevertheless India reached the Final, where they beat Great Britain 4–0 to win gold. India outscored the competition in their five games, ending with a 25–2 aggregate.

Women's Hockey Finals

1980	Zimbabwe-Czechoslovakia (round robin)
1984	Netherlands-West Germany (round robin)
1988	Australia 2, South Korea 0
1992	Spain 2, Germany 1
1996	Australia 3, South Korea 1
2000	Australia 3, Argentina 1
2004	Germany 2, Netherlands 1
2008	Netherlands 2, China 0

➜ *Ellen Hoog (left) and Sophie Polkamp (right) show off their gold medals after the Netherlands beat hosts China 2–0 in the women's Hockey Final at Beijing 2008.*

Pakistan breakthrough

Pakistan ended India's streak of six straight gold medals and 30 consecutive victories by winning the 1960 men's Final in Rome 1–0. India had outscored their opponents during those 30 games by 178 points to seven. The defeat ended India's streak of invincibility at the Games.

Pitching in

Synthetic pitches are mandatory for all international tournaments and for most national competitions. While hockey is still played on grass fields at some local levels and in lesser national divisions, it has been replaced by synthetic turf almost everywhere in the western world. Over the years, the game has become quicker, more skilful and, with the development of new techniques such as the Indian dribble, more exciting to watch.

Hawkes makes history

Australian midfielder Rechelle Hawkes competed in the Olympic Games for the first time in 1988 and won the first of her three women's Hockey gold medals as Australia eliminated the Netherlands 3–2 in the semi-finals and then hosts South Korea by 2–0 in the Final. At Barcelona 1992, Hawkes experienced a contrasting low point in her career when the Australians were upset 1–0 in the preliminaries by their Spanish hosts. She then led her country back to the top at Atlanta 1996. Australia entered the Final having enjoyed a 38-game unbeaten streak and then beat Korea 3–1. Four years later, in Sydney, Hawkes recited the Athletes' Oath at the Opening Ceremony ... and duly ended up with another gold medal. She is the only female Hockey player to have secured three medals (let alone three gold medals) and the only one to win medals 12 years apart.

➜ *Gold medals in 1988, 1996 and 2000 earned Rechelle Hawkes a place in the history books.*

Volleyball

Volleyball (both men's and women's tournaments) has been contested as an indoor sport at the Olympic Games since 1964. The United States and former Soviet Union lead the way in the men's tournament (with three wins apiece), while the latter are the only four-time winners in the women's event.

Tournament format

The Volleyball tournament format at the Olympic Games originally paralleled the one still employed in the sport's World Cup. All teams played against each other and then were ranked by wins, set average and points average. One disadvantage of this round-robin system is that medal winners could be determined before the end of the games, prompting a loss of focus on the outcome of the remaining matches. To cope with this situation, the competition was split into two parts by the introduction of a knock-out phase, consisting of quarter-finals, semi-finals and final. Since its creation, at Munich 1972, this system has become the standard for the Volleyball tournament at the Games, and is usually referred to as the 'Olympic format'.

➜ *The Soviet Union made a successful defence of their men's Volleyball crown at the 1968 Games in Mexico City.*

Eastern glory

The first two editions of the men's Volleyball tournament, at the Games of 1964 and 1968, were won by the Soviet Union. Four years later it was third time lucky for Japan, and in 1976 the introduction of a new offensive skill, the back row attack, helped Poland strike gold.

More and more

The number of teams involved in the Olympic Games has grown steadily since the first men's Volleyball tournament in 1964. From 1996 onwards, both men's and women's indoor events have involved 12 nations. Each of the five continental volleyball confederations has at least one affiliated national federation involved in the Games.

Taking turns

At Moscow 1980, many of the strongest teams belonged to the Eastern bloc, which meant that the boycott, led by the United States, did not have as great an effect on men's Volleyball as in some other sports. Not surprisingly, the Soviet Union won again, this time beating Bulgaria 3–1 in the Final. The roles were reversed in 1984, when the United States confirmed their new domination of the sport in the west by sweeping past Brazil. This time the Soviets were absent.

⬆ *Karch Kiraly shows his power at the net at the men's Volleyball tournament at Seoul 1988.*

Kiraly's double

'Karch' Kiraly of the United States is the only person to have won medals in both the indoor and beach versions of Volleyball at the Games. Known as the 'Thunderball in Volleyball', he was a fixture on the national team through much of the 1980s as a passer/outside hitter in the 'two-man' or 'swing hitter' serve reception system. Kiraly was in the USA teams that won gold medals at the 1984 and 1988 Games, the latter as team captain. He was also named the International Volleyball Federation's top player in the world in 1986 and 1988. In 1996, he won a gold medal in men's Beach Volleyball at the Atlanta Games. The nickname 'Karch' could be derived from the Hungarian 'Karcsi', which can be translated as 'Charlie'. It is a common derivative of Karoly, which is Charles. His last name, Kiraly, means 'King'.

Men's Volleyball gold, silver and bronze...

1964: Soviet Union–Czechoslovakia–Japan
1968: Soviet Union–Japan–Czechoslovakia
1972: Japan–East Germany–Soviet Union
1976: Poland–Soviet Union–Cuba
1980: Soviet Union–Bulgaria–Romania
1984: United States–Brazil–Italy
1988: United States–Soviet Union–Argentina
1992: Brazil–Netherlands–United States
1996: Netherlands–Italy–Yugoslavia
2000: Yugoslavia–Russia–Italy
2004: Brazil–Italy–Russia
2008: United States–Brazil–Russia

➡ *The United States took men's Volleyball gold for the third time at Beijing 2008.*

Giba's the man

Brazilian star Giba – full name: Gilberto Amaury de Godoy Filho – is arguably the most recognised men's Volleyball player among fans all over the world. Although by modern standards he is not that tall, at 6ft 4in, his charisma, skill and energy have more than made up for his lack of reach. After Brazil lost in the Final at Beijing 2008 some volleyball fans thought their run of success had come to an end. But, in 2010, Giba led Brazil to the world title – the perfect preparation for London 2012.

🔨 *The most famous name in men's volleyball, Brazil's Giba led his country to victory in every major competition in the game: eight South American Championships, three World Championships and to Olympic Games gold at Athens 2004.*

Women's Volleyball gold, silver and bronze...

1964: Japan–Soviet Union–Poland
1968: Soviet Union–Japan–Poland
1972: Soviet Union–Japan–North Korea
1976: Japan–Soviet Union–South Korea
1980: Soviet Union–East Germany–Bulgaria
1984: China–United States–Japan
1988: Soviet Union–Peru–China
1992: Cuba–Unified Team–United States
1996: Cuba–China–Brazil
2000: Cuba–Russia–Brazil
2004: China–Russia–Cuba
2008: Brazil–United States–China

Brazil out in front

Brazil have featured in more men's Volleyball competitions at the Games than any other country, having appeared in all 12, followed by Italy and the United States on nine each. Eleven nations have made just one appearance, the latest of them being Venezuela and Germany, who first took part in 2008 – Germany for the first time as a united country (West Germany having been represented in 1972).

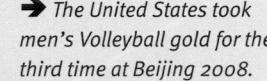

Beach Volleyball

Beach Volleyball originated in southern California and Hawaii around the 1920s but is now popular as far afield as eastern Europe, even in countries not known for their beaches: for example, landlocked Switzerland won the men's Beach Volleyball bronze medal in 2004.

Where it all began

At international level, the elite nations are the United States, Brazil and China. Along with Australia, they are the only winners of gold medals at Olympic Games in either men's or women's Beach Volleyball. The original purpose of the sport was to give bored surfers something to do when the surf was down. The major differences now between beach and indoor volleyball are that the former is played on sand instead of a hard floor and has two players per team rather than six. Plus, most players, even when not playing competitively, when the rules require it, prefer to play the beach version barefoot.

Class of his own

Ron Von Hagen is regarded as the Babe Ruth of men's beach volleyball. Von Hagen established standards and set records at a time when the sport was just beginning. He played in 54 tournaments from 1966 to 1972, never finishing lower than third place in any tournament he entered.

Men's Beach Volleyball gold, silver and bronze...

1996: Karch Kiraly and Kent Steffes (United States); Michael Dodd and Mike Whitmarsh (United States); John Child and Mark Hesse (Canada)

2000: Dain Blanton and Eric Fonoimoana (United States); Ze Marco de Melo and Ricardo Santos (Brazil); Axel Hager and Jorg Ahmann (Germany)

2004: Ricardo Santos and Emanuel Rego (Brazil); Javier Bosma and Pablo Herrera (Spain); Stefan Kobel and Patrick Heuscher (Switzerland)

2008: Todd Rogers and Phil Dalhausser (United States); Marcio Araujo and Fabio Luiz Magalhaes (Brazil); Ricardo Santos and Emanuel Rego (Brazil)

⬇ *Phil Dalhausser (centre left) and Todd Rogers (centre right) took gold at Beijing 2008.*

New arrival

Beach Volleyball was introduced into the Barcelona 1992 Olympic Games as a demonstration event, becoming a medal sport four years later. A total of 24 teams participate in each tournament. Teams qualify on the basis of their performance in FIVB events over the course of approximately 18 months leading up to the Games. There is a limit of two teams per country, and one spot is reserved for the Host Country and another for a randomly chosen wildcard country. In the event that any continent is not represented, the highest ranked team from that continent also qualifies for the tournament.

➡ *Karch Kiraly took his indoor Volleyball form to the sand to help the United States to the inaugural Beach Volleyball title at Atlanta 1996.*

Kiraly crosses over

Talk about versatility. Widely regarded as one of the best indoor men's volleyball players ever, leading the United States to gold in 1984 and 1988, 'Karch' Kiraly is considered the Michael Jordan of the sport, beating performers half his age. He has won at least one tournament in 24 of the 28 seasons he has played, spanning four different decades. He is the only person in the history of the Olympic Games to have won three men's Volleyball gold medals, and to have struck gold in both versions of the sport, having been part of the United States' indoor teams in 1984 and 1988 before winning on the sand in 1996 in Atlanta with Kent Steffes. He grew up in Santa Barbara, California, and learned the game from his father, Dr Laszlo Kiraly. He has claimed a title in 24 different states with 13 different partners.

Depression driven

The sport was given a boost in the United States by the Great Depression of the 1930s. Starved of cash, Americans flocked to the beaches in their hundreds to take part in what was virtually a no-cost pastime and a free source of entertainment. It was only a matter of time before the International Volleyball Federation had to recognise the sport and that breakthrough came in 1986.

No stroll across the sand

Beach Volleyball is one of the most spectacular of Olympic sports for the spectators, with players throwing themselves athletically around the court to keep the ball in play and to keep the action live. The court size is the same as the indoor version, as are the net dimensions. Each team is allowed three hits to return the ball and no player can hit the ball twice in a row. The sand must be at least 40 centimetres deep and no substitutions are allowed.

Doubling up

Kerri Walsh and Misty May-Treanor are the only pair to have successfully defended their women's Beach Volleyball title at the Games, adding the 2008 gold to their success four years earlier and being named 'the greatest beach volleyball team of all time'. They beat China's Jia Tian and Jie Wang 21–18 and 21–18. The victory was also the 100th of Walsh's career and the team's 19th consecutive tournament and 108th consecutive match win. Walsh became the fastest player, man or woman, to reach the 100-win milestone, having done it in just 141 career tournaments, eclipsing even May-Treanor, who had achieved the feat in her 153rd tournament.

➔ *Misty May-Treanor (left) and Kerri Walsh (right) won in 2004 and 2008.*

Fans flock to the beach

Eighteen teams competed in the first women's Beach Volleyball tournament at the 1996 Games in Atlanta, an event attended by more than 107,000 spectators. Brazil dominated, with Jackie Silva and Sandra Pires beating fellow Brazilians Monica Rodrigues and Adriana Samuel for the gold medal. Australians Natalie Cook and Kerri-Ann Pottharst won bronze.

↖ *Brazil's Sandra Pires (left) and Jackie Silva (right) won the first women's Beach Volleyball event in 1996.*

Women's Beach Volleyball gold, silver and bronze...

1996:	Jackie Silva and Sandra Pires (Brazil); Monica Rodrigues and Adriana Samuel (Brazil); Natalie Cook and Kerri Pottharst (Australia)
2000:	Natalie Cook and Kerri Potthurst (Australia); Adriana Behar and Shelda Bede (Brazil); Adriana Samuel and Sandra Pires (Brazil)
2004:	Kerri Walsh and Misty May-Treanor (United States); Shelda Bede and Adriana Behar (Brazil); Holly McPeak and Elaine Youngs (United States)
2008:	Kerri Walsh and Misty May-Treanor (United States); Tian Jia and Wang Jie (China); Xue Chen and Zhang Xi (China)

When the kit fits...

Women Beach Volleyball players have the option of playing in a one-piece uniform, but most prefer bikinis, which are more comfortable and allow for a greater range of motion. At the 2006 Asian Games, only one Muslim country fielded a team in the Beach Volleyball series, amid concerns that the uniform was inappropriate. Men Beach Volleyball players wear loose-fitting vests and shorts that hit mid-thigh.

Chapter Five
Cycling

Cycling's pride in its place among the foundation sports of the modern Olympic Games is justified by a glance at an oil painting in the Olympic Museum in Lausanne.

Painted by Charles de Coubertin – father of Pierre – it links the ancient Games with the modern. The goddess Athena is represented placing a laurel wreath on the head of a victorious modern athlete while cycling is among a handful of sports represented in the background.

Initially, Cycling at the Olympic Games was split between the Track contests and the Road Races. Mountain Bike competition 'arrived' only in 1996 in Atlanta – the same year professionals were formally allowed to compete for the first time. The 2008 Games in Beijing saw BMX Racing make its debut, a product of the need to enhance interest in the Games among young people worldwide.

Beijing 2008 also saw Great Britain's Cycling team enjoy unprecedented success. The 25-strong squad collected 14 medals (eight gold, four silver and two bronze) to top the Cycling medal table.

Chris Hoy was the first Briton to win three golds at a single Olympic Games in a century, while Rebecca Romero became the first British woman to win a medal in two different sports at the Games. Her gold in the women's Individual Pursuit outshone even her Rowing silver in the women's Quadruple Sculls in 2004.

Chris Hoy on his way to breaking the Games record with a time of 9.815 seconds during qualification for the men's Sprint event held at the 2008 Games in Beijing. Hoy went on to win the Sprint Final, added further gold medals in the Team Sprint and Keirin events and his efforts earned him not only a knighthood but also the accolade of becoming the most successful Scottish Olympian of all time.

Cycling — BMX

BMX Racing has been gaining in global prominence since the 1960s, with the International BMX Federation founded in 1981 and the first World Championships were staged 19 years later. Yet the landmark moment came when the International Olympic Committee approved its status as a full-medal sport in 2003 and it made its first appearance at Beijing 2008.

Golden 'Oldie'

French cyclist Anne-Caroline Chausson received the first ever gold medal for women's BMX Racing when she won the event at the 2008 Games in Beijing, at the Laoshan BMX Field. The women's Final was held 10 minutes before the men's. Thirty-year-old Chausson went into the event as the oldest woman taking part – and also as someone who had only just returned to BMX Racing after 14 years away. Chausson gave up the sport in 1993 to concentrate on downhill mountain bike racing, in which she won nine world titles. But she made a comeback in 2007, lured by BMX's imminent Games debut. Chausson not only performed faster than all the other women competing, but also almost all the men – her quickest 350-metre lap was timed at 35.976 seconds, in the final.

➘ She may have been the oldest competitor in the line-up, but age was no barrier for France's Anne-Caroline Chausson as she surged to women's BMX Racing gold at Beijing 2008.

Riding through the pain

Australia's Luke Madill was knocked out of the men's BMX Racing event at Beijing 2008 at the quarter-final stage, finishing seventh out of eight in his heat, but simply competing was prize enough. Just two years earlier he had broken his back while taking part in the Australian national championships. He was not alone: American Kyle Bennett rode in one of the 2008 semi-finals despite having dislocated his left shoulder in the quarter-final two days earlier, but missed out on the final by coming sixth out of eight.

Dangerous name

With its sharp bends, challenging bumps and breakneck pace, BMX Racing is not for the faint-hearted. Australian cyclist Jamie Hildebrandt has played up the potential dangers more than most, by officially changing his name to Kamakazi. This might have been the most memorable thing about his performance at the 2008 Games, however, as he finished sixth out of eight in his men's semi-final.

↑ Australian BMX racer James Hildebrandt/Kamakazi at Beijing 2008.

Speed King Artur

In the 2008 men's BMX Racing event both the gold medal and the fastest lap time were claimed by Latvia – but by different cyclists. While Maris Strombergs came out on top, Artur Matisons achieved a best time of 35.903 seconds in his quarter-final but was eliminated after finishing seventh out of eight in his semi-final, not even completing his final circuit of the track.

Magic maris

Maris Strombergs's triumphant ride in the Beijing 2008 final made him the first man ever to win a BMX Racing gold medal. The 21-year-old, who was also crowned BMX world champion that year, was Latvia's only gold medallist at Beijing 2008 – and only the second Latvian in history (after gymnast Igors Vihrovs in 2000) to win gold at the Games. Strombergs received further reward by being given the honour of carrying the Latvian flag at the Closing Ceremony of the 2008 Games.

Little and large

With a height of 1.91 metres, 2008 men's BMX Racing silver medallist Mike Day, a two-time world championship medallist from the United States, was the tallest participant in the men's event. The shortest was the man who took silver – his compatriot Donny Robinson, who is 1.65m tall.

Mountain Bike

Mountain Bike Racing is a relative newcomer to the sporting world – the Union Cycliste Internationale (UCI) recognised it as a sport as late as 1990 (when it sanctioned the world championship). It did not take long to achieve full-medal status at the Games, however: it made its first appearance at Atlanta 1996 and has been on the programme ever since.

Absalon supremacy

The superstar of Mountain Biking has been double Olympic champion Julien Absalon. The Frenchman successfully defended his title at the Beijing 2008 Games thanks to his commitment – in addition to skill and stamina – in his determination to search out any and every advantage he can gain from his equipment. His bike weighs less than 10kg due to its aerodynamic design and minimum number of gears. It's not for show, Absalon seeks the lightest vehicle he can muster to help him when he is forced to carry it on the toughest parts of a course. Absalon's compatriot Jean-Christophe Peraud improved from 11th in Athens to silver medallist at Beijing 2008 with Nino Schurter winning a photo finish for bronze against fellow Swiss Christoph Sauser ... two minutes after Absalon.

↘ *Julien Absalon of France hurtles around the Cross-Country course on his way to gold in the men's Mountain Bike event at the Beijing 2008 Games.*

Champ skates on thin ice

Mountain Biking's first men's Olympic champion might not have even taken up the sport at all had it not been for a childhood accident. Bart Brentjens, like many Dutch teenagers, took part in speed skating during the winter. When he was 13 years old he chose to skate on a particularly thin stretch of ice and fell into the freezing, dirty water. He picked up an infection via blisters on his feet which passed into his blood and then into the bone. Brentjens was hospitalised for seven weeks and was advised to cycle as part of his recovery due to being unable to walk far. He went on to win a World Championship and then came his moment of glory at Atlanta 1996.

Blazing Gunn-Rita

Gunn-Rita Dahle, who claimed the 2004 women's Olympic title at the Athens 2004 Games, was another champion who stumbled into the sport. The Norwegian was encouraged to give a mountain bike a whirl, two months later was crowned national champion and six months after first sitting on an `mtb` she signed a professional contract. A four-time world champion, Dahle took the race by the scruff of the neck at Athens 2004, storming into the lead on the first of the five 6km circuits and never relinquished it.

Roller-coaster ride

Hadleigh Farm will host the London 2012 Olympic Games Mountain Bike events. The highest point on the course is just 70 metres above sea level but the design requires riders to climb 50 metres therefore meeting the minimum elevation required for an Olympic cross country circuit. Competitors will make the climb and descend six times per lap – making it a real roller-coaster ride. The 550-acre site near Benfleet in Essex is overlooked by the 700-year-old ruins of Hadleigh Castle.

Spitz toughs it out

The Olympic discipline of Mountain Bike Cross-Country races are held over undulating circuits; a mixture of descents, forest roads, rocky paths and obstacles. The course distance varies and races can take up to two-and-a-half hours to complete. In the 2008 Games the weather on the day of the women's race over six laps of a tough 4.5km circuit was hot and humid. Only 18 of the 30 riders finished the race, among the retirements was defending champion Gunn-Rita Dahle who was two months pregnant at the time. The glory went to 36-year-old German Sabine Spitz, after one hour 45 minutes of hard graft.

↓ *Germany's Sabine Spitz on her way to winning the women's Mountain Bike event at Beijing 2008.*

Cycling – Road

Road Cycling was first contested at Athens 1896. The women's Individual Road Race has been contested since 1984. Two Road Races will be contested at London 2012: a 250km race for men, and a 140km equivalent for women. Time Trials on the road are also held, with riders setting off 90 seconds apart. Team races were contested from 1912 to 1956, with each country's best performers' average counted, while on-road team trials were held from 1960 to 1992.

A borrower be

Cycling featured at the inaugural Games in 1896 – a full seven years before the introduction of the Tour de France – with home country hero Aristidis Konstantinidis winning the men's Road Race through Athens. Yet Cycling would not return to the Games until 1912. In 1896, Konstantinidis completed his gruelling 87-kilometre (54-mile) ride from Athens to Marathon and back again in a winning time of 3:22.31 seconds despite falling off his bicycle at one point and reportedly having to borrow a replacement bike when his own broke. His luck ran out on the track in the 10km and 100km races, though – he finished fifth in the 10km after a collision with compatriot Georgios Kolettis and he was among the seven out of nine racers who failed to complete the 100km contest.

Individual Road Race winners
Men

1896	Aristidis Konstantinidis (Greece)
1912	Rudolph Lewis (South Africa)
1920	Harry Stenqvist (Sweden)
1924	Armand Blanchonnet (France)
1928	Henry Hansen (Denmark)
1932	Attilio Pavesi (Italy)
1936	Robert Charpentier (France)
1948	Jose Beyaert (France)
1952	Andre Noyelle (Belgium)
1956	Ercole Baldini (Italy)
1960	Viktor Kapitonov (USSR)
1964	Mario Zanin (Italy)
1968	Pierfranco Vianelli (Italy)
1972	Hennie Kuiper (Netherlands)
1976	Bernt Johansson (Sweden)
1980	Sergei Sukhoruchenkov (USSR)
1984	Alexi Grewal (USA)
1988	Olaf Ludwig (East Germany)
1992	Fabio Casartelli (Italy)
1996	Pascal Richard (Switzerland)
2000	Jan Ullrich (Germany)
2004	Paolo Bettini (Italy)
2008	Samuel Sanchez (Spain)

Women

1984	Connie Carpenter (USA)
1988	Monique Krol (Netherlands)
1992	Kathy Watt (Australia)
1996	Jeannie Longo (France)
2000	Leontien Zijlaard (Netherlands)
2004	Sara Carrigan (Australia)
2008	Nicole Cooke (Great Britain)

Leader of the pack

Not many races could be closer run than the 194-kilometre (121-mile) men's Road Race at Tokyo 1964, won by Italy's Mario Zanin. He finished in a time of 4:39:51.63 – only 0.2 seconds ahead of Denmark's Kjell Rodian. In fact, only 0.16 seconds divided the first 51 finishers, 26 of whom were all recorded at the third-best time of 4:39:51.74, though it was Belgium's Walter Godefroot who was awarded bronze.

What goes on tour

Spain's Miguel Indurain became the first Tour de France champion to add an Olympic Games gold, when he won the first men's Road Time Trial at the 1996 Games in Atlanta. That triumph completed a stunning winning run, after he claimed five consecutive Tour de France championships between 1991 and 1995. He was helped, though, by the fact that Atlanta 1996 was the first to admit professional cyclists – the only people, before then, allowed to enter the Tour de France.

← *Five-time Tour de France winner Miguel Indurain added a gold medal to his trophy haul at Atlanta 1996.*

Individual time trial winners
Men
1996 Miguel Indurain (Spain)
2000 Viatcheslav Ekimov (Russia)
2004 Tyler Hamilton (USA)
2008 Fabian Cancellara (Switzerland)

Women
1996 Zulfiya Zabirova (Russia)
2000 Leontien Zijlaard (Netherlands)
2004 Leontien van Moorsel (Netherlands)
2008 Kristin Armstrong (USA)

Krol's starring roles
Monique Krol of the Netherlands, winner of the women's Road Race in 1988, missed out on retaining her title when she could only finish third at Barcelona 1992. Yet her bronze medal there, four years after taking gold in Seoul, made her the first cyclist to win medals in the same individual Cycling event two Olympic Games in a row.

Jan the man
No male cyclist had clinched medals at the Games for both individual Road events and Road Time Trials until Jan Ullrich's triumph at the 2000 Games in Sydney. Ulrich, the 1997 Tour de France winner from Germany, took gold in the men's Road Race and silver in the men's Time Trial. Swiss cyclist Fabian Cancellara emulated Ullrich's feat at Beijing 2008, albeit with his medals the other way around – he won gold in the Time Trial and silver in the Road Race. Cancellara actually finished the Road Race in third place, but moved up a position when original silver medallist Davide Rebellin, from Italy, was demoted. Two women had already achieved such a double before Ulrich and Cancellara. At Atlanta 1996, France's Jeannie Longo secured gold in the Road Race and silver in the Time Trial, while Clara Hughes collected bronze in both events.

↑ *Germany's Jan Ullrich leads the field on his way to men's Road Race gold at Sydney 2000.*

Cycle of victory
As expected given the sport's popularity in the country, France hold the record for the most gold medals in the men's Team Road Race (an event which ran from 1912 until 1992) with four wins – in 1920, 1924, 1936 and 1956. The USSR (with three successive wins between 1972 and 1980) lie second on the all-time winners list alongside Italy (1932, 1960 and 1984).

Long-serving Longo
France's Jeannie Longo has competed in more Olympic Games than any other cyclist. The 2008 Games in Beijing were her seventh, Longo having first competed at Los Angeles 1984. She ended her career with four medals – one gold (from the Road Race in 1996), two silvers (the Road Race in 1992 and the Time Trial in 1996), and one bronze (from the Time Trial in 2000). Her final Games appearance saw her finish fourth in the 2008 Road Time Trial, just two seconds away from another bronze.

← *Seven Olympic Games brought Jeannie Longo four medals.*

Hughes better, Hughes best
Canada's Clara Hughes really was a woman for all seasons. At the 1996 and 2000 Summer Games in Atlanta and Sydney she competed as a cyclist – securing two bronzes, in the women's Road Race and the women's Time Trial. She was also an accomplished speed skater, winning women's 5km bronze at the 2002 Winter Olympics and then women's 5km gold and women's Team Pursuit silver four years later. Hughes was the first person to win more than one medal at both the Summer and Winter Games.

→ *Canada's Clara Hughes won two Cycling bronze medals in the Summer Games and a bronze and gold medal in the Winter Games – a unique feat.*

Cycling – Men's Track

Track Cycling has become more refined since the 1896 Games, when the Cycling events culminated in a gruelling 12-hour race. London 2012 will feature five track events (for men and women): Individual Sprint, Team Sprint, Team Pursuit, the Keirin and the Omnium, which involves six different races including sprints and time trials.

Chris chase

Chris Hoy has a strong claim to be the greatest male cyclist in the history of the Games, collecting four gold medals and a silver across the 2004 and 2008 Games – and with his sights set on even more at London 2012. The Scottish star won his first gold in Athens in 2004, in the 1km Time Trial. His winning performance set a new Games record – 1:00.711 – which will not be beaten since the event was removed from the schedule after Athens. Hoy responded by training in new disciplines, which paid off admirably at the 2008 Games in Beijing. His triumphs in the Individual Sprint, the Team Sprint and the Keirin made him the first British athlete to win three gold medals at one Games since swimmer Henry Taylor exactly 100 years earlier. He also set another Games record, his 9.815 seconds in the Individual Sprint. Within months of his Beijing glory, Edinburgh-born Hoy had been voted BBC Sports Personality of the Year and knighted in the Queen's New Year Honours List.

Hurley's early glory

The winner of even more golds in one Olympic Games than Chris Hoy, however, was the United States' Marcus Hurley. At the 1904 Games in St Louis he was victorious in the quarter-mile, third-mile, half-mile and one-mile races, as well as claiming bronze in the two-mile contest.

The feats of Flameng

France's Leon Flameng was rewarded for his sports-manship when Cycling first appeared at the modern Games in Athens in 1896. He took gold in the 100-kilometre track race, despite stopping during his 300 laps, getting off his bike and waiting to be caught up by a Greek opponent who had been delayed by mechanical difficulties. Flameng fell from his own bike close to the finish, but still ended in first place – and with a French flag tied to his leg. Also on the Athens track that summer, he added silver in the 10km race and bronze in the 2km Sprint.

↑ France's Leon Flameng (left) took the gold medal in the 100km race at the inaugural Modern Games in Athens in 1896.

Cycling Track: most medals

6: Bradley Wiggins (Great Britain, 2000–2008) – 3 gold, 1 silver, 2 bronze

6: Burton Downing (USA, 1904) – 2 gold, 3 silver, 1 bronze

5: Chris Hoy (Great Britain, 2000–2008) – 4 gold, 1 silver

5: Marcus Hurley (USA, 1904) – 4 gold, 1 silver

5: Daniel Morelon (France, 1964–1976) – 3 gold, 1 silver, 1 bronze

5: Jens Fiedler (Germany, 1992–2000) – 3 gold, 2 bronze

4: Jens Lehmann (Germany, 1992–2000) – 2 gold, 2 silver

3: Paul Masson (France, 1896) – 3 gold

3: Guido Fulst (Germany, 1992–2004) – 2 golds, 1 bronze

← Chris Hoy was Great Britain's star performer at the 2008 Games in Beijing, winning gold in the Individual Sprint, the Team Sprint and the Keirin.

Team Pursuit winners

1908 Great Britain (Benjamin Jones, Clarence Kingsbury, Leonard Meredith, Ernest Payne)
1912 Not included
1920 Italy (Arnaldo Carli, Ruggero Ferrario, Franco Giorgetti, Primo Magnani)
1924 Italy (Angelo de Martino, Alfredo Dinale, Aurelio Menegazzi, Francesco Zucchetti)
1928 Italy (Marco Cattaneo, Cesare Facciani, Mario Lusiani, Luigi Tasselli)
1932 Italy (Nino Borsari, Marco Cimatti, Alberto Ghilardi, Paolo Pedretti)
1936 France (Robert Charpentier, Jean Goujon, Guy Lapebie, Roger-Jean Le Nizerhy)
1948 France (Pierre Adam, Serge Blusson, Charles Coste, Fernand Decanali)
1952 Italy (Loris Campana, Mino de Rossi, Guido Messina, Marino Morettini)
1956 Italy (Antonio Domenicali, Leando Faggin, Franco Gandini, Valentino Gasparella)
1960 Italy (Luigi Arienti, Franco Testa, Mario Vallotto, Marino Vigna)
1964 Germany (Lothar Claesges, Karlheinz Henrichs, Karl Link, Ernst Streng)
1968 Denmark (Gunnar Asmussen, Mogens Jensen, Per Jorgensen, Reno Olsen)
1972 West Germany (Gunther Schumacher, Jurgen Colombo, Gunter Haritz, Udo Hempel)
1976 West Germany (Peter Vonhof, Gregor Braun, Hans Lutz, Gunther Schumacher)
1980 USSR (Viktor Manakov, Valery Movchan, Vladimir Osokin, Vitaly Petrakov)
1984 Australia (Michael Grenda, Kevin Nichols, Michael Turtur, Dean Woods)
1988 USSR (Viatcheslav Ekimov, Arturas Kasputis, Dmitry Nelyubin, Gintautas Umaras)
1992 Germany (Stefan Steinweg, Andreas Walzer, Guido Fulst, Michael Glockner, Jens Lehmann)
1996 France (Christophe Capelle, Philippe Ermenault, Jean-Michel Monin, Francis Moreau)
2000 Germany (Guido Fulst, Robert Bartko, Daniel Becke, Jens Lehmann)
2004 Australia (Graeme Brown, Brett Lancaster, Brad McGee, Luke Roberts)
2008 Great Britain (Ed Clancy, Paul Manning, Geraint Thomas, Bradley Wiggins)

Individual Sprint winners

1896 Paul Masson (France)
1900 Georges Taillandier (France)
1904 Not included
1908 Race declared void
1912 Not included
1920 Maurice Peeters (Netherlands)
1924 Lucien Michard (France)
1928 Roger Beaufrand (France)
1932 Jacobus van Edmond (Netherlands)
1936 Toni Merkens (Germany)
1948 Mario Ghella (Italy)
1952 Enzo Sacchi (Italy)
1956 Michel Rousseau (France)
1960 Sante Gaiardoni (Italy)
1964 Giovanni Pettenella (Italy)
1968 Daniel Morelon (France)
1972 Daniel Morelon (France)
1976 Anton Tkat (Czechoslovakia)
1980 Lutz Hesslich (East Germany)
1984 Mark Gorski (USA)
1988 Lutz Hesslich (East Germany)
1992 Jens Fiedler (Germany)
1996 Jens Fiedler (Germany)
2000 Marty Nothstein (USA)
2004 Ryan Bayley (Australia)
2008 Chris Hoy (Great Britain)

Games Records

SPRINT: Chris Hoy (Great Britain), 2008 – 9.815sec
INDIVIDUAL PURSUIT: Bradley Wiggins (Great Britain), 2008 – 4min 15.031sec
1KM TIME TRIAL: Chris Hoy (Great Britain), 2004 – 1min 0.711sec
TEAM PURSUIT: Ed Clancy, Paul Manning, Geraint Thomas, Bradley Wiggins (Great Britain), 2008 – 3min 53.312sec

Doubling up, twice over

Cheered on by his home crowd at the 1960 Games in Rome, Italy's Sante Gaiardoni became the first person to win gold in the 1km Sprint and 1km Time Trial events. He went into the Games as the reigning amateur world champion, adding the professional world title four years later.

Back in the saddle

Britain's Bradley Wiggins became the first cyclist to make a successful defence of a Pursuit title at the Games, winning the Individual Pursuit gold at the 2004 Games in Athens and again in Beijing four years later. In Athens he also won silver for the Team Pursuit and bronze for the Madison, making him the first Briton to win three medals in one Games since Mary Rand in 1964.

⬆ *Bradley Wiggins (left) leads Great Britain's Team Pursuit team to gold at the 2008 Games in Beijing.*

Cycling – Women's Track

Women did not contest Road Racing until Los Angeles 1984 and Track Racing had to wait four years for the first Individual Sprint (at Seoul 1988) and eight for the first Individual Pursuit (at Barcelona 1992). Concerns about an imbalance between male and female races (the men had seven races compared to the women's three in 2008) have been addressed at London 2012 – with five contests each.

Lion-hearted Leontien

Leontien van Moorsel's feats on the cycling track – and the road – are impressive enough, even before one takes into account her health struggles away from racing. The Dutch cyclist won four medals – including three golds – at the 2000 Games: gold in both women's individual races, and in the 3km Individual Pursuit, as well as silver in the track points race. She was one of only six athletes to complete a hat-trick of gold medals at that year's Games. At Athens 2004 she retained her women's Road Time Trial title and added bronze in the 3km Pursuit. Before such successes, however, she had had to win a fight against depression and anorexia that saw her lose 45 pounds in weight in the mid-1990s. She is one of only three cyclists to have won six medals at the Games. Britain's Bradley Wiggins won three golds (4km Individual Pursuit in 2004, the same event and the Team Pursuit in 2008), one silver (Team Pursuit in 2004) and two bronzes (Team Pursuit in 2000 and Madison in 2004). The United States' Burton Downing collected all six of his medals at the 1904 Games: golds in the 25-mile and two-mile races, silvers in the quarter-mile, third-mile and one-mile events, and a bronze in the half-mile contest.

➡ *The Netherlands' six-time Cycling medallist Leontien van Moorsel.*

So near, so far for Ferris

Australia's Michelle Ferris broke the Games record in the women's Sprint in Atlanta in 1996, completing a qualifier in 11.21 seconds. That time has not been beaten in any Games since – yet she still missed out on gold, finishing second behind Felicia Bellanger in the final. Ferris also finished a place behind Bellanger four years later in the women's 500m Time Trial – an event only staged at the 2000 and 2004 Games.

⬆ *An Olympic record but no gold medal for Michelle Ferris at Atlanta 1996.*

Individual Pursuit winners

1992 Petra Rossner (Germany)
1996 Antonella Bellutti (Italy)
2000 Leontien van Moorsel (Netherlands)
2004 Sarah Ulmer (New Zealand)
2008 Rebecca Romero (Great Britain)

Individual Sprint winners

1988 Erika Salumae (USSR)
1992 Erika Salumae (Estonia)
1996 Felicia Ballanger (France)
2000 Felicia Ballanger (France)
2004 Lori-Ann Muenzer (Canada)
2008 Victoria Pendleton (Great Britain)

Points Race (now discontinued)

1996	Nathalie Lancien (France)
2000	Antonella Bellutti (Italy)
2004	Olga Slyusareva (Russia)
2008	Marianne Vos (Netherlands)

500m Time Trial (now discontinued)

2000	Felicia Ballanger (France)
2004	Anna Meares (Australia)

Cycling Track: most medals

6: Leontien van Moorsel (Netherlands, 2000–2004) – 4 gold, 1 silver, 1 bronze

3: Felicia Ballanger (France, 1996-2000) – 3 gold

Ice Christa

Like Clara Hughes and Connie Carpenter-Phinney, East Germany's Christa Rothenburger won Olympic Games medals in both Speed Skating and Cycling – yet she is the only athlete to have claimed Summer and Winter Games medals in the same year. At Calgary 1988, she won silver in the 500km Sprint and gold in the 1000m. Seven months later, at the Summer Games in Seoul, she added a silver medal in the women's Sprint – having been persuaded in 1980 to take up Cycling by her coach and later husband Ernst Ludwig. She ended her career with two other Winter Olympics Speed Skating medals – gold in the 500m Sprint in Sarajevo in 1984 and bronze in the same event in Albertville eight years later.

→ *Christina Rothenburger (right) was on a roll in 1988*

Flying the flag

Two different countries – but the same athlete – won the first two sprint Cycling events contested by women at any Olympic Games. The race was introduced in Seoul in 1988, when Erika Salumae claimed gold for the USSR. Following the break-up of the Soviet Union, she competed for her native Estonia four years later when successfully defending her title in Barcelona. Salumae hardly put a foot wrong in becoming Estonia's first female gold medallist, as well as the country's first medallist since 1936 and the first gold medallist from any country formally separating from the Soviet Union. Alas, her Victory Ceremony was somewhat marred when organisers raised her country's flag the wrong way up – prompting Salumae to shake her head in amazement while standing on the podium, though she later insisted she minded the mistake 'only a little bit'.

⬇ *Erika Salumae (centre) took Individual Sprint gold (for the USSR) at Seoul 1988 and defended her title (for Estonia) at Barcelona 1992.*

Romero's conquests

Rebecca Romero became only the second woman to win medals in two different sports at a Summer Games when she clinched Cycling gold for the Individual Pursuit at Beijing 2008. She had earlier won a silver medal for Rowing at the 2004 Games in Athens, in the Quadruple Sculls event. But she switched to track cycling after a back injury forced her to give up rowing. Romero went to Beijing as the first Brit even to compete in two different sports at Summer Games. She hoped to defend her Cycling title at the 2012 Games in London – especially since she grew up in the south London borough of Sutton – but was disappointed when the Individual Pursuit was dropped from the programme.

→ *Britain's Rebecca Romero powered to Individual Pursuit gold at Beijing 2008.*

Chapter Six
Equestrian

Equestrian has changed immensely since its debut at the 1900 Olympic Games in Paris. There, five nations competed in five different equestrian events, with Belgium becoming the most successful country when they won Jumping and the Long Jump gold.

After its inaugural appearance, there was a 12-year gap before horse and rider made a return to the Games, at Stockholm in 1912, in accordance with the wishes of Count Clarence von Rosen of Sweden, Master of the Horse to the King of Sweden.

By this time a more modern structure of events had been introduced, featuring a programme of Dressage, Eventing and Jumping, while events such as the Vault and Polo have long since disappeared from the Games agenda. There remained an elitist feel to the contest, however, and only military men were allowed to compete in Equestrian events until Helsinki 1952.

Nowadays Equestrian is regarded as a symbol of equality, with men and women competing on equal terms. It is also the only Games discipline in which humans and animals are permitted to compete together, the only stipulation being that all horses must be at least seven years old and the same nationality as their rider.

As we shall see, the Games have spawned a number of equine and human stars, and Equestrian at the Games has featured competitors from all walks of life including royalty, prisoners of war and national heroes.

Such is the appeal of Equestrian that gold medallists have come from five continents, while scientific advances and changes in attitude have greatly improved safety for both horse and rider.

Hinrich Romeike punches the air after leading Germany to team gold in the Show Jumping competition at the 2008 Games held in Hong Kong. Australia finished in second place, with Great Britain picking up the bronze medal.

Dressage

Dressage competition at the Games remained an exclusive club open only to male cavalry officers until Helsinki 1952, when both male and female civilians were finally gained admittance. Today, as a sport that is open to all, Dressage lays claim to being the fastest-growing Equestrian event at the Games.

King of the castle

Stockholm 1912 saw the debut of Dressage as a sport at the Olympic Games. The event was dominated by the host nation, with Carl Bonde and his white-faced steed Emperor leading a triumvirate of Swedish medallists. Such was Sweden's superiority that all six of its riders finished in the top eight of a truly international field of 21 competitors. Bonde later claimed further Games success, winning the silver medal at Amsterdam 1928, before he won the title of 'King of the Castle', when he inherited the spectacular Tudor castle of Tjolöholm in Fjärås, Sweden.

Out of sight but not mind

The Olympic Dressage competition at the 1956 Games did not take place in the Host City of Melbourne. Strict quarantine laws made taking horses to Melbourne in November impractical, and all of the Equestrian events took place in Stockholm the preceding June. As at Stockholm 1912, the Dressage events were won by Swedish riders, with Henri Saint Cyr and his mount Juli winning the Individual event as well as forming part of the triumphant gold medal-winning team. At the medal ceremony for the Individual event, Saint Cyr helped silver medallist Lis Hartel on to the medal podium.

Women's late start

Women were not allowed to compete in Dressage at the Olympic Games until Helsinki 1952. At those Games, Lis Hartel made the first mark for women when claiming a silver medal in the Individual event. Some 20 years later, at the 1972 Games in Munich, West Germany's Liselott Linsenhoff went one better, becoming the first woman to win an individual gold medal at the Games in any Equestrian event, when she captured the Individual Dressage crown. That particular competition featured 33 riders, of which 21 were women.

Beating adversity

Lis Hartel is arguably the highest profile competitor in the history of Dressage at the Olympic Games, and her legacy lives on. The Dane became the first woman in Equestrian history to win a medal at the Games when she won silver medals at the Individual Dressage in 1952 and 1956. What made her achievement all the more remarkable was that she competed despite having been paralysed below the knees as a result of contracting polio at the age of 23. Just eight years later, and walking on crutches, Hartel won her first silver in Helsinki. Her determination raised the profile of disabled sports and she played a major role in starting the movement for therapeutic riding schools.

⬇ *Denmark's Lis Hartel (left) – pictured with Henri Saint Cyr (centre) – defied disability to win two silver medals in Dressage (in 1952 and 1956).*

Kaiser Klimke

German Reiner Klimke holds the distinction of having been the most successful equestrian at the Olympic Games, as a member of West Germany's dominant Dressage team for three decades. In all Klimke won six gold and two bronze medals. He made his debut at Rome 1960, and four years later in Tokyo he secured his first team gold medal aboard Dux. He also featured in winning West German teams at Mexico City 1968 and at Montreal 1976, before claiming double gold at Los Angeles 1984. Riding Ahlerich, Klimke won the Individual Dressage competition and helped West Germany to team gold both at these Games and at Seoul four years later, his last appearance in an Olympic Games career that spanned 28 years.

Age before glory

The 2008 Games in Beijing saw the remarkable Japanese rider Hiroshi Hoketsu back in the saddle at the age of 67. Hoketsu had first appeared at the 1964 Games in Tokyo, when he took part in the Jumping. A former company director at Johnson and Johnson, Hoketsu quit his job in 2003 to concentrate on his latest bid for Games success in the Dressage event. Riding the chestnut mare Whisper 115, he finished ninth in the Team Competition and 35th in the Individual Competition and was the oldest competitor at the Games. Hoketsu's accomplishments were very much in keeping with the Olympic Games protocol – he was first and foremost a businessman, who retained an interest in his horses. Indeed, rumours abound that he would have been equally adept in the sailing competitions, as his family were allegedly descendants of pirates who operated in the Inland Sea during the Middle Ages.

German gold

The Team Dressage event at the Games was completely dominated by Germany over a 24-year period. The German run of gold medals started with West Germany's victory at Montreal 1976 but was then interrupted when Germany boycotted the Moscow Games four years later. West Germany returned to clinch gold at Los Angeles 1984, the first of five consecutive victories in the event that climaxed with another win at Sydney 2000. This meant that the Germans had won the six successive Team Dressage events they had competed in. The 2000 team were led by Isabell Werth, who collected her fourth Olympic Games gold medal.

⬆ *Germany's Isabell Werth won four gold medals in Dressage.*

Writing on the wall...

Mystery shrouds the origins of the letters that adorn the 20 x 60 metre Dressage arena, which first appeared during the Olympic Games in the 1920s. Certain movements have to take place in the vicinity of specific letters and serve to guide the judges on just how much control the rider has of the horse. Although their debut came at the Olympic Games, two of the more plausible explanations for the letters pre-date the modern Games: one is that they were the initials of the first cities that the Romans conquered; while another theory is that the letters come from the time of the Old German Imperial Court, when courtiers representing the various dignitaries would be positioned around the stable yard in a strict order with the horses ready to ride.

◀ *Japan's Hiroshi Hoketsu made his second appearance at the Games, at Beijing 2008, 44 years after he had made his first.*

Eventing

Eventing made its debut at Stockholm 1912. The competition has been through many format changes down the years, one of which saw Dressage completely dropped from the Eventing programme at the Antwerp 1920 Games, only to return in Paris four years later.

↑ Competitors jump a fence during the Team Three-Day Event competition at the 1912 Games in Stockholm. Hosts Sweden took gold.

Clocking out

The Eventing competition at Athens 2004 was marred by confusion and controversy. During the Jumping phase, German rider Bettina Hoy twice passed between the start flags, first during her warm-up and then in the competition, blissfully unaware of the impact this had on the clock, which needed to be restarted. The ground jury realised the mistake and gave Hoy the 14 time penalties she would have received had her time started with the first, premature pass between the start flags. This dropped both Hoy and her German team out of the medals, when they had looked poised for Individual and Team gold respectively. The German team lodged an initially successful objection to the technical appeal committee and the gold medals were reinstated. However, the French team, backed by the British and Americans, argued to the Court of Arbitration of Sport that the technical committee should not have revoked the time penalties for Hoy's score and the original decision was upheld, resulting in France claiming the gold medal.

Welfare state

The Eventing competition at the Olympic Games has proven a breeding ground for innovations in horse welfare. The 1936 Games in Berlin saw new rules introduced to help protect horses from the use of performance-altering drugs, especially stimulants and sedatives. The same event brought in a new elimination rule for horses that were deemed exhausted or lame following the endurance test.

Cool riders

The Olympic Games have often introduced scientific advances to sport and the 1996 Games in Atlanta were no exception. They provided the setting for a new experiment to cool the horses down after the cross-country phase, including the deployment of misting fans, and added an additional hold during Phase C to ensure the horses were cooling properly. The competition also featured an extensive study of the effects on the horses of heat and of different methods of cooling. This was the first instance of an extensive veterinary study being conducted in conjunction with the Games.

Golden Australia

Few Olympians can match the determination of Bill Roycroft in the Team Competition at the 1960 Games in Rome. One of only five Australians to have competed at five separate Games, Roycroft's performance in Rome laid the foundations for a golden era for the Australian Equestrian team at the Games. During the cross-country phase, Roycroft took a heavy fall from his mount Our Solo. Reports vary as to the extent of his injuries – some suggested that he broke his neck – but they appeared to have cost his country the gold medal. However, Roycroft had other ideas and, after discharging himself from hospital the following day, rode a faultless round in the Jumping, which helped Australia to win its first Eventing gold medal.

↑ Bettina Hoy's error at the start of her stadium-jumping round cost Germany the Team Eventing gold medal at the 2004 Games in Athens.

Singing for their...

Competing in Three-Day Eventing at the Games has given riders varying degrees of gravitas. Great Britain's Mary King has bankrolled her Games successes – team silver in 2004 and bronze in 2008 – with a number of different jobs, including working in a butcher's shop, in a kitchen and as a gardener. Team-mate William Fox-Pitt built a reputation teaching the rich and famous how to ride, with pop star Madonna among his clientele.

⬆ *Mary King (riding Call Again Cavalier) in action during the Cross Country section of the Team Event at the 2008 Games, in which her team, Great Britain, took bronze.*

Royalty reigns

Although women were allowed to compete in the Eventing competitions from the 1952 Games onwards, it was not until Tokyo 1964 that American Helena du Pont became the first female participant. Subsequent Games have enjoyed a royal seal of approval, with Princess Anne, the daughter of Queen Elizabeth II, competing as part of the Great Britain Eventing team at Montreal 1976. The Princess is so far the only member of the British royal family to have competed at an Olympic Games. Her own daughter, Zara, became world eventing champion in 2006, but had to miss out on Beijing 2008 because of injury to her horse Toytown.

Kiwi inspiration

One of the most successful of all Three-Day Eventing riders at the Olympic Games is New Zealand's Mark Todd. Regarded as a pioneer of three-day eventing in his home country, Todd made his Games debut at Los Angeles 1984, winning the Individual gold medal aboard his most famous horse, Charisma. The pair were possibly the most formidable partnership in the history of Eventing at the Games, retaining their gold medal four years later in Seoul, before Charisma was retired. As a result largely of Todd's success, the sport continued to grow in New Zealand, and those 1988 Games also yielded a bronze medal in the Team competition. Todd followed up with further bronze in the Individual competition at Sydney 2000, and then announced his retirement. However, the lure of the Games proved irresistible and Todd returned to competition at Beijing 2008.

More than a sport

For triple Olympic Games gold medallist Adolph Dirk Coenraad van der Voort van Zijp, taking part in the Eventing competition at Paris 1924 must have paled into insignificance beside what later ensued in his life. He was born into a Dutch patrician family and became a military man, reaching the rank of lieutenant in the Second Regiment of the Hussars by 1924. As such, Van der Voort van Zijp was permitted to compete in Paris, where he won Individual and Team gold medals, and he went on to help the Dutch team to retain gold in Amsterdam four years later. When the Second World War broke out and the Nazis invaded Holland, Van der Voort van Zijp took part in the Battle of the Grebbeberg in May 1940 and, after being captured, he was detained, with other notables, as a prisoner of war in Germany.

⬇ *Mark Todd took Individual Three-Day Eventing gold at the 2000 Games in Sydney.*

Jumping

Although an Individual Jumping event was contested at the 1900 Games in Paris, the current programme (of both Team and Individual events) did not take place until Stockholm in 1912, although it has featured at every Games since. Germany lead the way in both the Individual event (with five gold medals) and in the Team event (with eight successes).

Mighty Foxhunter

Great Britain's solitary gold medal at Helsinki 1952 came courtesy of its Jumping team, captained by the inimitable Harry Llewellyn and his mount Foxhunter. Llewellyn had previously been a successful jump jockey, finishing second in the 1936 Grand National on Ego. At the Games, a disastrous final morning had seen the British team slip to sixth position, with Llewellyn claiming that lack of sleep was partly to blame for his abject performance. An hour's sleep at lunchtime brought redemption, and the final afternoon phase saw the pair record the clear round that secured gold. The press treated Llewellyn as though he had single-handedly saved the honour of British sport, while both Winston Churchill and the new queen, Elizabeth II, sent telegrams of congratulation. Foxhunter was retired in 1953, but his name lives on in the form of the Foxhunter Trophy, awarded to the most promising horses and riders of each new generation.

⬇ *Colonel Harry Llewellyn guides Foxhunter to a clear round at Helsinki 1952 to guide Great Britain to a memorable Team Jumping gold medal.*

Stamp of fame

The giant chestnut Big Ben holds a special place in Canadian hearts. Born in Belgium and later sold to Canadian equestrian Ian Millar, he won 40 showjumping Grand Prix events and two consecutive World Cups. He competed at two Olympic Games as part of the fourth-placed teams at Los Angeles 1984 and Seoul 1988. Few Olympians can have been more acclaimed: Big Ben has been honoured with his own stamp by Canada Post; was inducted into the Ontario Sports Legends Hall of Fame; had a statue erected and a book written about him; and is one of only two horses, along with the legendary racehorse Northern Dancer, inducted into the Canadian Sports Hall of Fame.

Double clears

It took a genuine Touch of Class for an equine competitor to transcend human endeavour at the Olympic Games. That was the name of the former racehorse that entered showjumping legend in 1984. The bay mare, with rider Joseph Fargis, won the Individual Jumping gold medal and was part of the victorious US team at Los Angeles 1984, posting the first double clear rounds in Games history into the bargain. Her golden exploits resulted in Touch of Class becoming the first non-human USOC Female Equestrian Athlete of the Year and she was inducted into the Show Jumping Hall of Fame in 2000.

⬆ *A Touch of Class, ridden by Joseph Fargis, helped the United States team to a well-received Team Jumping gold at Los Angeles in 1984.*

Wall games

The life and times of Humberto Mariles Cortés could fill an entire book alone. The Mexican became his nation's first-ever gold medallist when, riding his home-bred horse Arete, he won the Individual competition at London 1948. Doubling up as a member of the jubilant Mexican team, Cortés deployed a bold approach: in the final round his horse jumped into the water obstacle, incurring faults, in what appeared to be a deliberate move. The tactic duly gave Arete the balance he needed to clear the following large wall – the only horse to do so. Cortés met a tragic end: he was imprisoned in Paris in 1972, having been caught drug-trafficking, and died in his cell later that year.

Nishi Memorial

An Olympian whose exploits came to be exploited in the movies was Japanese rider Takeichi Nishi, an aristocratic cavalry officer who won the gold medal in the Individual Competition at the Los Angeles 1932 Games. Riding Uranus, 'Baron Nishi' became – and remains to this day – the only equestrian from his country to strike gold. During the Second World War he took part in the defence of Iwo Jima with a tank regiment and died there in 1945, possibly during a mass suicide. His life was recorded for posterity in the Clint Eastwood film *Letters from Iwo Jima*.

Saudi success

The dawn of a new century also marked the rise of a new power in Jumping at the Games, with Khaled Al-Eid recording a rare medal for Saudi Arabia at Sydney 2000. The country had first entered the Jumping competition four years before, and by Sydney the team had improved under the guidance of Brazilian equestrian legend Nelson Pessoa, whose own son Rodrigo won an Olympic Games gold medal. In winning bronze, Al-Eid defied the label 'rank outsider' that had been bestowed by one news bulletin, attributing his success to patient training and the savvy accuracy of his mount Khashm al-'Aan.

↑Khaled Al-Eid (on Khashm Al-'Aan) secured Saudi Arabia's first-ever equestrian medal when he took Individual Jumping bronze at Sydney 2000.

↙ At Mexico City in 1968, William Steinkraus (shown here as a 16-year-old) became the first American to win Individual gold in an Equestrian event.

Here comes the cavalry

William C. Steinkraus is a six-time Olympian who in 1968 became the first American to win an Olympic Games individual gold medal in Equestrian sport, by triumphing in the Jumping in Mexico City. Educated at Yale, Steinkraus served with the US Cavalry during the Second World War before embarking on a career in equestrian, first competing at the 1952 Games in Helsinki as a member of the US bronze medal-winning team. He remained on the US team at every subsequent Olympic Games through to 1972 and is perhaps best remembered for his association with the former unsound racehorse called Snowbound, his willing partner in Mexico.

Chapter Seven
Gymnastics

Gymnastics at the Games consists of three separate disciplines: Artistic, Rhythmic and Trampoline. In Artistic events, a gymnast is judged on performances on a series of apparatus. The Rhythmic discipline is solely for female competitors and requires graceful and athletic movements to music using different hand-held implements. Trampolinists are graded on skills exhibited in their routines on the sprung surface.

The Artistic side of the sport is recognised as one of the mainstays of the Games programme, with the likes of Olga Korbut and Nadia Comaneci having become worldwide celebrities after their stunning performances in 1972 and 1976 respectively. The combination of grace, power, agility and nerve makes Artistic Gymnastics one of the hottest tickets at any Games and ensures the sport has a massive global audience.

Gymnastics in some form has been a part of every celebration of the modern era. The first gold medal was claimed by the German men's Parallel Bars team at Athens 1896, when the first individual champion was Carl Schuhmann in the Vault. Those first Games saw only men involved in five individual Artistic apparatus contests, team events on the Parallel Bars and Horizontal Bars, plus an idiosyncratic Rope Climbing discipline. Women made their Gymnastics debut in 1928, Rhythmic Gymnastics came on to the scene in 1984 and Trampoline was first staged at Sydney 2000.

Because individuals are able to claim multiple medals at each Games from the various Team, All-Around and apparatus finals, the top Artistic gymnasts have been among the most decorated of all participants at the Olympic Games.

The United States' Nastia Liukin produced a dazzling floor display to edge out compatriot Shawn Johnson by 0.6 points to claim gold in the women's Artistic Individual All-Around competition at Beijing 2008.

Men's Artistic Gymnastics

Men's Artistic Gymnastics is one of the few sports to have been contested at every Olympic Games since Athens 1896. Gymnasts from Russia (in all its guises – as the Soviet Union and as the Unified Team in 1992) have been the most successful over the years, capturing almost 25 per cent of the total medals available.

Ever present

The men's Individual All-Around competition is the only Gymnastics event to have been staged at every Olympic Games since Paris 1900. The leading performers from the Team Competition qualify for the All-Around Final. The gymnasts perform a routine in each of the six disciplines – Floor, Horizontal Bar, Parallel Bars, Pommel Horse, Rings and Vault. Formerly the marks gained were added to their scores from the team round. Now the champion is the man with the highest overall tally in the pressure-cooker atmosphere of the final.

↑ *The Unified Team's Vitaly Scherbo dominated the men's Gymnastics competition at Barcelona 1992, winning six of eight available gold medals*

Super Scherbo

Vitaly Scherbo won an unprecedented six of the eight possible Gymnastics gold medals at Barcelona 1992. Owing to the fall of the Soviet Union, Belarussian Scherbo was part of the 'Unified Team' made up of the individual republics that had yet to achieve formal recognition by the IOC. He won four of the individual apparatus finals – Rings, Horizontal Bar, Parallel Bars and Vault – to add to his All-Around and Team honours. Only swimmers Mark Spitz and Michael Phelps have ever won more gold medals in a single Games.

Stukelj finds secret to long life

Leopon Stukelj lived most of his life as one of the elder statesmen of gymnastics. Born in what is now Slovenia in 1898, the All-Around champion at the 1924 Games lived to within four days of his 101st birthday and nearly saw in his third century. He attended the 1996 Games in Atlanta and was presented to the crowd at the Opening Ceremony as the oldest living gold medallist. At the age of 97 he walked jauntily to the presentation platform to join the likes of Carl Lewis, Bob Beamon, Nadia Comaneci and Vitaly Scherbo.

↘ *Aleksandr Dityatin in action at the Moscow 1980 Games.*

Aleksandr the great

In 1980, at the height of Soviet bloc domination of Gymnastics at the Games, Aleksandr Dityatin delighted the Moscow crowd with an awesome series of displays to claim Individual All-Around gold. Dityatin also made history by becoming the first male gymnast to claim medals in each of the eight competitions open to him at one Games. He went on to win three gold medals at the 1981 World Championships, but then retired through injury.

Close shave

At Los Angeles 1984, Japan's Koji Gushiken held off the challenge of home favourite Peter Vidmar to claim Individual All-Around gold by the slenderest of margins: 0.025 points. Remarkably, Gushiken was a lowly fifth going into the final. Even Gushiken's obvious competitive spirit could not prevent China from romping away with the Team title at Beijing 2008 when, as coach, he guided Athens 2004 winners Japan to silver. However, the indefatigable old warrior vowed that he would learn from the heavy defeat and 'be up for the next challenge'.

Handy Andrianov

The most prolific medal winner in the history of men's Gymnastics at the Games is the 1976 Individual All-Around champion, Nikolay Andrianov. The Soviet superstar won 15 medals across three Games from 1972 to 1980, a tally that included seven gold, five silver and three bronze medals. However, it could all have been so different, as Andrianov only established himself in the powerful USSR team after being called up as a late substitute for the 1971 European Championships. He won six medals there and never looked back.

⬆ *The Soviet Union's Nikolay Andrianov won an unprecedented 15 medals – seven of them gold – in three appearances at the Games.*

Champion Chukarin

Viktor Chukarin was the star turn at Helsinki 1952, having overcome great suffering to compete. Chukarin was a prisoner of the Nazis during the Second World War, but after his release made up for lost time by dedicating himself to gymnastics. He went on to defend the title in Melbourne four years later and was rewarded by the Soviet Union with the post of head of gymnastics at the renowned Institute of Physical Culture in Lvov.

⬇ *Viktor Chukarin heads to gold in the Parallel Bars at Melbourne 1956.*

Tiny Kato a big star

Sawao Kato, the 1968 and 1972 Individual All-Around champion, was a diminutive 5ft 3in, but made up for his lack of stature with absolute composure and stunning skill. In 1968 he had a stirring battle for the gold medal with the Soviet Union's Mikhail Voronin, but at the troubled Munich Games four years later no one could match him. Kato won 12 medals at the Games, including eight golds, and is Japan's most successful Olympian. He was head judge in the Gymnastics competition at the Athens 2004 Games.

Roll up! Roll up!

Italian Alberto Braglia was the first man to win successive Individual All-Around golds when he followed up his title at London 1908 with a similar success in Stockholm four years later. Braglia opted to join a circus as an acrobat as his next challenge, but he returned to the Olympic Games as his country's chief coach at Los Angeles 1932. Braglia led his charges to second in the medal table, still the best showing by the Azzurri at a Games.

Olympic Games men's Individual All-Around gold-medal winners

Date (host)	Score/Points	Winner
1900 (Paris)	302.000 pts	Gustave Sandras (FRA)
1904 (St Louis)	69.800 pts	Julius Lennard (AUT)
1908 (London)	317.000 pts	Alberto Braglia (ITA)
1912 (Stockholm)	135.000 pts	Alberto Braglia (ITA)
1920 (Antwerp)	88.350 pts	Giorgio Zampori (ITA)
1924 (Paris)	110.340 pts	Leon Stukelj (YUG)
1928 (Amsterdam)	247.500 pts	Georges Miez (SUI)
1932 (Los Angeles)	140.625 pts	Romeo Neri (ITA)
1936 (Berlin)	113.100 pts	Alfred Schwarzmann (GER)
1948 (London)	229.700 pts	Veikko Huhtanen (FIN)
1952 (Helsinki)	115.700 pts	Viktor Chukarin (URS)
1956 (Melbourne)	114.250 pts	Viktor Chukarin (URS)
1960 (Rome)	115.950 pts	Boris Shakhlin (URS)
1964 (Tokyo)	115.950 pts	Yukio Endo (JPN)
1968 (Mexico City)	115.900 pts	Sawao Kato (JPN)
1972 (Munich)	114.650 pts	Sawao Kato (JPN)
1976 (Montreal)	116.650 pts	Nikolay Andrianov (URS)
1980 (Moscow)	118.650 pts	Aleksandr Dityatin (URS)
1984 (Los Angeles)	118.700 pts	Koji Gushiken (JPN)
1988 (Seoul)	119.125 pts	Vladimir Artemov (URS)
1992 (Barcelona)	59.025 pts	Vitaly Scherbo (UNI)
1996 (Atlanta)	58.423 pts	Li Xiaoshuang (CHN)
2000 (Sydney)	58.474 pts	Alexei Nemov (RUS)
2004 (Athens)	57.823 pts	Paul Hamm (USA)
2008 (Beijing)	94.575 pts	Yang Wei (CHN)

Team champions

The first medals to be decided in Gymnastics competitions at the Games are those for Team honours. During qualifying, five of a team's six gymnasts perform on all six items of apparatus, with the highest four marks counting. The scores determine which teams advance to the final and which individual gymnasts reach the All-Around and apparatus finals. In the final, three of each team compete on each apparatus with all scores counting. The team with the most points wins.

China – the new power

In 2008, on home soil, China won Team gold for the second time in three Games, to add to seven of the previous world titles in the event. Coach Huang Yubin described the display in Beijing as 'perfect'. The Chinese had won their first-ever men's Team gold at Sydney 2000 but had failed to build on the achievement at Athens 2004, losing to arch-rivals Japan and only finishing fifth. In 2008 the pressure was intense in the National Indoor Arena, but Zou Kai, Yang Wei, Xiao Qin, Li Xiaopeng, Huang Xu and Chen Yibing were all triumpant.

⬆ *Considered the best Gymnastics team in history, the Soviet Union eased to Team All-Around gold at the 1988 Games in Seoul.*

Soviet strongmen

The 1988 Soviet Union men's squad is widely recognised as the greatest Gymnastics team in the Games' history. They recorded six perfect 'ten' scores, including three by Dmitri Bilozertchev, who three years earlier had broken his left leg in 42 places in a road accident. Valeri Lyukin achieved the highest possible score on the Pommel Horse and Parallel Bars, while Vladimir Artemov was awarded ten for his work on the Horizontal Bar. Both Lyukin and Artemov subsequently emigrated to the United States. The margin of the Soviet's victory in Seoul was all the more impressive as East German Holger Behrendt and Japanese duo Daisuke Nishikava and Koichi Mizushima also achieved the ultimate score, each on the Rings. 'It is the best display of team gymnastics I have ever seen,' said Peter Vidmar, a member of the United States team that won the gold medal four years earlier in Los Angeles.

⬆ *China's men's team delighted the home crowd when it stormed to Team All-Around gold at the 2008 Games in Beijing.*

The ultimate team player

Japan was the powerhouse of men's gymnastics in the 1960s and 1970s. At the 1976 Games in Montreal, 'the land of the rising sun' was going for a fifth straight Team title. However, disaster struck when Shun Fujimoto injured himself on the Floor, sustaining a broken kneecap. Showing incredible team spirit and will to win, Fujimoto hid the extent of his injury and completed his final two events. On the Rings he scored 9.7, executing a dismount despite his ailment. His score helped the Japanese earn yet another gold.

Child star

The first modern Olympic Games in 1896 saw team events held for each individual apparatus rather than across multiple disciplines. Unlike today, there was no age restriction on competitors. Dimitrios Loundras was 10 years and 218 days old when he won a silver medal in the team Parallel Bars.

⬅ *Shun Fujimoto produced one of the most courageous performances in sporting history at Montreal 1976 when he defied a broken kneecap to compete in the final two rounds to help Japan to men's Team All-Around gold.*

Simply Fin-tastic

Finland were the foremost nation at London 1948, picking up the men's Team championship with a collection of six gold, two silver and two bronze medals. Among the Finnish team was the remarkable Heikki Savolainen, for whom this was the fifth out of six Olympic Games in a career stretching from Amsterdam 1928 (where he won a bronze medal in the Pommel Horse competition) to Finland's own Games at Helsinki in 1952, in which he took the Olympic Oath on behalf of the competitors and claimed a Team bronze. In the Pommel Horse competition at London 1948, Savolainen had the same score as team-mates Veikko Huhtanen and Paavo Aaltonen, and uniquely for Gymnastics at the Games each was awarded a gold medal. London 1948 was the heyday of Finnish gymnastics; they have only won five Gymnastics medals since, the last coming in 1968.

Old man Manilo

Italy's Manilo Pastorini is still the oldest Gymnastics gold medallist more than 90 years after he was a member of the champion team of 1920. Pastorini was 41 years and 117 days when he struck gold in Antwerp as part of the victorious Italian squad. Pastorini, though, was a relative pup compared to one of the bronze medallists in that competition, France's Lucien Demanet was 45 years and 266 days old. Demanet remains the oldest Gymnastics medallist at the Games and, like Pastorini, will surely hold on to the accolade in perpetuity.

⬆ *Romania's mission to take Team gold for the first time at Athens 2004 failed when they slipped from first to third in the final round...*

Selariu's costly slip

At Athens 2004, Romania, who had never won men's Team gold at the Games, were leading going into the final piece of apparatus. The narrow margins of victory and defeat in this technical sport were then summed up by the luckless Razvan Selariu falling off the Horizontal Bar, which allowed Japan to snatch the title, their first in the event for 28 years.

⬆ *A wooden leg proved no handicap for George Eyser (centre): the United States' athlete picked up three gold medals at St Louis 1904.*

Eyser overcomes handicap

At St Louis 1904, United States won the first men's Team title at the Games. George Eyser was a leading member of that United States squad, also winning gold in the Parallel Bars and Vault competitions. Eyser's achievements were all the more remarkable ... because he had a wooden leg.

Olympic Games men's Team Competition gold-medal winners

Date (host)	Score/Points	Winner
1904 (St Louis)	374.430 pts	United States
1908 (London)	438.000 pts	Sweden
1912 (Stockholm)	265.750 pts	Italy
1920 (Antwerp)	359.885 pts	Italy
1924 (Paris)	839.058 pts	Italy
1928 (Amsterdam)	1718.625 pts	Switzerland
1932 (Los Angeles)	541.850 pts	Italy
1936 (Berlin)	657.430 pts	Germany
1948 (London)	1358.300 pts	Finland
1952 (Helsinki)	575.400 pts	Soviet Union
1956 (Melbourne)	568.250 pts	Soviet Union
1960 (Rome)	575.200 pts	Japan
1964 (Tokyo)	577.950 pts	Japan
1968 (Mexico City)	575.900 pts	Japan
1972 (Munich)	571.250 pts	Japan
1976 (Montreal)	576.850 pts	Japan
1980 (Moscow)	589.600 pts	Soviet Union
1984 (Los Angeles)	591.400 pts	United States
1988 (Seoul)	593.350 pts	Soviet Union
1992 (Barcelona)	585.450 pts	Unified Team
1996 (Atlanta)	576.778 pts	Russia
2000 (Sydney)	231.919 pts	China
2004 (Athens)	173.821 pts	Japan
2008 (Beijing)	286.125 pts	China

Individual apparatus champions

There are six apparatus disciplines. The Floor exhibits tumbling and strength skills. The Horizontal Bar, 2.5 metres above the ground, sees swings, releases and twists. The Parallel Bars involves swings, balances and releases performed on two bars 42 centimetres apart. The Pommel Horse sees gymnasts perform on top of a gym 'horse' with two rings attached. The Rings (suspended at 5m) tests strength, power and flexibility. The Vault sees gymnasts sprinting down a runway and leaping from a springboard to perform twists, somersaults and a landing.

Men's Horizontal Bar gold-medal winners

Date	Winner
1896	Hermann Weingartner (GER)
1904	Anton Heida (USA); Edward Hennig (USA)
1924	Leon Stukelj (YUG)
1928	Georges Miez (SUI)
1932	Dallas Bixler (USA)
1936	Ale Saarvala (FIN)
1948	Josef Stalder (SUI)
1952	Jack Gunthard (SUI)
1956	Takashi Ono (JPN)
1960	Takashi Ono (JPN)
1964	Boris Shakhlin (URS)
1968	Akinori Nakayama (JPN); Mikhail Voronin (URS)
1972	Misuo Tsukahara (JPN)
1976	Misuo Tsukahara (JPN)
1980	Stojan Deltshev (BUL)
1984	Shinji Morisue (JPN)
1988	Vladimir Artemov (URS); Valery Liukin (URS)
1992	Trent Dimas (USA)
1996	Andreas Wecker (GER)
2000	Alexei Nemov (RUS)
2004	Igor Cassina (ITA)
2008	Zou Kai (CHN)

Japan's Tsukahara makes his mark

Innovation is celebrated in gymnastics, with new techniques and moves named after their instigators. Perhaps the most famous example is the legendary Japanese Misuo Tsukahara, who claimed back-to-back Horizontal Bar titles at the 1972 and 1976 Games and is still the only man to have retained that crown. Tsukahara appeared to be fearless and both his somersault dismount from the high bar and his complex cartwheel vault were added to the Gymnastics skills manual in his honour.

↑ Misuo Tsukahara performs his legendary dismount from the Horizontal Bar at Munich 1972.

Blanik breaks the mould

Only one non-Chinese male gymnast claimed a title at Beijing 2008. Leszek Blanik secured Poland's first-ever Gymnastics gold at the Games with a supreme display of vaulting beyond even the impressive hosts. The only one who could match Blanik was Thomas Bouhail of France, who equalled Blanik's score but was denied victory on a tie-break analysis of the judges' marks.

➜ Leszek Blanik took a surprise gold at Beijing 2008.

Men's Floor gold-medal winners

Date	Winner
1932	Istvan Pelle (HUN)
1936	Georges Miez (SUI)
1948	Ferenc Pataki (HUN)
1952	William Thoresson (SWE)
1956	Valentin Muratov (URS)
1960	Nobuyuki Aihara (JPN)
1964	Franco Menichelli (ITA)
1968	Sawao Kato (JPN)
1972	Nikolay Andrianov (URS)
1976	Nikolay Andrianov (URS)
1980	Roland Bruckner (GDR)
1984	Li Ning (CHN)
1988	Sergey Kharkov
1992	Li Xiaoshuang (CHN)
1996	Ioannis Melissanidis (GRE)
2000	Igors Vihrovs (LAT)
2004	Kyle Shewfelt (CAN)
2008	Zou Kai (CHN)

Men's Parallel Bars gold-medal winners

Date	Winner
1896	Alfred Flatow (GER)
1904	George Eyser (USA)
1924	August Guttinger (SUI)
1928	Ladislav Vacha (CZE)
1932	Romeo Neri (ITA)
1936	Konrad Frey (GER)
1948	Michael Reusch (SUI)
1952	Hans Eugster (SUI)
1956	Viktor Chukarin (URS)
1960	Boris Shakhlin (URS)
1964	Yukio Endo (JPN)
1968	Akinori Nakayama (JPN)
1972	Sawao Kato (JPN)
1976	Sawao Kato (JPN)
1980	Aleksandr Tkachev (URS)
1984	Bart Conner (USA)
1988	Vladimir Artemov (URS)
1992	Vitaly Scherbo (UNI)
1996	Rustam Sharipov (UKR)
2000	Li Xiaopeng (CHN)
2004	Valery Goncharov (UKR)
2008	Li Xiaopeng (CHN)

↑ *Nobody could touch Japan's Sawao Kato on the Parallel Bars at Munich 1972 and Montreal 1976.*

Kato first bar none

Japan's Sawao Kato won a record eight Gymnastics gold medals across three Games from 1968 to 1976. He remains the only man to have successfully defended the Parallel Bars title.

Men's Rings gold-medal winners

Date	Winner
1896	Ioannis Mitropoulos (GRE)
1904	Herman Glass (USA)
1924	Francesco Martino (ITA)
1928	Leon Stukelj (YUG)
1932	George Gulack (USA)
1936	Alois Hudec (CZE)
1948	Karl Frei (SUI)
1952	Grant Shaginyan (URS)
1956	Albert Azaryan (URS)
1960	Albert Azaryan (URS)
1964	Takuji Hayata (JPN)
1968	Akinori Nakayama (JPN)
1972	Akinori Nakayama (JPN)
1976	Nikolay Andrianov (URS)
1980	Aleksandr Dityatin (URS)
1984	Koji Gushiken (JPN), Li Ning (CHN)
1988	Holger Behrendt (GDR), Dmitry Bilozertchev (URS)
1992	Vitaly Scherbo (UNI)
1996	Yuri Chechi (ITA)
2000	Szilveszter Csollany (HUN)
2004	Dimosthenis Tampakos (GRE)
2008	Chen Yibing (CHN)

Fantastic Finns

The Pommel Horse Competition at the 1948 Games in London produced the only three-way tie for a gold medal in the history of Gymnastics at the Games. All three men hailed from Finland.

Men's Pommel Horse Gymnastics gold-medal winners

Date	Winner
1896	Louis Zutter (SUI)
1904	Anton Heida (USA)
1924	Josef Wilhelm (SUI)
1928	Hermann Hanggi (SUI)
1932	Istvan Pelle (HUN)
1936	Konrad Frey (GER)
1948	Paavo Aaltonen (FIN); Veikko Huhtanen (FIN); Heikki Savolainen (FIN)
1952	Viktor Chukarin (URS)
1956	Boris Shakhlin (URS)
1960	Eugen Ekman (FIN); Boris Shakhlin (URS)
1964	Miroslav Cerar (YUG)
1968	Miroslav Cerar (YUG)
1972	Viktor Klimenko (URS)
1976	Zoltan Magyar (HUN)
1980	Zoltan Magyar (HUN)
1984	Li Ning (CHN); Peter Vidmar (USA)
1988	Dmitry Bilozertchev (URS); Zsolt Borkai (HUN); Lubomir Geraskov (BUL)
1992	Gil-Su Pae (NKO); Vitaly Scherbo (UNI)
1996	Li Donghua (SUI)
2000	Marius Urzica (ROM)
2004	Teng Haibin (CHN)
2008	Qin Xiao (CHN)

Men's Vault gold-medal winners

Date	Winner
1896	Carl Schuhmann (GER)
1904	George Eyser (USA); Anton Heida (USA)
1924	Frank Kriz (USA)
1928	Eugen Mack (SUI)
1932	Savino Guglielmetti (ITA)
1936	Alfred Schwarzmann (GER)
1948	Paavo Aaltonen (FIN)
1952	Viktor Chukarin (URS)
1956	Helmut Bantz (GER); Valentin Muratov (URS)
1960	Takeshi Ono (JPN); Boris Shakhlin (URS)
1964	Haruhiro Yamashita (JPN)
1968	Mikhail Voronin (URS)
1972	Klaus Koste (GDR)
1976	Nikolay Andrianov (URS)
1980	Nikolay Andrianov (URS)
1984	Lou Yun (CHN)
1988	Lou Yun (CHN)
1992	Vitaly Scherbo (UNI)
1996	Alexei Nemov (RUS)
2000	Gervasio Deferr (ESP)
2004	Gervasio Deferr (ESP)
2008	Leszek Blanik (POL)

Women's Artistic Gymnastics

From Comaneci to Korbut, women's Gymnastics has produced some of the most legendary names in the Games' history. Team competitions were contested for the first time at Amsterdam 1928, with individual competitions introduced at Helsinki 1952. The Soviet Union were the dominant force over the years, winning 33 gold medals.

Ten-up Nadia

Nadia Comaneci of Romania became the Games' youngest women's All-Around Gymnastics champion in 1976 when she astounded the world with her skill at the tender age of 14 in Montreal. She followed up with first places in the Balance Beam and Uneven Bars apparatus finals, achieving an unprecedented seven perfect 'ten' scores. No gymnast had previously been awarded a single ten in the Gymnastics Competition at the Games. Comaneci raised standards to a new level and her prowess led to revisions of the judging criteria.

← Nadia Comaneci's performance on the balance beam at the 1972 Games in Munich sent shockwaves around the sporting world.

Latynina on cloud nine

Larisa Latynina of the Soviet Union, the 1956 and 1960 Individual All-Around champion, won nine Gymnastics gold medals in her Games career, a record for a female competitor in any sport. No one has exceeded that tally, although swimmer Mark Spitz and athletes Carl Lewis and Paavo Nurmi have equalled it. With her overall total of 18 medals, however, Latynina is out on her own. Her grace and artistry evolved from her training as a ballet dancer from the age of 11.

All-around champions

The women's Individual All-Around title is awarded to the gymnast with the highest score across all four women's disciplines – Floor, Balance Beam, Uneven Bars and Vault. The leading performers from the Team event, up to a maximum of two per nation, qualify for the Individual All-Around Final, in which they perform the four routines. The marks gained used to be added to their scores from the Team round, but in recent years the champion has been decided solely on performances in the final. The champion is the competitor with the most points.

Caslavska triumphs

Vera Caslavska was the first Gymnastics superstar. Representing Czechoslovakia at Mexico City 1968, just two months after her country had been invaded by the Soviet Union, the charismatic Caslavska defeated all the mighty Soviet squad in her successful defence of the Individual All-Around title she had won at Tokyo 1964. Her amazing career over those two Games brought 11 medals. Caslavska was forced into hiding when Soviet tanks rolled into Prague, but at the Games she gained inspiration from the strife back home. Afterwards she presented the four gold medals she had won in Mexico to her country's ousted leaders.

Retton's dramatic victory

The 1984 Olympic Games at Los Angeles were boycotted by most of the Eastern European nations, including the awesome Soviet team. Their absence allowed the United States to claim the women's Individual title through the charismatic Mary Lou Retton – but only just. In an incredible finish, Retton needed to score a perfect 'ten' in her exercise to deny Romania's Ecaterina Szabo. She achieved it and became a national hero.

↑ Mary Lou Retton produced a perfect final routine at the 1984 Games in Los Angeles to edge out Romania's Ecaterina Szabo for the gold medal.

Height matters

Half-way through the women's All-Around competition at the 2000 Games in Sydney, Australian gymnast Allana Slater questioned whether the vaulting horse was the correct height. She was right: the apparatus was 5 centimetres below the prescribed height of 125cm. The horse was raised and gymnasts who had already vaulted at the wrong height were offered the opportunity to retake their vault. It was too late for many, though, as the likes of Svetlana Khorkina had failed on the incorrectly set horse and had subsequently crumbled in other disciplines under the extra pressure of knowing that a further mistake would ruin their chances of victory.

Keeping it in the family

Nastia Liukin, the 2008 Individual All-Around champion, was following in a proud family tradition that crossed not only eras but also political history when she came first in Beijing. Both her parents were champion gymnasts. Liukin's father, Valery, was a member of the 1988 Soviet Union team in Seoul and won gold medals in the Team and Individual Horizontal Bar events. Her mother is former world rhythmic champion Anna Kotchneva. Liukin emigrated to the United States in 1992 aged two and was coached to success by her father at his gymnastics academy in Texas.

⬆ *Nastia Liukin followed in her father Valery's footsteps when she took gold in 2008; he had been part of the Soviet Union's golden team in 1988.*

Kim proves a point

Nellie Kim defied the opinion of Soviet gymnastics legend Larisa Latynina (who, when Kim was a child, said she had no future in the sport) to become one of the most celebrated gymnasts of all time. In her much-storied battle with Nadia Comaneci at Montreal 1976, she took three gold medals (in the Team All-Around, the Vault and the Floor – in the latter, she became the first gymnast in history to achieve the first perfect score of ten). She also took silver in the Individual All-Around event, despite becoming the first gymnast to record a perfect ten score on the vault. Four years later, at Moscow 1980, she shared gold with Comaneci in the Floor and won the fifth gold medal of her Olympic Games career in the Team All-Around.

Patterson peaks to deny Khorkina

At Athens 2004, American Carly Patterson ensured that Svetlana Khorkina would be remembered as arguably the greatest gymnast never to have won the Individual All-Around title at the Games. Khorkina had won the World Championship on three occasions, but in 1996 and 2000 had failed to achieve the ultimate prize in the sport. This was her last chance. Khorkina led at the half-way stage, but slipped back to second after the Balance Beam, allowing 16-year-old Patterson to swoop.

⬆ *Russia's Svetlana Khorkina was a three-time world champion who never managed to hit golden heights at the Olympic Games.*

Women's Individual All-Round Competition gold-medal winners

Date (host)	Points	Winner
1952 (Helsinki)	76.780 pts	Mariya Gorokovskaya (URS)
1956 (Melbourne)	74.933 pts	Larisa Latynina (URS)
1960 (Rome)	77.031 pts	Larisa Latynina (URS)
1964 (Tokyo)	77.564 pts	Vera Caslavska (CZE)
1968 (Mexico City)	78.250 pts	Vera Caslavska (CZE)
1972 (Munich)	77.025 pts	Lyudmila Turishcheva (URS)
1976 (Montreal)	79.275 pts	Nadia Comaneci (ROM)
1980 (Moscow)	79.150 pts	Yelena Davydova (URS)
1984 (Los Angeles)	79.175 pts	Mary Lou Retton (USA)
1988 (Seoul)	79.662 pts	Yelena Shushunova (URS)
1992 (Barcelona)	39.737 pts	Tatyana Gutsu (UNI)
1996 (Atlanta)	39.255 pts	Lilia Popkopayeva (UKR)
2000 (Sydney)	38.642 pts	Simona Amanar (ROM)
2004 (Athens)	38.387 pts	Carly Patterson (USA)
2008 (Beijing)	63.325 pts	Nastia Liukin (USA)

Team champions

Team honours in women's Gymnastics at the Olympic Games are decided on a similar basis to the men's equivalent. During qualifying, five of the six gymnasts on each team perform on each apparatus, with the highest four marks counting. The scores determine which teams advance to the final and which individual gymnasts reach the Individual All-Around and apparatus finals. In the final, three of each team compete on each apparatus, with all three scores counted. The team with the highest overall tally wins the gold medal.

⬇ The Netherlands' gymnasts delighted the home crowd by taking the inaugural team title at the 1928 Olympic Games in Amsterdam.

Soviet might

For 40 years teams from the Soviet Union dominated women's Gymnastics at the Olympic Games. From 1952 through to 1988 the line-up of gymnastic talent drawn from the 15 republics won the women's Team title every time they turned up. In 1992, the Unified Team (the coming together of the majority of the 15 while each was not formally recognised by the IOC) continued the tradition, but then the break-up of the old superpower meant that none of its constituents, now independent nations, had the resources to lift the title. Russia, Ukraine and Belarus are all very competitive, but none has the strength of the Soviets. A good illustration is the extraordinary 1976 Soviet team, which even the inspired Romanian Nadia Comaneci could not prevent from retaining the Team title. Its three biggest stars were Lyudmila Turishcheva (born in Grozny, currently Russia), Olga Korbut (Grodno, Belarus) and Nelli Kim (Leninabad, Tajikistan). In recent years that awesome trio would have been competing in different teams, which just goes to show that sometimes there is no escaping the fact that politics and sport are inextricably linked.

➡ A sign of their power: at the 1976 Games in Montreal, Soviet gymnasts Ludmila Tourischeva (left) with a silver medal and Nelli Kim (right) with gold pushed the legendary Nadia Comaneci into bronze in the Floor Competition.

Comaneci the spark

Nadia Comaneci was the catalyst behind Romania's challenge to the Soviet dominance. The gymnast, famed for her string of perfect scores at Montreal 1976, led the Romanians to their first Team silver medal that year, and her legacy led to them lifting the title in 1984, when the Soviets were absent – ironically beating a United States team led by Comaneci's former coach Bela Karolyi. Romania's time came again in 2000 and 2004. In Sydney it was Andreea Raducan (who was allowed to keep her team gold despite being disqualified from the Individual event after failing a drugs test) and Simona Amanar who were the main contributors, and four years later in Athens Catalina Ponor and Monica Rosu took up the mantle.

Tragic first champions

The Team title was the first of the women's events to be accorded medal status, at the 1928 Games in Amsterdam. There was delight for the hosts as the Dutch became the first-ever women's Gymnastics Team champions. However, within 15 years four of the 12-strong line-up were dead – Ans Polak, Jud Simons, Helena Nordheim and Estella Agsteribbe all perished during the Second World War in Nazi concentration camps. Elka de Levie was the only Jewish member of the team to survive the Holocaust.

Really youthful

Gymnastics was notorious for making stars out of children, but in recent years a minimum age limit of 15 has been in force. There was no such rule at Amsterdam 1928, when 11-year-old Luigina Giavotti helped Italy to the silver medal in the women's Team Competition. Giavotti is the youngest women's Gymnastics medallist at the Games.

Ageless Seymour

Ethel Seymour was 46 years and 222 days old when she won a bronze medal as part of the Great Britain team at the 1928 Games in Amsterdam. Old enough then to have been silver-medal winner Luigina Giavotti's grandmother, she remains the oldest medallist in the history of women's Gymnastics at the Olympic Games.

⬇ *Great Britain's Gymnastics team perform their bronze medal-winning routine at the 1928 Olympic Games in Amsterdam.*

⬆ *The United States team take the plaudits after winning Team gold at the 1996 Games in Atlanta. It remains the country's last taste of victory in the competition.*

US steps up

The United States were second-raters in the women's Gymnastics Team Competition during the years of Soviet domination. A bronze medal at the 1992 World Championships provided a hint of change, and then, on home soil at Atlanta 1996, the US won its first women's Team title, with Shannon Miller and Kerri Strug leading the way. Despite individual success for Carly Patterson and Shawn Johnson in 2004 and 2008 respectively, there has been no team gold since, as the Romanians and then the Chinese showed just a little more strength in depth.

Individuals carry teams

Czechoslovakia and Hungary owe their success in the Team Competition to the inspiration provided by two incredible individuals. The Czechs won three successive Team silvers in the 1960s with the peerless Vera Caslavska as their leader. Hungary had been a force in the 1950s thanks to the example set by quadruple gold-medal winner Agnes Keleti. Neither country has been on the women's Team podium since 1972.

Chinese resent age slur

China's women gymnasts were slower than the men to challenge at world level, but are now one of the leading powers. The world team title in 2006 was a forerunner to their landing a first Team title at the Games at Beijing 2008. The success was called into question by media reports that some of the team were under 15, the minimum age for participation in the Games. In particular, the slight He Kexin was said to be only 14 at the time, but the Chinese authorities produced documentation that they said proved she was 16.

Women's Team Competition gold-medal winners

Date (host)	Score/Points	Winner
1928 (Amsterdam)	316.750 pts	Netherlands
1932 (Los Angeles)	Not held	
1936 (Berlin)	506.500 pts	Germany
1948 (London)	445.450 pts	Czechoslovakia
1952 (Helsinki)	527.030 pts	Soviet Union
1956 (Melbourne)	444.800 pts	Soviet Union
1960 (Rome)	382.320 pts	Soviet Union
1964 (Tokyo)	380.890 pts	Soviet Union
1968 (Mexico City)	382.850 pts	Soviet Union
1972 (Munich)	380.500 pts	Soviet Union
1976 (Montreal)	390.350 pts	Soviet Union
1980 (Moscow)	394.900 pts	Soviet Union
1984 (Los Angeles)	392.020 pts	Romania
1988 (Seoul)	395.475 pts	Soviet Union
1992 (Barcelona)	395.666 pts	Unified Team
1996 (Atlanta)	389.225 pts	United States
2000 (Sydney)	154.608 pts	Romania
2004 (Athens)	114.283 pts	Romania
2008 (Beijing)	188.900 pts	China

Individual apparatus champions

Women compete in four disciplines: the 10-centimetre-wide Balance Beam, which tests the gymnast's acrobatic and dancing skills; the Floor, a combination of tumbling and moves to music; the Uneven Bars, in which gymnasts perform a routine on bars set at heights of 241cm and 161cm and 130–150cm apart; and the Vault, where gymnasts run, twist and turn in the air and perform a landing.

Super Szabo

In the Soviet Union's absence, the 1984 women's Gymnastics competition developed into a match between the United States and Romania. Home favourite Mary-Lou Retton took the All-Around title, but Romania won the Team title and Ekaterina Szabo stole the show in the apparatus finals, winning the Floor and Vault Competitions, plus sharing the Balance Beam crown with team-mate Simona Pauca. Szabo's four golds equalled the record for a woman gymnast at one Games.

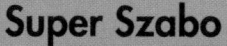
← *Although she missed out on the All-Around title to Mary Lou Retton, Ekaterina Szabo struck gold a record four times at the 1984 Games.*

Share of the glory

Women's Gymnastics at the 1956 Games was dominated by the Warsaw Pact countries and by two performers in particular. Only one medal went outside the Soviet bloc as Hungary's Agnes Keleti and the USSR's Larissa Latynina annexed the five individual gongs. All-Around champion Latynina, who was also part of the victorious Soviet team, won the Vault, with Keleti claiming Balance Beam and Uneven Bars honours. On the Floor the judges could not split them, so the gold was shared and Keleti, aged 35, became the Games' oldest women's Gymnastics champion.

Captivating Korbut

Arguably the first gymnast to earn worldwide stardom was Olga Korbut. At just 17, Korbut stole the show at the 1972 Games in Munich. Her impish displays on the Floor earned her a gold medal to add to that for her virtuoso Balance Beam routines, which were rated the best on show. Korbut was edged out into silver by East German Karin Janz in the Uneven Bars, but her standing back flip to catch on the apparatus was considered a move before its time. The Soviet star's nerve, coupled with a flashing smile, brought a brief thaw to the Cold War.

↑ *Olga Korbut won three gold medals at the 1972 Olympic Games: on the Balance Beam, on the Floor and as part of the victorious Soviet team.*

Women's Balance Beam Competition gold-medal winners

Date (host)	Points	Winner
1952 (Helsinki)	19.220 pts	Nina Bocharova (URS)
1956 (Melbourne)	18.800 pts	Agnes Keleti (HUN)
1960 (Rome)	19.283 pts	Eva Bosakova (CZE)
1964 (Tokyo)	19.449 pts	Vera Caslavska (CZE)
1968 (Mexico City)	19.650 pts	Natalya Kuchinskaya (URS)
1972 (Munich)	19.400 pts	Olga Korbut (URS)
1976 (Montreal)	19.950 pts	Nadia Comaneci (ROM)
1980 (Moscow)	19.800 pts	Nadia Comaneci (ROM)
1984 (Los Angeles)	19.800 pts	Simona Pauca (ROM)
		Ekaterina Szabo (ROM)
1988 (Seoul)	19.924 pts	Daniela Silivas (ROM)
1992 (Barcelona)	9.975 pts	Tatyana Lysenko (UNI)
1996 (Atlanta)	9.862 pts	Shannon Miller (USA)
2000 (Sydney)	9.825 pts	Liu Xuan (CHN)
2004 (Athens)	9.787 pts	Catalina Ponor (ROM)
2008 (Beijing)	16.225 pts	Shawn Johnson (USA)

Women's Floor Competition gold-medal winners

Date (host)	Points	Winner
1952 (Helsinki)	19.360 pts	Agnes Keleti (HUN)
1956 (Melbourne)	18.733 pts	Agnes Keleti (HUN)
		Larissa Latynina (URS)
1960 (Rome)	19.583 pts	Larissa Latynina (URS)
1964 (Tokyo)	19.599 pts	Larissa Latynina (URS)
1968 (Mexico City)	19.675 pts	Vera Caslavska (CZE)
		Larisa Petrik (URS)
1972 (Munich)	19.575 pts	Olga Korbut (URS)
1976 (Montreal)	19.850 pts	Nellie Kim (URS)
1980 (Moscow)	19.875 pts	Nellie Kim (URS)
		Nadia Comaneci (ROM)
1984 (Los Angeles)	19.975 pts	Ekaterina Szabo (ROM)
1988 (Seoul)	19.937 pts	Daniela Silivas (ROM)
1992 (Barcelona)	10.000 pts	Lavinia Milosovici (ROM)
1996 (Atlanta)	9.887 pts	Lilia Popkopayeva (UKR)
2000 (Sydney)	9.850 pts	Elena Zamolodchikova (RUS)
2004 (Athens)	9.750 pts	Catalina Ponor (ROM)
2008 (Beijing)	15.650 pts	Sandra Izbasa (ROM)

Women's Uneven Bars Competition gold-medal winners

Date (host)	Score / Points	Winner
1952 (Helsinki)	19.400 pts	Margit Korondi (HUN)
1956 (Melbourne)	18.966 pts	Agnes Keleti (HUN)
1960 (Rome)	19.616 pts	Polina Astakhova (URS)
1964 (Tokyo)	19.332 pts	Polina Astakhova (URS)
1968 (Mexico City)	19.650 pts	Vera Caslavska (CZE)
1972 (Munich)	19.675 pts	Karin Janz (GDR)
1976 (Montreal)	20.000 pts	Nadia Comaneci (ROM)
1980 (Moscow)	19.875 pts	Maxi Gnauck (GDR)
1984 (Los Angeles)	19.950 pts	Ma Yanhong (CHN)
		Julianne McNamara (USA)
1988 (Seoul)	20.000 pts	Daniela Silivas (ROM)
1992 (Barcelona)	10.000 pts	Li Lu (CHN)
1996 (Atlanta)	9.850 pts	Svetlana Khorkina (RUS)
2000 (Sydney)	9.862 pts	Svetlana Khorkina (RUS)
2004 (Athens)	9.687 pts	Emilie Lepennec (FRA)
2008 (Beijing)	16.725 pts	He Kexin (CHN)

Just perfect

Before 1976, no male or female gymnast had ever achieved Gymnastics perfection at the Olympic Games. At Montreal 1976, Nadia Comaneci scored seven perfect tens, including two on the Uneven Bars. It was on this apparatus that she made history by being awarded her first maximum on 18 July 1976. Her feat was replicated by fellow Romanian Daniela Silivas in 1988.

⬆ *It may have taken a technicality to separate them, but China's He Mexin edged out Nastia Liukin of the US to take gold in the Uneven Bars in 2008.*

He just makes it...

Chinese gymnast He Kexin was adjudged to be the winner of the 2008 women's Uneven Bars Competition thanks to the sport's complex rules. He Kexin and American Nastia Liukin were locked together after both recording scores of 16.725 and, incredibly, identical tallies of 7.700 and 9.025 from the two judging panels. Rather than letting them share the gold, however, the International Federation invoked their analysis of 'lowest variance', which showed that the Chinese gymnast had a slightly more even spread of scores from the various judges.

Women's Vault Competition gold-medal winners

Date (host)	Points	Winner
1952 (Helsinki)	19.200 pts	Yekaterina Kalinchuk (URS)
1956 (Melbourne)	18.833 pts	Larissa Latynina (URS)
1960 (Rome)	19.316 pts	Margarita Nikolayeva (URS)
1964 (Tokyo)	19.483 pts	Vera Caslavska (CZE)
1968 (Mexico City)	19.775 pts	Vera Caslavska (CZE)
1972 (Munich)	19.525 pts	Karin Janz (GDR)
1976 (Montreal)	19.800 pts	Nelli Kim (URS)
1980 (Moscow)	19.725 pts	Natalya Shaposhnikova (URS)
1984 (Los Angeles)	19.875 pts	Ekaterina Szabo (ROM)
1988 (Seoul)	19.905 pts	Svetlana Boginskaya (URS)
1992 (Barcelona)	9.925 pts	Lavinia Milosovici (ROM)
		Henrietta Onodi (HUN)
1996 (Atlanta)	9.825 pts	Simona Amanar (ROM)
2000 (Sydney)	9.731 pts	Elena Zamolodchikova (RUS)
2004 (Athens)	9.656 pts	Monica Rosu (ROM)
2008 (Beijing)	15.650 pts	Hong Unjong (NKO)

Rhythmic Gymnastics

Only women compete in Rhythmic Gymnastics, with individual competitors executing choreographed movements to music using five types of apparatus: rope, hoop, ball, clubs and ribbon. In the Group Competition teams of six gymnasts complete one routine with five ribbons and another with three hoops and two balls. Two panels of judges award points for each performance.

Fung the first

In Rhythmic Gymnastics more than most sports the rare absence of Eastern Europeans has a devastating effect on the pecking order. Such a phenomenon happened in 1984, when the withdrawal from the Olympic Games of the Soviet Union and most of the Warsaw Pact countries drastically lowered the quality of the Rhythmic field. Thus the fact that the first Rhythmic Gymnastics gold was won by a Canadian remains an anomaly. Lori Fung from Vancouver edged to the top of the podium ahead of Romania's Doina Stainculescu. In the World Championships the following year, Fung could only finish ninth.

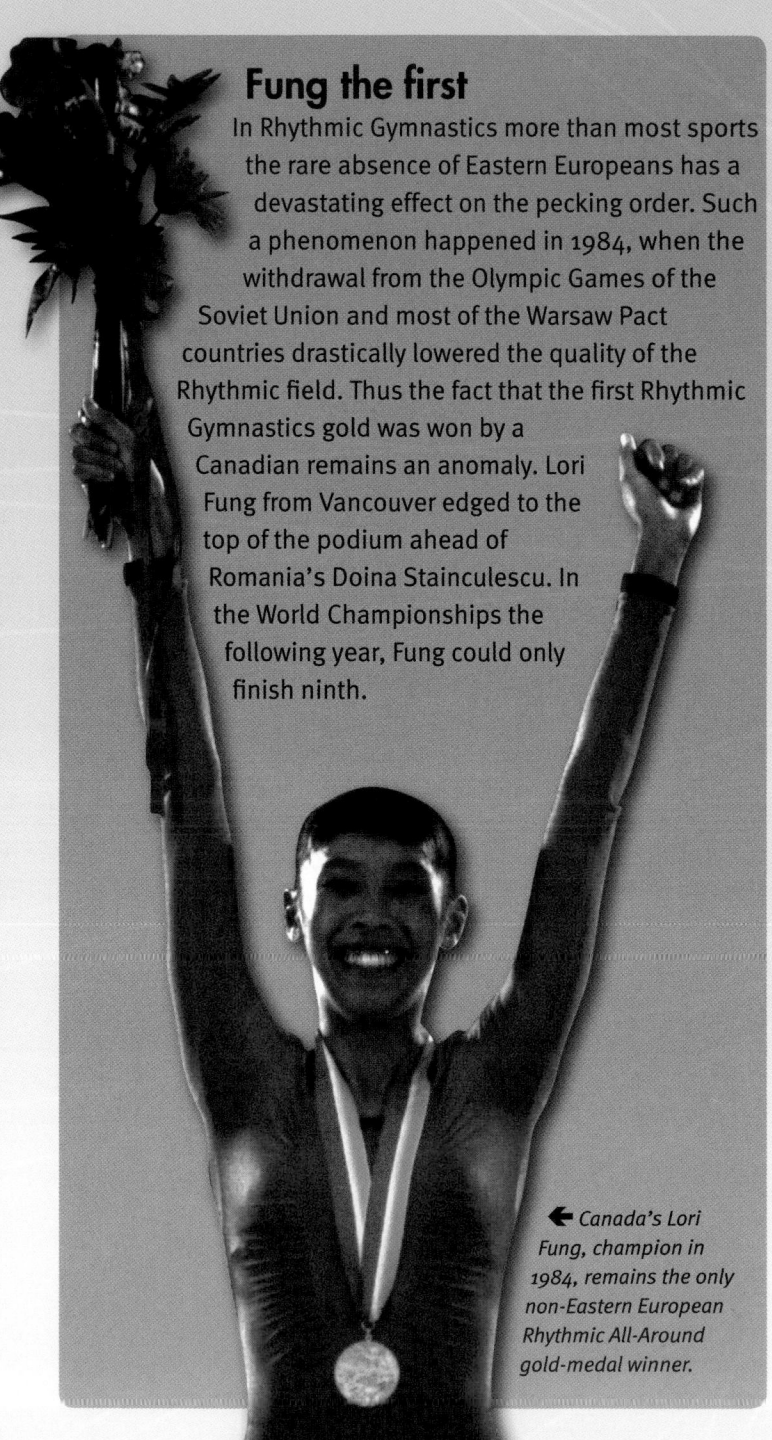

← *Canada's Lori Fung, champion in 1984, remains the only non-Eastern European Rhythmic All-Around gold-medal winner.*

The apparatus

Rope: Made of hemp or a synthetic material, the rope must be proportional to the gymnast's height. It can be swung and circled during the routine, which requires jumping and explosive movements.

Hoop: Made of plastic or wood, the hoop has an interior diameter of 80–90 centimetres and must weigh at least 300 grams. Favoured movements include rolls over the body or on the floor, rotations around the hand, throws and catches and passing over or through the hoop. It offers the greatest variety of movements and technical skills. Any vibration of the hoop in the air is penalised.

Ball: Made of rubber or a synthetic material, the ball is 18–20cm in diameter and weighs 400g. It is thrown, caught, bounced and rolled over the body or on the floor, but no grip is allowed as the movement should be 'flowing and sensuous'.

Clubs: Made of wood or a synthetic material, the clubs are 40–50cm long, weigh 150g each and are circled, thrown, caught and tapped.

Ribbon: Made of satin and at least 6m long, the ribbon is held by a stick to enable the gymnast to circle, spiral, throw and catch. Any knots in the ribbon are penalised.

Rhythmic Group Competition gold-medal winners

Date (host)	Score/Points	Winner
1996 (Atlanta)	38.933 pts	Spain
2000 (Sydney)	39.500 pts	Russia
2004 (Athens)	51.100 pts	Russia
2008 (Beijing)	35.550 pts	Russia

Late developer

Rhythmic Gymnastics began in the former Soviet Union in the 1940s before being officially recognised as a competitive event in 1961. It became part of the Games programme in Los Angeles in 1984, and the Group Competition was introduced 12 years later at the Atlanta 1996 Games.

⬆ *A slip-up for Russia's Yanina Batyrchina – she dropped the ribbon – cost her a chance of a Rhythmic Gymnastics All-Around gold medal at the 1996 Games.*

Ribbon ruins it

Just as one punch in Boxing or a throw in Judo can mean instant heartbreak for a potential gold medallist, so a dropped ribbon can do the same in Rhythmic Gymnastics. In 1996, Russia's Yanina Batyrchina was duelling for the title with Ekaterina Serebryanskaya of Ukraine going into the final discipline. Alas for Batyrchina, the stick tied to the satin slipped through her fingers and her chance had gone. Serebryanskaya was not faultless herself with the ribbon, but her errors were not as cataclysmic as Batyrchina effectively 'dropped the baton'. Serebryanskaya became the first Rhythmic gymnast to hold the European, World and Olympic Games All-Around gold medals at the same time, a feat equalled by Russia's Alina Kabayeva eight years later.

Russia on top

Russia dominates Rhythmic Gymnastics, with its gymnasts taking gold at the last three Olympic Games. Evgeniya Kanaeva became the third successive Russian winner at Beijing 2008, when identical scores of 18.850 with the rope and hoop and a superb club routine earned her the highest rating of any display in the Final – 18.950. It was a performance to make the inhabitants of Kanaeva's home city of in Western Siberia very proud, coming four years after another woman from Omsk won the silver in the Individual competition – Irina Tchachina. Inna Zhukova of Belarus won the silver this time round, and Ukraine's Anna Bessonova claimed the bronze to ensure that all the Individual medallists came from former Soviet Union nations.

Rhythmic Individual All-Around Competition gold-medal winners

Date (host)	Points	Winner
1984 (Los Angeles)	57.950 pts	Lori Fung (CAN)
1988 (Seoul)	60.000 pts	Marina Lobach (URS)
1992 (Barcelona)	59.037 pts	Alexandra Timoshenko (UNI)
1996 (Atlanta)	39.683 pts	Ekaterina Serebryanskaya (UKR)
2000 (Sydney)	39.632 pts	Yulia Barsakova (RUS)
2004 (Athens)	108.400 pts	Alina Kabaeva (RUS)
2008 (Beijing)	94.575 pts	Evgenia Kanaeva (RUS)

Little Miss Perfect

Perfection is always sought in sport, but rarely achieved. According to the judges at the 1988 Games in Seoul, Rhythmic gymnast Marina Lobach achieved it. The Belarussian (competing under the Soviet flag) received a perfect 'ten' for all of her routines during the qualifying and the final rounds of the All-Around Competition. Others were also given the ultimate score during the finals, but none could match Lobach over both phases of the event. Her score of 60.000 is her sport's equivalent of a hole-in-one at golf or a 147 in snooker. Silver medallist Adriana Dunavska came so close to glory (59.950), but you just can't beat perfection. Lobach was a phenomenon – the youngest Rhythmic Gymnastics champion at the Games, she retired the following year at the grand old age of 19.

Old at 21

The sheer flexibility required to compete at the highest level in Rhythmic Gymnastics means that athletes are already too old for it at a time when they would be nowhere near their peak in other sports. At the 2000 Games, Yulia Barsakova became the oldest gold medallist in the sport at the age of 21. Her big moment came at the expense of the woman who would succeed her four years later in Athens – Alina Kabaeva. Kabaeva made a mistake during the hoop discipline and Barsukova took full advantage.

➡ *Yulia Barsakova (centre) is the oldest All-Around champion – aged 21.*

Trampoline

The trampoline was invented in 1935 by Americans George Nilsen and Larry Griswold. They bolted together an iron frame and attached a piece of canvas to it using springs. The name comes from the Spanish word 'trampolin', meaning springboard. Trampoline became a mainstream competitive activity when the International Trampoline Federation merged with the International Gymnastics Federation in 1999.

Karavaeva kicks it off

One of the trampoline's inventors, George Nilsen, then 86 years old, was there to see Russia's Irina Karavaeva enter the record books as the inaugural women's Individual gold medallist in the sport, thanks to her success at Sydney in 2000. Ukraine's Oxana Tsyhuleva took silver and Canada's Karen Cockburn bronze before admitting to an unusual phobia for a trampolinist: 'It's an adrenaline rush. I'm actually afraid of heights... But it's a different feeling on the trampoline.' Germany's Anna Dogonadze led after the qualification round, but bounced off the trampoline during her final routine.

He makes Chinese breakthrough

He Wenna won China's first-ever gold medal in Trampoline at the conclusion of the 2008 women's competition in Beijing. She finished ahead of Canadian Karen Cockburn by 0.80 points. Ekaterina Khilko struck a blow for Uzbekistan by claiming the bronze, the country's first medal in Trampoline. Germany's Anna Dogonadze, the 2004 gold medallist, fell mid-way through her routine and finished fourth, while Sydney 2000 winner, Russia's Irina Karavaeva, came fifth.

↑ Alexander Moskalenko in action in the men's Trampoline Final at the 2004 Games in Athens. The legendary Russian added a silver medal to the gold he had won at Sydney four years earlier.

↖ In 2008, He Wenna became China's first-ever Trampoline champion at the Games.

Magnificent Moskalenko

The foremost competitor in the history of trampoline has been Alexander Moskalenko. The Russian 'king of spring' dominated the sport in the 1990s and early 2000s, winning five world titles and the first men's Olympic Games title at Sydney 2000. He won the 1990 and 1992 World Championships and then, at the age of 22, decided to retire, unable to find 'the right motivation'. His absence did not last long, as he came back to secure the 1994 global crown before once again leaving the scene. The news that Trampoline would make its Olympic Games debut in 2000 was too much of a lure for Moskalenko, and he prepared by claiming a fourth world title in 1999. Sydney was then the stage for the greatest display in the sport's history as Moskalenko utterly outclassed the opposition in the final, winning by the enormous margin of 2.40 points in a sport where often fractions of a point make the difference. He concluded a career that compares to any of the all-time greats in other sports by claiming the 2001 World Championship and the 2002 European title, after which he was only denied the 2003 world crown on a tie-break and also narrowly lost in the final at the 2004 Games in Athens.

New kids on the block

Trampolinists are judged by a panel on the technical difficulty and execution of their moves. There are two phases to each competition, qualification and final. The qualification round has two routines. The first must include special requirements, the second is voluntary. The top eight from these two routines qualify for the Final. Scores from the qualification round do not carry over to the final, which has one voluntary routine, with the highest scorer declared the winner. Synchronised Trampoline, a feature of the World Games, has yet to make its Olympic Games debut.

China's Lu doubles up

The day after He Wenna's triumph, Lu Chunlong followed her example to become the first Chinese man to win the men's Individual Trampoline title. Lu, the top qualifier for the final, scored 41.00 to win gold, showing superior style while executing a slightly easier routine than Jason Burnett, who won the silver. Burnett fulfilled the toughest display of all the finalists to earn the best result in the sport for a Canadian man. Lu's team-mate Dong Dong, at 19 the youngest competitor in the final, took bronze.

↑ *Irina Karavaeva's defence of her women's Individual title ended abruptly when she finished 15th out of 16 in qualifying at Athens 2004.*

Greek tragedy for Karavaeva

Reigning women's Individual champion Irina Karavaeva endured a disastrous defence of her title at the 2004 Games in Athens. The Russian finished in 15th place, second last, at the end of the qualifying routines to miss out on the chance to progress to the final. Germany's Anna Dogonadze claimed gold, with the then world champion Karen Cockburn from Canada having to settle for silver and China's Huang Shanshan taking bronze. Dogonadze became the first non-Russian to win Trampoline gold at the Olympic Games, although her heritage ties her to the former Soviet Union. She was born in Mtskheta, the former capital of Georgia, and represented that country from 1992 to 1997. Prior to Georgia's independence, she had competed under the Soviet banner, but on marrying her former coach she became a German citizen.

Nikitin nicks it

At the 2004 Games in Athens, Ukraine's Yuri Nikitin claimed the men's title by the narrowest of margins. Nikitin finished just 0.3 points ahead of five-time world champion Alexander Moskalenko from Russia.

↙ *Ukraine's Yuri Nikitin took the men's Individual title at Athens 2004.*

Women's Individual Trampoline gold-medal winners

Date (host)	Score/Points	Winner
2000 (Sydney)	38.900 pts	Irina Karavaeva (RUS)
2004 (Athens)	39.600 pts	Anna Dogonadze (GER)
2008 (Beijing)	37.800 pts	He Wenna (CHN)

Men's Individual Trampoline gold-medal winners

Date (host)	Score / Points	Winner
2000 (Sydney)	41.700 pts	Alexander Moskalenko (RUS)
2004 (Athens)	41.500 pts	Yuri Nikitin (UKR)
2008 (Beijing)	41.000 pts	Lu Chunlong (CHN)

Chapter Eight
Martial arts and combat sports

George Orwell once said that serious sport is 'war minus the shooting'. The author might have been describing the ferocity displayed at the Olympic Games inside the boxing ring, fencing sale or dojo, or on the wrestling mat, where some of the hardest-fought sporting contests are staged every four years.

Statues and paintings found in archaeological digs demonstrate that some form of wrestling has been known as a sport in Japan and China, Babylon and Egypt in antiquity. The ancient Greeks also practised it, as Homer has an account of a wrestling match in the *Iliad*.

Thus Wrestling was included in the first modern Olympic Games in 1896. The international Freestyle and Greco-Roman styles, as introduced at the Games, became the universally accepted version of the sport.

Boxing traces its history back to the ancient Greeks, to around 686 BC. Yet, despite professional pugilism's popularity in Victorian times, the amateur sport was omitted from the first two modern Games, the official attitude being that it was ungentlemanly and practised by the dregs of the population. That view was revised by 1904 and since 1920 Boxing has been one of the highlights of every Olympic Games.

Combat sports introduced to the Olympic Games have often reflected the culture of a particular Host City. Thus in 1964, when Tokyo staged the Games, Judo made its bow. Taekwondo, the Korean martial art, was introduced at Seoul 1988.

The 2012 Games in London will witness a significant change in the Boxing programme, as women's events will be staged at the Games for the first time.

Great Britain's James DeGale (blue) gains the upper hand during his Middle Weight semi-final victory over Ireland's John Sutherland (red) at the Beijing 2008 Games. The London-born southpaw went on to win gold and had turned professional by the end of the year.

Boxing

With the exception of 1912 (because Swedish law banned the sport at the time), boxing has been contested at every Olympic Games since 1904. Several of the sport's all-time greats – including Mohammad Ali, Joe Frazier, George Foreman and Lennox Lewis – have used their gold-medal-winning exploits as a springboard to greatness on the professional circuit.

Ali's shining light

Muhammad Ali, the gold-medal winner at Light Heavy Weight at the 1960 Games in Rome, remains one of the all-time Games greats. Ali, then a brash 18-year-old boxing under his original name, Cassius Clay, was the outstanding boxer of those Games, and his subsequent career underlined that gold-medal success as an amateur can be a springboard to a professional career. Ali is such an iconic sporting figure (so much so that he is widely regarded as one of the most recognisable figures of the 20th century), that it was perhaps unsurprising, although no less emotional, when he was chosen to light the cauldron at the Opening Ceremony of the Atlanta 1996 Games.

⬆*Cassius Clay proves too strong for Australia's Tony Madigan in the semi-finals of the Light Heavy Weight event at the 1960 Games in Rome.*

Savon the successor

Following his retirement, Teofilio Stevenson became Cuba's national boxing coach. His team's star performer was Felix Savon, who went on to match his hero by winning Super Heavy Weight gold in 1992, 1996 and 2000. Savon was formidable, standing 6ft 5in (1.96 metres) tall and with a reach of more than 2m. Savon dominated amateur boxing from 1986, when he won the first of his six world titles, until his retirement after Sydney 2000, at the age of 33.

Lennox Lewis's springboard

The big boys who have won Boxing medals at the Olympic Games have regularly featured future professional world champions among their ranks. The 1988 Super Heavy Weight final was a gripping contest between two future heavy weight champions of the world, with Lennox Lewis, then representing Canada, defeating Riddick Bowe, of the USA. Other medallists who have gone on to win professional world titles include Joe Frazier and George Foreman, both of the USA, who won the Heavy Weight gold medal in 1964 and 1968 respectively, and Wladimir Klitschko, of Ukraine, who won Super Heavy Weight gold at Atlanta 1996. Ingemar Johansson, the only Swede ever to hold the professional world heavy weight title, won the silver medal at Helsinki 1952. He was probably glad of the opportunity to box at all: Sweden's national ban on boxing had seen the sport excluded altogether in 1912 when the Games were held in Stockholm.

⬇ *Joe Frazier finds the target against Hans Huber en route to the Heavy Weight gold medal at Tokyo 1964.*

Stevenson's amateur ethos

Three-time gold medallist Teofilio Stevenson of Cuba consistently refused all entreaties to turn pro, famously declining one offer of US$2m. He said: 'Professional boxing treats a fighter like a commodity, to be bought and sold and discarded when no longer of use.' Such was Stevenson's domination of the Heavy Weight competition from 1972 that it was not until he met Hungary's Istvan Levai in the semi-final of the 1980 tournament in Moscow that another boxer was able to last the full three rounds with him. Even then, Levai spent nine minutes back-pedalling away from the Cuban's punch. Denied the possibility of a fourth gold medal by Cuba's boycott of the 1984 Games, Stevenson won his last amateur world title in 1986, aged 34.

→ *Cuba's Teofilo Stevenson won three Heavy Weight gold medals between 1972 and 1980, but always resisted the lure of professional boxing.*

Weights and measures

The growing size and stature of the population in general has seen regular adjustments made to the weight categories in Boxing at the Games. For instance, in 1904, when Boxing was contested for the first time, the Heavy Weight division was open to anyone weighing 11 stone 4 pounds (72 kilograms) or more. By the time of the Athens 2004 Games a century later, Heavy Weights were boxers weighing between 81 and 91kg, with the biggest category by now Super Heavy Weights, for the giants of more than 14 stone (89 kg). There has been a Super Heavy Weight category since Los Angeles 1984. The Light Heavy Weight category has remained unchanged since Helsinki 1952, for boxers weighting between 75 and 81kg (a little more than 12½ stone).

↑ *The USA's Tyrell Biggs (left) and Yugloslavia's Salihu Aziz square off in the first-ever Super Heavy Weight competition at Los Angeles 1984.*

British hat-trick

The 1908 Olympic Games, the first time the event was staged in London, saw an achievement that cannot be repeated in 2012: all three Heavy Weight boxing medallists came from Great Britain. Albert Oldman won the final with a knockout in just two minutes, beating his compatriot Sydney Evans, while Fred Parks took the bronze medal by defeating the other losing semi-finalist. In order to participate in the Games, Oldman had to take time off from his day job, as a policeman in the City of London. It is understood that afterwards he never encountered much trouble while walking his beat. Today, nations are only allowed to enter one boxer in each weight division. Since 1952, bronze medals have been awarded to each of the losing semi-finalists.

Ali's medal journey

The story of Muhammad Ali's Olympic Games gold medal has, in just half a century, entered into folklore, and is seen by some as symbolising how sport in general, and the Olympic Games in particular, have helped to improve race relations. Ali loved his medal. On his return to Louisville, Kentucky, in the Deep South of the United States, he kept his medal with him at all times, even sleeping with it. But what he could not do with his medal was take it with him into a whites-only restaurant in the home town that had given him a hero's welcome on his jubilant return from Rome 1960. After a confrontation with the restaurant owner and a white gang, Ali was so disgusted with his treatment that he tossed the medal into the Ohio River. Nearly 50 years later, in recognition of Ali's stance for human rights, the International Olympic Committee presented its former champion, by now badly affected by Parkinson's disease, with a replacement gold medal in a special ceremony during the 1996 Games in Atlanta.

Style standard

The Middle Weight and Welter Weight boxers at the Olympic Games have consistently been seen as among the most stylish boxers in the tournament, possessing the swiftest of hands and providing the best examples of the sweet science. At every Games since 1936, a trophy named the Val Barker Cup – in honour of the first general secretary of the World Amateur Boxing Federation (AIBA) – has been awarded to a boxer chosen from the entire tournament who displays the best style and technique. The recipients of the Val Barker have usually been gold medallists in their division, and they regularly feature the winners of the Middle Weight or Welter Weight class.

All that glitters – but never gold

After turning professional, Roy Jones Junior went on to enjoy a fabulous 20-year career. Regularly named as the world's best 'pound-for-pound' boxer, he won world titles at every weight division from middle to heavy weight. Before that, the 19-year-old Jones had won the Val Barker Cup, as the most stylish boxer at Seoul 1988 – even though he did not win the gold medal. Boxing at Light Middle Weight, Jones met South Korea's Park Si-hun in the final and landed 86 punches to his opponent's 32. Park even apologised for the verdict which led to a change in the scoring system. Jones put the disappointment behind him to turn professional seven months later. Within a further four years he had seized the first of his world titles. In Washington DC, Jones defied the pain from a broken right hand to outpoint Bernard Hopkins and secure the IBF Middle Weight crown.

⬆ *The shock can be seen in their faces as Park Si-hun (right) is declared the winner against Roy Jones (left) in the Light Middle Weight Final at Seoul 1988.*

Tipping the scales

The weight limits in the Middle Weight division at the Olympic Games have been altered frequently over the past century. Since 2004, the Middle Weight division has been for boxers between 69 and 75 kilograms. The Light Middle Weight category was first contested at the 1952 Games in Helsinki, but was dropped after Sydney 2000. Since the 2004 Games, the Welter Weight division has been for boxers weighing between 64 and 69kg. The Light Welter Weight division, which from 1952 until 2008 was contested by boxers weighing between 60 and 64kg, has been dropped from the programme for 2012. With three new weight divisions for women being introduced, the IOC is still maintaining a strict limit on the total number of competitors at the Games.

Sweet Sugar

One of the most renowned champions in Boxing history at the Olympic Games is Sugar Ray Leonard, winner of the Light Welter Weight gold medal at Montreal 1976. Leonard turned professional just months after his golden moment, and went on to become the first professional boxer ever to earn more than US$100 million in his career. Leonard's bouts with Roberto Duran, Tommy Hearns and Marvin Hagler have become the stuff of sporting legend, and helped install the American as 'The Boxer of the Decade' for the 1980s.

➔ *Sugar Ray Leonard won Light Welter Weight gold at Montreal 1976.*

Papp perfection

The Boxing tournament at Melbourne 1956 will always be remembered for the feat of the Hungarian Laszlo Papp. Having won the Middle Weight title at London 1948, Papp won the new Light Middle Weight title in 1952 and retained it at Melbourne 1956. That made him the first boxer ever to win three gold medals at the Games, a feat that was unique until Teofilio Stevenson matched it in the 1970s. In his amateur career, Papp scored 55 first-round knockouts. In the 1956 Light Middle Weight Final, Papp defeated José Torres, the Puerto Rican fighting under the flag of the United States, who would go on to become light heavy weight world champion as a professional.

↑ *Hungary's Laszlo Papp won three successive gold medals between 1948 and 1956 – the first of two boxers to achieve the feat.*

Best of British

Born on 1 June 1982, Harry Mallin, a London policeman by profession, was the British ABA Middle Weight champion in 1919 and 1920 and had his first taste of the Olympic Games at Antwerp 1920. He cruised through to the final, in which he faced Art Preud'Homme – a French-Canadian soldier who had won all of his previous bouts by knockout – and the Englishman won the fight on points to take gold. At Paris 1924, Mallin began the defence of his title at the Velodrome d'Hiver with two straightforward victories, won a controversial quarter-final fight against French hero Roger Brousse, out-pointed Belgium's Joseph Beecken in the semi-final, before beating compatriot John Elliot on points in the final. In doing so, Mallin had become the first boxer, at any weight, to defend a title at the Games and remains the only British boxer in history to have won two Boxing gold medals.

↖ *James DeGale ended Great Britain's 40-year wait for Middle Weight gold at the 2008 Games in Beijing.*

Patterson steps up

Floyd Patterson, who would later become the youngest-ever professional world heavy weight champion, won Middle Weight gold at the 1952 Games. During his pro career, he would twice encounter the silver medallist in the Heavy Weight division at those Games, Ingemar Johansson, winning once and losing once to the Swede for the world heavy weight title.

DeGale's breakthrough

Middle Weight British boxers have struggled to make their mark at the Olympic Games. James DeGale, the Middle Weight champion at Beijing 2008, was the first British boxer to win Middle Weight gold for 40 years. The last British Middle Weight champion before him was Chris Finnegan, who struck gold at the 1968 Games in Mexico City, despite having been put on the floor in his first bout, against Titus Simba of Tanzania. Even in his semi-final, Finnegan came close to defeat, being given two standing counts of eight in his contest with Al Jones of the United States. Yet still the hard-working British hod carrier battled his way through to the final, where he won a majority points decision over the Soviet Union's Aleksei Kiselov.

Endurance test

Winning medals in Boxing is among the most gruelling and demanding of all the challenges offered by the Olympic Games. The competition lasts almost the entire duration of the Games and culminates in two days of finals, completed only just before the Olympic Flame is extinguished in the stadium at the Closing Ceremony. In some cases, boxers have to get through three bouts before reaching the semi-finals, giving them sometimes less than 48 hours for recovery and the repair of any cuts or injuries sustained along the way.

Stretching the limit

Amateur boxing was always used to be contested over three rounds, each of three minutes. Recently, in the tournaments at the 2000, 2004 and 2008 Games, the contests lasted four rounds, each of two minutes, as the sport sought to minimise damage to boxers through exhaustion and blows to the head. Boxing experts, however, felt that the traditional format of three-minute rounds demanded more stamina from the contestants, and in London the Boxing tournament will revert to that format for men. Women will continue to box four two-minute rounds.

Simple in St Louis

The International Olympic Committee continues to recognise St Louis 1904 as the Games at which Boxing made its debut. In the Boxing tournament staged at St Louis, many of the contests were simply one-off, straight finals. This helped Oliver Kirk to claim a unique place in history as the only boxer to win in two weight divisions at a single Games. Kirk, of the United States, beat another American, Frank Haller, for the Feather Weight title, and at Bantam Weight, he stopped George Finnegan in the third round.

Marvellous McTaggart

Dick McTaggart, one of 18 children from a family in Dundee, is widely regarded as Britain's finest ever boxer at the Olympic Games. The 21-year-old Scot won the Light Weight gold medal at Melbourne 1956, where he also received the Val Barker Cup as the tournament's most stylish boxer. McTaggart boxed again at the 1960 Games in Rome, winning the bronze medal, and at Tokyo in 1964, where he was eliminated in his second bout. In both 1960 and 1964, McTaggart was beaten by Polish boxers, first Kazimierz Pazdzior and later Jerzy Kulej, who both went on to win gold medals. McTaggart's career achievements included five ABA titles, a Commonwealth Games gold medal and the European Championship, and he won 610 of his 634 bouts. He never turned professional.

↑ *Scotland's Dick McTaggart picked up two medals (one gold, the other bronze) at three appearances at the Games between 1956 and 1964.*

Wrong target

Spanish Featherweight Valentin Loren has gone down in infamy for his performance in the Boxing tournament at the 1964 Games. The referee, Hungarian Guorgy Sermer, stepped in and disqualified Loren in round two of his first-round bout for repeated holding and punching with an open glove. The Spaniard was so furious with the decision that, according to some ringside observers, he landed his first punch with a proper fist on the referee's nose. Loren duly received a lifetime ban from international boxing.

← *Spain's Valentin Loren flattens referee Guorgy Sermer at the 1964 Games – it was his last action in an international boxing ring.*

→ Oscar De La Hoya (USA), still a teenager, celebrates winning Light Weight gold at the 1992 Olympic Games in Barcelona.

Safety features

All modern amateur boxers now wear headguards, while their large, padded gloves have white areas in the scoring area, with the aim of scoring a point with each punch they land successfully on their opponent's head or upper body. Other safety measures in amateur boxing include an age limit: senior boxers can be no younger than 17 and no older than 34. Boxers are also banned from wearing beards.

Ten for 2012

At London 2012, the Boxing competition will feature ten men's weight categories, from Light Fly Weight (46–49 kilograms) to Super Heavy Weight (over 91kg). Light Fly Weight is the lightest weight division contested at the Games, with a limit of 49kg, or a little over 7 stone 7 pounds. The weight category was first fought at Mexico City 1968, where the champion was Francisco Rodriguez, the first Venezuelan ever to win an Olympic Games gold medal.

Great Gunn

Amateur boxing's age rule makes it impossible for Richard Gunn, the Feather Weight champion when the Games were first held in London in 1908, to lose his record as the oldest ever Boxing champion in history. Gunn was 37 in 1908. He had been British amateur champion from 1894 to 1896, but had retired because of a lack of competition and only came out of retirement for the 1908 Games. With the gold medal duly won, Gunn retired once more, this time for good, having lost one bout in 15 years.

Ultimate Oscar winner

One of the greatest boxers of all time, amateur or professional, was Oscar De La Hoya, the Los Angelino who, as a teenager, won the Light Weight gold medal at the 1992 Olympic Games in Barcelona. A year beforehand, De La Hoya had pledged to his mother, who was dying from cancer, that he would win the Boxing gold medal. At the Games, duly inspired, De La Hoya would drop to his knees after each of his victories and point to the sky. De La Hoya won the Light Weight Final by beating Marco Rudolph, the German who had beaten him in the World Championship final a year before. The triumph at the Games set up De La Hoya for a professional career in which he dominated the lighter weight divisions for the rest of the decade.

Women enter the ring

Women's Boxing at London 2012 will feature as a full medal event for the first time, with medals in Fly Weight (48–51 kilograms), Light Weight (57–60kg) and Middle Weight (69–75kg). At the 2010 World Championships, the winners of the titles in those weight categories were Mary Kom (India), Yun Kum Ju (North Korea) and Mary Spencer (Canada). With ten categories contested at those championships, staged in Barbados, 21 countries won medals.

← Women's world middle weight champion Mary Kom (right) will be among the favourites for gold at London 2012.

Fencing

Fencing is one of just five sports – with Athletics, Cycling, Gymnastics and Swimming – to have been an ever-present in every modern Games since 1896. Fencing also has a unique place in Games history, because, at the first two Games of the modern era, in Athens in 1896 and Paris in 1900, amateurs and professionals were allowed to compete. There are three forms of Fencing at the Games: Epée, Foil and Sabre.

Setting the rules

Fencing's international governing body was not formed until 1913, and at the early Games, as with so many sports, the competition rules set by the International Olympic Committee and the local organisers often had a formative influence on many facets of the event. Since it was commonplace at the turn of the 20th century for fencing masters and their pupils to enter parallel competitions, it seemed almost natural to allow both to compete in the first two Games, in Athens and Paris. Contests had no time limits until the 1930s, when one match lasted seven hours. In modern fencing, the bout lasts for three rounds, each of three minutes.

Judges wired in

In the days before automatic electronic scoring revolutionised fencing, matches depended on the sharp eyes and quick wits of a set of expert judges. Two side judges stood behind and beside each fencer, watching for hits made by that fencer. A 'director' observed from several feet away. He would end each action by calling 'Halt!' and then poll the judges. If the judges differed, or abstained, the director could overrule. Judges began to be replaced in Fencing at the 1936 Olympic Games in Berlin, when an electrical scoring system was used for the Epée, with a buzzer and lights indicating if a competitor had made a touch. The foil was scored electronically from the time of the 1956 Games in Melbourne, but the sabre, with its cut and thrust style, had to wait until the 1988 Games in Seoul before it, too, had automated scoring. As well as reducing the possibility of judges being open to any accusations of bias, the introduction of electronic scoring (and with it the possibility of more accurate scoring with faster actions previously unseen by the human eye) allowed fencers to perform subtler, lighter touches, and more touches to the back and flank than had been the case beforehand. A touch of a mere 15 milliseconds is now enough for a fencer to register a score.

⬇ *Hungary's Aladar Gerevich (right) registers a point against Italy's Gastone Darè in the men's Individual Sabre at London 1948. The Hungarian went on to collect Individual and Team gold.*

A question of honour settled by a duel

When the French and Italian Foil teams competed at the 1924 Games in Paris, a disputed call by a judge led to an extraordinary incident: a real duel, and possibly one of the last to be fought in the 20th century. After the Games, the Italian team issued a statement that accused the Italian-born Hungarian fencing master, Italo Santelli, of supporting a competition judge's decision in favour of one of the Hungarians. When he heard of the insult, Santelli, although 60 years old, issued a challenge to the captain of the Italian team, Adolfo Cotronei. Government permission was required before the duel could be fought, and Santelli's son, Giorgio, stepped in for his ageing father. Using sabres, but not electronic scoring equipment, Santelli jnr was declared the winner after three minutes of duelling and honour was satisfied.

Six-hit Gerevich

Aladar Gerevich, the Individual Sabre gold medallist the last time that the Olympic Games were staged in London, in 1948, won a total of seven golds, one silver and two bronze in a Games career that began at Los Angeles in 1932. All but one of Gerevich's golds came in the Team Sabre competition, from 1932 through to his final Games, in Rome in 1960, when the Hungarian was 50 years old. It makes Gerevich the Olympian who has recorded the most consecutive victories – six.

Fencing equality

Since the 1992 Olympic Games in Barcelona, there have been ten Fencing events contested, and at London 2012 there will again be five events for men and five for women fencers. The Fencing events (for both men and women) at the 2012 Games will be: Individual and Team Foil, Individual Epée (the team event being dropped from the programme), and Individual and Team Sabre.

⬆ Hungary's current President, Pal Schmitt, won two Team Épée gold medals (in 1968 and 1972).

Zhdanovich breaks in

Given that the sport drew heavily upon its traditions in the French school, and its strong Italian influence, perhaps it shouldn't have come as a surprise that the men's Foil events at the early Games were dominated by French and Italian fencers. It wasn't until the 1960 Games, staged in Rome, that the Franco-Italian duopoly of the event finally came to an end, with Viktor Zhdanovich of the Soviet Union winning gold (to become the first Soviet fencer to win an Olympic Games gold medal), his compatriot Yuri Sisikin taking silver and American Albert Axelrod claiming bronze.

Pals' progress

Fencing has always been a rich source of medals for the Hungarians at the Olympic Games. Aladar Gerevich's team-mate Pal Kovacs, who beat him to the Individual Sabre gold medal in 1952, had a similarly long and illustrious career, winning six gold medals and a bronze at five Games between 1936 and 1960. Pal Schmitt, a Team Epée gold medalist for Hungary at both Mexico City 1968 and Munich 1972, and was elected as his country's President in August 2010.

⬇ Aladar Gerevich (right) collected ten medals (seven of them gold) in six appearances at the Games.

Magical Magyars

In Team Sabre competition at the Games, Hungary's men went unbeaten between 1928 and 1960 – one of the longest winning streaks in Olympic Games history. In all, the Hungarian Sabre teams won 46 matches at the Games and seven gold medals. After losing the title in 1964, Hungary did not win the Team Sabre gold medal again until 1988.

Nadi spans the war

In the early part of the last century, Nedo Nadi did much to establish Italy's precedence in the salle. As an 18-year-old in 1912, Nadi won his first title in the Individual Foil in Stockholm. War then intervened, but Nadi emerged from it a stronger fencer; at Antwerp in 1920, in the absence of several European teams, including the Hungarians, he not only retained his foil title but also won five of the six available gold medals, three of those with his team-mates. His victory in the Individual Sabre left his brother Aldo nursing the silver medal.

◤ At one stage hailed as the greatest living fencer, Italy's Nedo Nadi won five of the six Fencing gold medals on offer at Antwerp 1920: in the Individual Foil and Sabre events and the Team Épée, Foil and Sabre events.

Fencing for the Fatherland

Women fencers have competed at the Olympic Games since Paris 1924, when 33-year-old Ellen Osiier, of Denmark, became the Games' first woman Fencing champion. Osiier beat Great Britain's Gladys Davies to the gold medal in the Individual Foil after winning all 16 of her bouts in Paris. At the next Olympic Games, in Amsterdam in 1928, the Individual Foil was won by Helene Mayer, of Germany, at the age of 17. Eight years later, and by now living in the United States, Mayer was included in the German Fencing team again for the 1936 Games staged in Hitler's Germany, despite her being Jewish. This time Mayer, who had placed fifth in the 1932 competition in Los Angeles, picked up a silver medal.

Family business

There is often a strong family aspect to Fencing events at the Games. Here is one example. Albert Bogen competed for Austria at the 1912 Games in Stockholm (picking up a medal in the Team Sabre) and for Hungary at the 1928 Games in Amsterdam (a Jew, he had moved to Hungary). His daughter, Erne Bogen, won a bronze medal for Hungary in the women's Individual Foil at the 1932 Games in Los Angeles. Erna later married one of Hungary's greatest Olympians, seven-time Sabre gold medallist Aladar Gerevich. To maintain the family tradition, Erna and Aladar's son, Pal, won bronze medals in the Team Sabre in 1972 and 1980 – a third generation of his family to win an Olympic Games medal.

⬆ *Hungary's Erna Bogen (right) finished behind Great Britain's Heather 'Judy' Guinness (left, silver) and Austria's Ellen Preis (centre, gold) to claim women's Individual Foil bronze at the 1932 Games in Los Angeles.*

⬅ *Denmark's Ellen Osiier became the Games' first-ever women's Fencing champion when she beat Great Britain's Gladys Davies to win the Individual Foil event at the 1924 Games in Paris.*

Silver linings

Before Gillian Sheen won her gold medal at the 1956 Games, British fencers had won six silvers. Three of those had come in the men's Team Epée event. Great Britain's individual medals had all been won by women: Gladys Davies (1924), Muriel Freeman (1928) and Judy Guinness Penn-Hughes (1932) – and all the medals were won in the Individual Foil.

Latin links

Given that the two countries are often credited as being the birthplace of modern fencing (national fencing schools abounded in the two countries in the late 19th and early 20th centuries), it comes as little surprise that France and Italy dominate Fencing's all-time medal table. Since 1896, the two countries' have won 86 gold medals between them – with Italy leading the way with 45 to France's 41. France lead the way on the overall medals count, however, with 115 (41 gold, 40 silver, 34 bronze) to Italy's 114 (45 gold, 38 silver, 31 bronze). Both countries took home two gold medals at the 2008 Games in Beijing: France in the Team Épée and the Team Sabre; and Italy in the men's Individual Épee (Matteo Tagliariol) and the women's Individual Foil (Valentina Vezzali).

The French have a word for it...

Fencing has a vocabulary all of its own, much of it derived from ancient French. Thus a contest is termed a 'bout', with a specific number of hits as the target for victory; a 'barrage' is a fight-off to determine a result, or qualifier, in the event of a tie. Given the sport's deadly origins, it may be reassuring to know that in fencing there is an offence called 'brutality', when a fencer performs with an unacceptable level of force or violence. A fencing sword has a forte and a foible. The foible is the flexible part of the blade furthest away from the hilt, while the forte is the wider, stiffer part of the blade closer to the hilt.

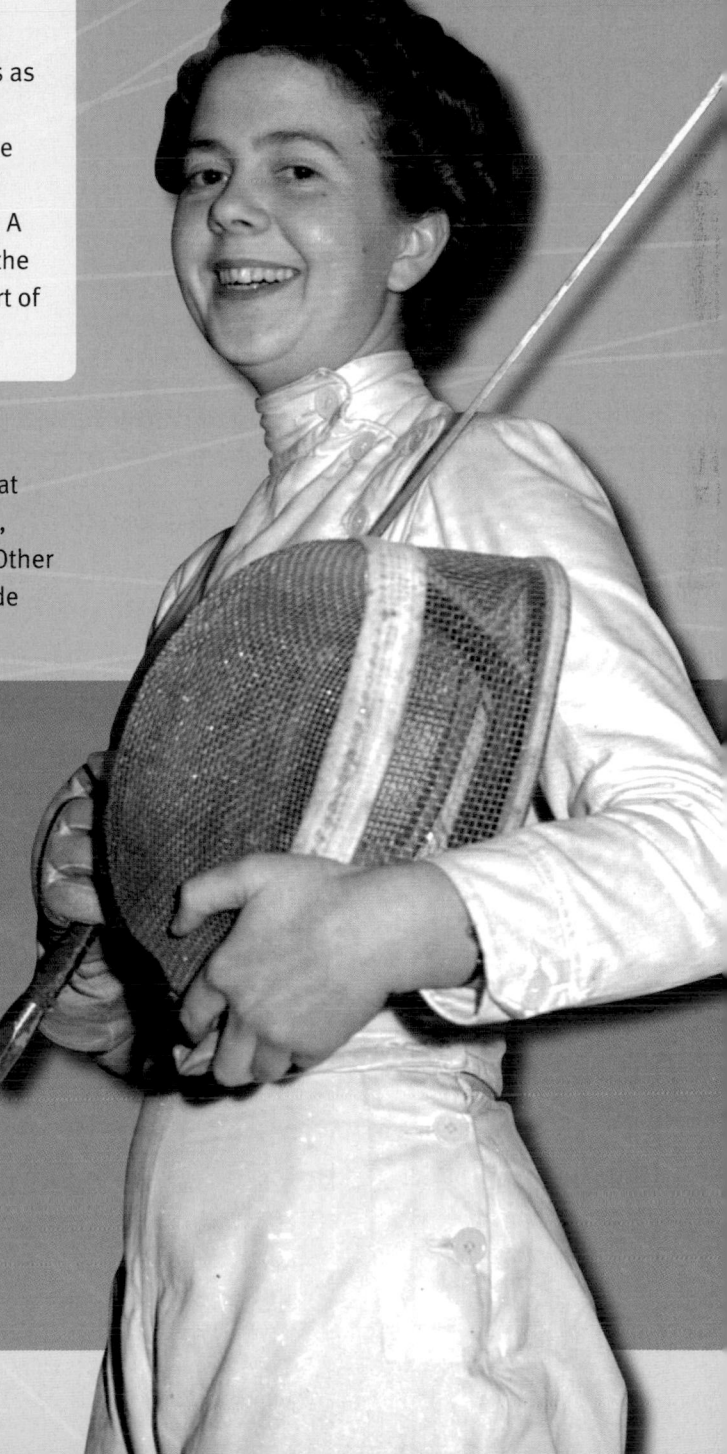

Excellence at ExCel

The Fencing events at the 2012 Olympic Games in London will be staged at ExCel, in the heart of Docklands, which has staged major sporting events, including world championship boxing and the annual London Triathlon. Other sports being staged alongside the Fencing at ExCel at London 1012 include Boxing, Judo, Table Tennis and Taekwondo.

Sheen's gold

In the history of the modern Olympic Games, Britain has won but a solitary Fencing gold, won by Gillian Sheen, a 28-year-old dental surgeon from London, who took the Individual Foil title in Melbourne in 1956. Sheen managed to edge into the final by defeating the world champion, Lídia Dömölky-Sákovics, of Hungary, in a barrage to decide the fourth place in her semi-final pool. In the final, Sheen lost her first bout to Olga Orban-Szabo, of Romania, but won her other six bouts to finish equal first with the Romanian. The gold medal was decided on a barrage between these two and, despite having already lost to Orban earlier, Sheen managed to win by four touches to two at the second attempt. Sheen would compete again at the 1960 Games in Rome, before marrying and moving with her husband to live and work in New York.

➜ *Gillian Sheen became a national star when she took women's Individual Foil gold at Melbourne 1956. She is the only fencer from Great Britain to have struck Fencing gold.*

Judo

Judo is a modern martial art and combat sport that was invented in 1882 by Kano Jigoro in Japan; the object is to throw, or take down, one's opponent to the ground with one of a number of possible moves. It was contested for the first time at Tokyo 1964 and (with the exception of Mexico City 1968) has been ever-present at the Games ever since. A women's event has been running since Barcelona 1992.

Parisi wins for Europe

Born in the Frosinone province in central Italy, Angelo Parisi was brought up in London and had to have a change of nationality rushed through government departments in 1970 so he could represent Britain at the European Junior Championships, which he won. After taking a bronze medal at the 1972 Games in Munich, he married a French girl and switched nationalities again. Parisi's fluent throwing style could uproot the most stubborn of opponents and he won the Heavyweight title for France at the 1980 Games in Moscow, as well getting as a silver medal in the Open classes in 1980 and 1984.

⬆ *Italian-born Angelo Parisi won a bronze medal for Great Britain at Munich 1972 and gold for France at Moscow 1980.*

Geesink puts an end to Japan's monopoly

In 1961, for the first time since the event started in 1956, the Dutchman Anton Geesink became the first judo fighter to defeat a Japanese fighter at the World Championships, winning the open (unlimited weight) category. Three years later, when Tokyo staged the Olympic Games, the Japanese won three weight divisions and were desperate to add a fourth in the Open category. In the final, Geesink, 1.98 metres tall and weighing more than 120 kilograms, towered over Akio Kaminaga, only 1.70m although weighing 102kg. Geesink, who had defeated Kaminaga in the preliminaries, managed to hold down the Japanese fighter to take gold. It was a pivotal moment in the sport: the landscape of international judo had changed for ever.

⬆ *1961 world champion Anton Geesink (Netherlands) denied Japan a whitewash of Judo gold medals when he won the Open category at the 1964 Games in Tokyo.*

Gold on one leg

Built, as one opponent remarked, 'like a refrigerator with a head on top', Yasuhiro Yamashita was the outstanding heavyweight in the world from 1977 until his retirement in 1985, being unbeaten in 203 consecutive bouts, including four world titles. However, Japan boycotted the 1980 Games in Moscow and he had to wait four years, until 1984, for the supreme title, the Olympic Games gold medal. Yamashita was expected to cruise to victory in Los Angeles, but he tore a right calf muscle early on and had to limp for the rest of the tournament. In the final, Egyptian Mohammed Ali Rashwan lasted barely a minute before being held down. A fully fit Yamashita would have made the contest even shorter.

Adams felled at the last

Neil Adams — coached at the same London club, the Budokwai, as Angelo Parisi — was possibly the finest-ever stylist apart from the Japanese. Although European champion four times and world champion in 1981, he only managed to collect two silver medals at the Olympic Games, losing in the Moscow 1980 -71kg final to Ezio Gamba and the Los Angeles 1984 -78kg final to Frank Wieneke of West Germany. In the latter, Wieneke cleverly made a half-hearted attack and, as Adams pulled his shoulder back, the Briton left himself open to a superb left seionage (shoulder throw) and was hurled to the mat.

➔ *Great Britain's Neil Adams was a supreme stylist but fell at the final hurdle at the 1980 and 1984 Games and had to be content with silver.*

Sadness to happiness

In 1992, Spain's Miriam Blasco was the favourite to win the -57kg class at the Olympic Games in Barcelona. She was the 1991 world and European champion. But a few weeks before the Games, her coach, Sergio Cardell, was killed in a car crash. She wore his black belt for the final against Great Britain's Nicola Fairbrother. It was a desperately close contest, Blasco scoring with a leg attack only for Fairbrother later to get in a position to affix a strangle, which the referee did not believe was going to be completed. Blasco won the gold medal, but the rivals became close friends, later entering into business together running a judo centre in Spain.

No short cut

At the 2000 Games in Sydney, Debbie Allan was among the favourites for the Featherweight title. On the morning of the event, the Briton weighed in under the 52-kilogram limit on the practice scales, but it was discovered that paper had been inserted in the mechanism. After the scales were recalibrated, she was found to be overweight. In a desperate attempt to make the weight before the time limit expired, she began vigorously exercising, stripped naked and even had her hair cut off. But she was still 50 grams overweight and was barred from competition.

⬇ *Japan's Ryoko Tani won the women's -48kg events in 2000 and 2004.*

A real-life comic-book character

No female Japanese judo fighter has ever inspired as much fascination in her country as Ryoko Tani, whose resemblance to the comic-book character 'Yawara-chan' made her a celebrity. A bronze medallist at the age of 16 in 1992, she was favourite for the -48kg in 1996, having been unbeaten for four years, but she lost to a wild-card entry from North Korea, Kye Sun-hui, in the biggest upset in the history of the sport. Four years later in Sydney, with Japanese cameramen surrounding the mat, she took the coveted title at last — and went on to retain it at Athens 2004.

Taekwondo

A relative newcomer to the Games programme, Taekwondo appeared twice as a demonstration sport (in 1988 and 1992) before it became a full-medal sport at the 2000 Games in Sydney. South Korea have been the dominant force in the event, winning nine of the 24 gold medals contested. At London 2012 men and women will each compete in four categories – -58kg, -68kg, -80kg and +80kg and -49kg, -57kg, -67kg and +67kg respectively.

Controversial start for Steve

Steve Lopez was the first person to win a Taekwondo title at the Olympic Games. This was at the Sydney 2000 Games in the Featherweight division, when Lopez met Korea's Sin Joon-Sik. The Korean was ahead until Lopez scored with a back kick. At the scheduled end of the bout, the referee awarded the bout to the American stating the Korean had been penalised for two half-points during the contest. In fact, the rules stated that the bout should have continued until one fighter had scored. The referee was suspended for a year, but Lopez kept what proved merely the first of two Olympic and five world titles. His world title success in 2005 was notable because both his brother Mark and sister Diana also collected gold medals at the same championships in Madrid.

↗ *Two-time gold-medal winner Steve Lopez was a controversial champion at the 2000 Games.*

Iranian auction

Iranian Hadi Saei Bonehkohal, a triple world champion, was one of the favourites for the Featherweight (Under 68kg) title in Sydney but he lost to Korea's Sin Joon-Sik in the semi-final. Three years later an earthquake flattened his home town of Bam, and the competitor, a former national sportsman of the year in Iran, auctioned his medal collection to help the victims. He was, therefore, without any trophies when he arrived in Athens for the 2004 Games – but he soon had the best trophy of all. In the final, he defeated Huang Chich Hsiung of Chinese Taipei to take the gold medal.

↑ *Iran's Hadi Saei Bonehkohal launches an attack on Chinese Taipei's Huang Chih Hsiung on his way to gold in the Lightweight Final in 2004.*

Bronze medal for Afghanistan

Afghanistan won their first Olympic medal in any sport when Rohullah Nikpai took bronze in the men's 58kg competition at the Beijing 2008 Games. Nikpai beat world champion flyweight Juan Antonio Ramos of Spain in the repechage. Afghanistan president Hamid Karzai immediately called to congratulate Nikpai. He also awarded him a house at the government's expense.

First for Taiwanese

Chen Shih-Hsien became a celebrity in Chinese Taipei when she beat Cuba's Yanelis Labrada to win the Flyweight (Under 49kg) gold medal in Athens in 2004. In doing so, she became the first competitor in any sport from her country to win an Olympic Games title, although she was followed a few minutes later by her compatriot Chu Mu-Yen, also in Taekwondo. At the Victory Ceremony, the Chinese Taipei Olympic Flag was flown rather than the country's national flag because of an original ruling by the International Olympic Committee at the behest of the Chinese government. She said afterwards: 'I am a single girl who has wandered around for ten years. My parents now want me to settle down.'

➔ *Chen Shih-Hsien (right) of the Chinese Taipei made history when she won the women's Flyweight Taekwondo event at Athens 2004.*

Stevenson Proves Appealing

British Heavyweight Sarah Stevenson, competing in her third Olympic Games in 2008, caused a major upset in the Over 67kg class when she defeated China's double Olympic champion Chen Zhong. In the second round, she seemed to have lost by a point to her Chinese opponent, although the Doncaster fighter believed she had scored with a last-second kick to the face, which had not been registered. Gary Hall, Britain's Performance Director, filed a protest and the appeal was upheld. Zhong went out while Stevenson continued in the competition. After the drama, it was no surprise that she then lost to Mexican Maria Espinoza, the eventual gold medallist, but she did take bronze with an easy victory over Noha Abd Rabo of Egypt.

Champion Chu

Chu Mu-Yen won the gold medal in the Flyweight (Under 58kg) category at Athens 2004, Chinese Taipei's first-ever gold in the Olympic Games. He went into the Athens 2004 Games as the World Champion, having claimed that title at Garmisch–Partenkirchen in 2003, and the World Student Games (Universiade) at Daegu in the same year. A student at the University of Pittsburgh in the United States, he earned an MSc, masters degree, in Occupational Therapy in December 2008, four months after claiming bronze at the Beijing 2008 Games. Chu's girlfriend, Yan Shun-chun lost in the semi-final of the Under 49kg category to gold medallist Wu Jingyu of China and then in the bronze medal match to Daynellis Montejo of Cuba.

Vietnamese join in

Vietnam finally joined the long list of countries to have won Olympic Games medals when Tran Hieu Ngan took silver in Taekwondo at the 2000 Games in Sydney. Two years earlier, Ngan had taken a bronze medal in the Southeast Asian Games and a gold medal in the Asian Championships, but her performance in Sydney made her a national celebrity. The 26-year-old Ngan, whose father, the owner of a confectionery shop, had died a week before the Games opened, lost 2–0 in the Featherweight (Under 57kg) Final to Jung Jae-Eun, the reigning world champion.

⬅ *Sarah Stevenson is dismayed after her defeat to Zhong Chen in the women's +67kg quarter-finals at Beijing 2008. Zhong won the match but Stevenson later received an reprieve after an appeal proved successful.*

Wrestling – Freestyle

Freestyle Wrestling, which unlike Greco-Roman Wrestling allows the use of legs in both offence and defence, has been contested at every Games since St Louis 1904 by men and since Athens 2004 by women. The United States have been the sport's most successful country, winning 108 medals, 46 of them gold.

Unbeaten champion

No other international wrestler has had a record as perfect as that enjoyed by Osamu Watanabe who, in a brief but glorious career, won the featherweight title at the 1962 and 1963 World Championships, finished first in the 1962 Asian Games and then competed at the 1964 Games in Tokyo amid huge expectation. The 24-year-old from Hokkaido, the island renowned for producing fighters, captured gold without conceding a point. He had won 186 consecutive bouts and retired after the Games.

Banging the gong

British heavyweight Ken Richmond got a bronze medal at the 1952 Games in Helsinki and finished fourth equal in Melbourne four years later. Richmond, who was also picked, although never fought, for Great Britain in Judo, was desperately unlucky in Helsinki, losing on a split decision to the Georgian Arsen Mekokishvili, the eventual gold medallist. Yet Richmond's face and physique would become better known than those of any of his contemporaries: he was the man who was seen banging the gong at the start of the J. Arthur Rank films.

⬇ *A bronze medallist at the 1952 Games, Great Britain's Kenneth Richmond achieved greater fame on the silver screen.*

Bobby dazzler

In 1964, the Japanese were confident that they would dominate both Judo and Wrestling when Tokyo hosted the Olympic Games. However, Dutchman Anton Geesink ended their hopes of a clean sweep in Judo and, in Wrestling, they suffered an equal ignominy, when Denis McNamara, a 38-year-old London policeman, pinned the Japanese heavyweight Masanori Saito after 1:23.00 to silence the crowd, which included Emperor Hirohito. Saito had to cut off his pigtail in penance for bringing disgrace on his country. McNamara damaged a thumb in a subsequent bout and eventually finished fifth.

⬆ *London policeman Denis McNamara silenced a partisan Tokyo crowd when he beat Masanori Saito in the early rounds of the Heavyweight competition at the 1964 Games. He went on to finish fifth.*

Ultimate American winner

Dan Gable was not only one of history's outstanding freestyle wrestlers, but was also a stunningly successful coach. The Iowa-born-and-raised American lost only six of his 308 bouts in a career climaxed by his victory in the Lightweight division at the 1972 Games in Munich, despite a ravaged left knee and a deep cut over his left eye. Gable's ferocious training routine included taking a pack of cards, turning each one over and doing the number of press-ups equivalent to the figures on the card – he would see how often he could go through the pack. Gable then moved into coaching, leading Iowa University to 15 victories in the National Collegiate Championships. In 1984, he coached the US Olympic team to seven gold and two silver medals in Los Angeles.

The greatest pin?

When Werner Dietrich, the 120-kilogram super-heavyweight German known as 'The Crane of Schifferstadt', competed at Munich 1972, he wanted to be the first wrestler to win medals in five successive Games, having already won a record total of five competing in both Freestyle and Greco-Roman. His first bout in front of his home crowd in Munich was against the American Chris Taylor, who weighed a monstrous 195kg. After 13 seconds, the German produced a magnificent suplex, bending backwards as the American lent on his chest and then turning the airborne Taylor on to his back for a pin – an extraordinary feat. However, Dietrich's Games ended with him finishing fifth.

Medved the magnificent

Between 1962 and 1972, Ukraine's Alexander Medved missed out on the Olympic Games or world title only once, when he drew a bout with Turkey's Ahmet Ayik in the 1965 World Championships and forfeited the gold medal through having more bad marks. Otherwise he was supreme, moving up from Light Heavyweight to Heavyweight and finally to Super Heavyweight, and winning three consecutive gold medals. He was described by British contemporary Ron Grinstead as 'the Muhammad Ali of the sport – like Ali he has terrific strength but is very skilful as well'. His final triumph in the Super Heavyweights, weighing only 108 kilograms and outweighed by most of his rivals, was at Munich 1972. He announced his retirement by kissing the mat.

Making amends

When women's Freestyle Wrestling was introduced to the Games' programme in 2004, the Japanese, with their background in Judo, were expected to win most of the titles. It wasn't to be. Heavyweight Kyoko Hamaguchi was controversially beaten in a preliminary bout before bouncing back to take bronze and, in the Flyweights, Chiharu Icho picked up a silver. Thirty minutes later, however, Chiharu's younger sister, Kaori, won Middleweight gold, Saori Yoshida won the Lightweights, and Japan ended up capturing half the titles.

The family man

Daniel Igali was born in Nigeria, where his father had four wives and 21 children. After competing at the 1994 Commonwealth Games at Victoria, Canada, he stayed in the country to seek refugee status and, due to the political unrest in Nigeria at the time, was accepted. He was guided by Maureen Matheny, even though she was suffering from cancer. At the 1999 World Championships, he won lightweight gold and was able to show her the medal before she died. The following year, he took the Olympic Games title.

↑ *Nigeria-born Daniel Igali won Freestyle Wrestling gold for Canada in the 69kg category at Sydney 2000.*

↙ *Dave Schultz (left) on his way to gold in the 74kg category at the 1984 Games in Los Angeles.*

Golden brothers

The United States' Dave Schultz won Welterweight gold at the 1984 Games in Los Angeles while brother Mark took the Middleweight title. Displaying immense ability, Dave overwhelmed the opposition, and although most communist countries were not present, he was the 1983 world champion and probably would have triumphed anyway. He retired three years later, but in 1993, inspired by the prospect of competing at Atlanta 1996, started wrestling again. Sadly, however, the man who was top-ranked American at the time, was shot dead in January 1996 by squad sponsor John Du Pont.

Wrestling — Greco-Roman

Greco-Roman Wrestling, despite its name, has its origins in 19th century France, was contested at the inaugural Modern Games in 1896 and has been a constant presence at the Olympic Games (as a men-only sport) since London 1908. Unlike Freestyle Wrestling, competitors make any holds below the waist.

All for nothing

There must be huge sympathy for the winner of the longest Wrestling bout in Olympic Games history. Estonia's Martin Klein fought Finland's Alfred Asikainen for 11 hours in the fierce sun of the outdoor arena in the semi-final of the Middleweight class in 1912. Klein was actually representing Russia, because Estonia was then part of the Czarist Empire, as was Finland, his opponent's country. Although there were regular breaks, the continuous struggle was an enormous strain on both competitors. Eventually, Klein pinned the Finn to end the bout and earn himself a place in the final against Sweden's Claes Johanson. However, Klein was so exhausted that he could not take part, and the Swede was declared the winner.

⬇ *Russia's Martin Klein (left) and Finland's Alfred Asikainen in their epic 11-hour battle in the Middleweight semi-final at the 1912 Games.*

The rolling Swede

Carl 'Calle' Westergren is a unique figure in Greco-Roman Wrestling at the Games, taking three titles between 1920 and 1932, all at different weights and despite being beaten in the first round in 1928, when he refused to continue after losing his first-round bout to Finland's Onni Penninen. He won his first gold medal at Middleweight in 1920 at the age of 24, then moved up to Light Heavyweight successfully four years later and finally to Heavyweight for his last gold medal in Los Angeles. He once recalled that when he stood on the edge of the mat, he used to put his thumbs inside his suit and say to himself: 'Considering how strong I feel today, no one can beat me.' His speciality move was the 'Westergren Roll', with which he used to tip opponents over.

⬆ *Sweden's Carl Westergren (pictured left) was one of the early stars of Greco-Roman Wrestling. The Malmo-born star won three gold medals at three different weights at three Olympic Games (in 1920, 1924 and 1932).*

Time after time

Wrestling officials at the 1912 Games in Stockholm must have been a patient lot. They not only had to officiate at the match between Klein and Asikainen (which lasted 11 hours) but also the final of the Light Heavyweights between Sweden's Anders Ahlgren and Finland's Ivar Boling, which went on for nine hours before being abandoned with no winner declared. The rules at the time stated that someone had to win to get the gold medal, so instead of two gold medals being awarded to the wrestlers for their efforts, both received silver medals.

A brother's inspiration

Few gold-medal winners were more emotional at the 1984 Games in Los Angeles than Jeff Blatnick, a 110-kilogram American. In 1977, he had lost his brother Dave in a motorcycle accident and, in 1982, Jeff himself was diagnosed with Hodgkin's lymphoma, a form of cancer. He had his spleen and appendix removed and underwent radiation therapy – three weeks later he was wrestling again. In the Super Heavyweight Final, he defeated Sweden's Thomas Johannson. After his victory, watched by his parents, Blatnick sank to his kees, made the sign of a cross and told reporters: 'Thinking about Dave helped me keep my mind in perspective.'

➡ *Jeff Blatnick battled his way to a memorable and popular victory in the Super Heavyweight category at the 1984 Games in Los Angeles.*

Pole with an eye for the ladies

Poland's Kazimierz Lipiern had a series of ferocious Featherweight battles with Ukraine's Nelson Davydyan during the 1970s and, after losing to him in the 1975 World Championships, gained revenge by taking the gold medal in Montreal ahead of Davydyan the following year. Afterwards, Lipiern recommended wrestlers not to drink alcohol or smoke. To this the Hungarian bronze medallist Lazlo Reczi added: 'And no women.' Lipiern responded: 'That is taking sacrifices too far. Women are good to wrestle with too.'

The power of faith

When Yury Melnichenko, a Jew living in the Ukraine, visited Jerusalem in 1991, he placed a paper in the 'Wailing Wall' stating that his ambition was to become champion at the Olympic Games. Five years later, having transferred his allegiance to Kazakhstan because of the superior training environment there, he stormed through the early rounds of the Bantamweight division in Atlanta. Then, in the decisive bout with American Dennis Hall, who had upset him in the World Championships in Prague in 1995, Melnichenko scored three points for a lift and throw just 90 seconds into the match, stretched his lead to four points and hung on to win a memorable gold.

➘ *Russia's Alexandr Karelin in action at Atlanta 1996.*

Karelin – the real fridge magnet

Russian Aleksandr Karelin is the greatest Greco-Roman wrestler in history. He won three successive Super Heavyweight titles and was unbeaten in international competition for 13 years until, at the 2000 Games in Sydney, while still recovering from an injury, he was beaten in the final by American Rulon Gardner. At Atlanta 1996, when he won his third title at the Games, he was called 'the bouncer in the meanest bar in Hell'. At 1.93 metres tall and weighing 125 kilograms, he was so robust that once, when the lift broke down at his block of flats in Siberia, he carried a fridge up eight flights of stairs. An exponent of the reverse body lift, he locked hands under an opponent's prone body, lifted him to waist height and hurled him to the mat.

Chapter Nine
Multi-event sports

Modern Pentathlon was created by the founder of the modern Olympic Games, Baron Pierre de Coubertin. He wanted an event that echoed the classic pentathlon event held at the ancient Greek games. His 'modern' pentathlon drew on the story of a soldier delivering a message. In order to make sure that the message got through, he had to ride, shoot, fence, swim and, finally, run.

It was introduced at the 1912 Games in Stockholm and will celebrate 100 years as a sport at the Games at London 2012. A women's competition has been part of the programme since 2000. In 2012, the Modern Pentathlon will effectively be made up of four events. After the fencing, swimming and riding, the competition now concludes with the combined event (shooting and running).

Triathlon is in every way the new kid on the block at the Olympic Games. Although there had been attempts at something similar in the early 20th century, the first triathlon as it is known now was held only in the mid-1970s. Its popularity grew so rapidly that it was accepted as a full medal sport less than 30 years later and it made its debut at the 2000 Games in Sydney.

The brutal combination of swim-bike-run has persuaded many to make the switch from other sports. Distances vary from competition to competition, with the gruelling 'iron man' among the most testing. The competition at the Games features a 1.5-kilometre swim, a 40km cycle ride and a 10km run. All three elements happen sequentially, with no break in between.

A three-time world champion and the winner of gold at the 2006 Commonwealth Games in Melbourne, Australia's Emma Snowsill confirmed her status as the world's no.1 woman triathlete when she took gold in the women's Triathlon at Beijing 2008 in a new Games record time – 1:58:27.66.

Modern Pentathlon

Invented by Baron Pierre du Coubertin, the father of the Modern Games, Modern Pentathlon – the word 'modern' distinguishes the event from the Ancient Games' original pentathlon – has been contested at every Games since 1912 (and by women since 2000). Athletes contest fencing, swimming, riding and the combined event (shooting and running).

↑ Second World War hero George S. Patton finished fifth in the Modern Pentathlon at the 1912 Games.

Patton too accurate

The American pentathlete who finished fifth in the first competition at Stockholm 1912 was none other than George S. Patton junior. As General Patton, he commanded the 7th Army during the Second World War invasion of Sicily and later led the 3rd Army across France after the Normandy landings. Patton, a graduate of the West Point military academy, was a lieutenant at the time of his Games participation. It was shooting, strangely, that proved to be his weakest discipline. Patton always maintained he would have won gold had one of his shots not been ruled a miss. He insisted his shot had gone through an existing hole in the target.

Onishenko out

In 1976, Soviet competitor Boris Onishenko was disqualified in the biggest scandal to hit the sport. Before the fencing phase of the competition, he had tampered with the handle of his épée so that it could register a hit when no contact had been made. This was discovered after he had recorded a hit during his bout with Great Britain's Jim Fox. Onishenko, a silver medallist at the 1972 Games, was thrown out of the competition. That opened the way for Poland's Janusz Peciak to take gold in the Individual event. It also put the Soviet team out of the running for the Team event, in which Great Britain took gold.

Hall's unique double

Swedish athletes enjoyed huge success in the Modern Pentathlon's early years. The competition was dominated by members of the military, and every gold medal from 1912 to 1956 was won by a Swedish competitor. The 1952 winner, Lars Hall, a carpenter from Gothenburg, was the first non-military winner. He enjoyed a stroke of good fortune on the way. He arrived late for the shooting phase, but was allowed to take part because a protest had delayed the competition. Hall was back in action at Melbourne 1956, when he won the gold medal once more and remains the only man to have won the event twice.

Magnificent Magyars

A Team event was held in Modern Pentathlon from 1952 until 1992. This competition was run concurrently with the Individual event and the winners were calculated by adding the combined scores of three participating pentathletes from each nation. Hungary were the first Team champions and won the competition on four occasions. The Soviet Union also won four gold medals. Despite objections, each victorious team was only given one medal to be shared between the three members.

Courting trouble

American pentathlete Orben Greenwald, a World Championship Team silver medallist in 1975, faced a court martial for insubordination shortly before the 1976 Games in Montreal. Incredibly, the charge was brought by his team manager, one Colonel Donald Johnson. Although the matter was eventually dropped, Greenwald was not allowed to compete.

Seven-up Soviet

Pavel Lednev, with seven medals in a career spanning four Games between Mexico City 1968 and Moscow 1980, can stake a claim as the most successful competitor in Modern Pentathlon, even though he never won the Individual title. Lednev was a member of the gold medal-winning Soviet Union team in both 1972 and 1980, but, despite winning four Individual medals, his best performance in Individual competition came at the 1976 Games in Montreal, when he finished in the silver-medal position.

← Sweden's Lars Hall, a carpenter from Gothenburg, became the Modern Pentathlon's first non-military winner at the 1952 Games.

Double gold

Hungary's gold medal-winning team in the Rome 1960 Games featured two individual champions. Ferenc Nemeth won his prize at the same Games, but Andras Balczo had to wait a further 12 years for his personal moment of glory. He finally became Individual champion at the 1972 Games in Munich, aged 34.

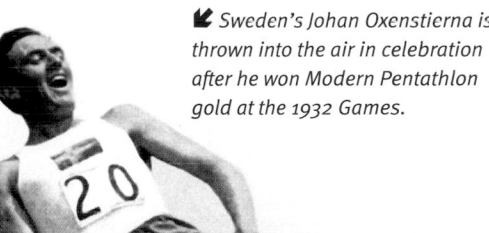

↙ Sweden's Johan Oxenstierna is thrown into the air in celebration after he won Modern Pentathlon gold at the 1932 Games.

Arresting practice

At the 1932 Games in Los Angeles, Sweden's Johan Oxenstierna decided to fire some practice shots in nearby woods shortly before the pistol shooting was to begin. A suspicious local police officer raced over and threatened to arrest him. Eventually, when he realised that the Swede was a genuine competitor, the officer was persuaded to wait until after the competition. Oxenstierna went on to take the gold medal.

Man with All the Answers

Bjorn Ferm kept himself occupied during breaks in the long and exhausting fencing section of the Modern Pentathlon competition at the Mexico City 1968 Games by reading a detective novel. Ferm, an economics student from Jönköping in Sweden, eventually completed the cross-country course four seconds inside the target time to take the gold medal.

Grut the great

The 1948 champion was Willie Grut, a Swedish army captain. He finished first in riding, fencing and shooting. At the Winter Games held earlier that year in St Moritz, Grut had finished second in a demonstration Winter Pentathlon event, which included alpine and cross-country skiing, shooting, fencing and equestrian sport. Not surprisingly, he was voted Sweden's sportsman of the year.

One-day wonders

At the 1996 Olympic Games in Atlanta, the Modern Pentathlon was conducted over a single day for the first time. Previously it had been held over five gruelling days, except in 1920, 1984 and 1992, when the competition took place over four days.

Doctor knows best

Great Britain's Stephanie Cook put her career as a doctor on hold to prepare for the first women's Modern Pentathlon competition at the 2000 Olympic Games in Sydney. This was held on the last day of the Games and Cook, an outstanding runner, made up 49 seconds on American Emily de Riel to win gold. De Riel had been her team-mate at Oxford University.

↖ A stunning performance in the running section saw Great Britain's Stephanie Cook claim gold at Sydney 2000.

Order, order...

The order in which the five sports are contested in Modern Pentathlon has been changed many times. Perhaps the most radical alteration will come in 2012, when the competition will end with a combined event (shooting and running). Introduced at senior level for the 2009 World Championships, the pentathletes will have to run three 1000m legs, each punctuated by a stop in which they have to shoot at five targets on a shooting range.

Triathlon

Although World Championships in the sport have been staged every year since 1989, Triathlon had to wait until Sydney 2000 before it made its first appearance at the Games. The events are contested over international distances (1.5km swim, 40km cycle and 10km run).

Parisian approval

The decision to introduce Triathlon as a full-medal sport at the Games was taken in Paris at the 103rd session of the International Olympic Committee held in 1994. The International Triathlon Union itself had only been formed five years before.

Gold Hawaii

Switzerland's Brigitte McMahon was the first triathlete to win an Olympic Games gold medal. Initially a Swiss swimming champion, she was bitten by the Triathlon bug while working in Hawaii as a teaching assistant at the university. At the 2000 Games in Sydney she left it late to make her surge to gold and her final victory margin was only two seconds ahead of home favourite and long-time race leader Michellie Jones of Australia.

Canada's Simon Whitfield put a crash in the cycle ride behind him to win men's Triathlon gold at the 2000 Games in Sydney.

Taking to the water

The inaugural women's Triathlon at the Games was one of the first medals to be decided on the opening day of competition at Sydney 2000. Competition began with a swim in Sydney Harbour and the event helped introduce the landmarks of the Host City to millions of television viewers worldwide. The Sydney police estimated that nearly 500,000 spectators lined the streets to watch the cycling and running in the women's event on one day and the men the next.

⬇ *The 2000 Games got off to a spectacular start when the women's Triathlon got under way in Sydney Harbour.*

Switch in time

New Zealand's Hamish Carter was a rower at school who switched to triathlon when he realised he would never be tall enough to row at senior level. His main rival at the 2004 Games was compatriot and sometime training partner Bevan Docherty, then reigning world champion. Carter was only 33rd after the swim, but had an excellent cycle ride and dismounted to find himself among a small leading group with Docherty. With 1km to go, the Kiwis were out on their own, before Carter escaped to win by seven seconds.

Lucky 13 for Whitfield

Canada's Simon Whitfield was ranked only 13th in the world at the time of his men's Triathlon triumph at Sydney 2000. He had decamped to Australia for three years to train during the Canadian winter and actually held joint citizenship in both countries. After the swim and cycle ride he was in 28th place, but in the run he picked his way through the field and overtook the eventual silver medallist Stefan Vuckovic of Germany less than 100 metres from the finish. His victory helped him fulfil a childhood ambition that he had since he competed in his first triathlon aged 12. He had decided he wanted to do something that would merit inclusion in the *Encyclopaedia Britannica*. Whitfield also won men's Triathlon silver at Beijing 2008.

Married bliss

Katherine Allen, winner of the 2004 women's Triathlon, hailed from Geelong in Australia. On a backpacking holiday in Europe, she visited Austria, where she met and later married Austrian triathlete Marcel Dichtler. She became an Austrian citizen and qualified to represent them at Athens 2004. After the swim in the Aegean she was only 44th, but moved up to 28th (albeit some three minutes behind the leaders) after an encouraging bike ride. Her performance in the run was superb, however, and she finally took the lead from Australia's Loretta Harrop in the last 200 metres to win by 6.72 seconds.

← *Katherine Allen (representing Austria, for whom she qualified through marriage) produced a scintillating run to claim women's Triathlon gold at the 2004 Olympic Games in Athens.*

Paying the price

The men's Triathlon at Beijing 2008 was still wide open with less than 300 metres to go. The leading group included Sydney 2000 champion Simon Whitfield and Athens 2004 silver medallist Bevan Docherty (New Zealand), who made the break for the line. The unfancied German Jan Frodeno, not noted for his sprint finish, went with him and burst through to take a surprise gold medal. Frodeno was originally from Cologne, but had spent his childhood in South Africa. There he had watched the 2000 Olympic Games on television and was inspired to take up the sport seriously. He sold his bike to raise the air fare back to Germany to compete in his home country.

Snowsill beats the odds

Australia's Emma Snowsill overcame personal tragedy and serious injury to win gold at the 2008 Games in Beijing. Her boyfriend, fellow triathlete Luke Harrop, was killed by a car in a hit-and-run accident while training in 2002. The following year she became world champion, but suffered a stress fracture of the femur, which ruled her out of contention for the Australian team at the 2004 Games in Athens. She bounced back to win the World Championships in 2005, took the 2006 Commonwealth title and then won the world title again to seal her place in Beijing. There she led as the field completed the bike ride, and she eventually had such a lead that she was able to pause to grab an Australian flag from a fan before crossing the line a minute ahead of her nearest rivals.

Three in one...

Although the sport was not invented until the 1970s, all three elements were performed simultaneously during the 1908 Games in London. This was possible because the White City Stadium, where the Games were held, featured not only a running track (536 metres in length) but also a 600m cycle track and a 50m swimming pool. On certain days, events in all three sports were scheduled at the same time.

Carry on ... in the heat

At the 2004 men's Triathlon in Athens, Great Britain's Marc Jenkins had his prospects of a medal ended by a crash mid-way through the cycling leg. With broken spokes his bike was impossible to ride. He refused to retire from the race, but the wheel was so badly buckled that he was forced to carry his bike on his shoulders in blistering heat for nearly two kilometres to the next repair point. When he eventually completed the race he received a standing ovation from the crowd, even though he finished in last place and some 15 minutes behind the winner.

→ *Great Britain's Marc Jenkins feels the heat during the men's Triathlon at Athens 2004.*

Chapter Ten
Racket sports

Tennis was one of the original sports at the first modern Olympic Games at Athens in 1896. It was the first sport to embrace women participants and was a fixture in the early years of the Games. Indoor and outdoor events were both part of the programme, but the sport was removed from the roster in 1924.

There were moves to bring it back in the 1960s, but the advent of the open era in tennis created difficulties because the Olympic Movement insisted on a strict amateur code at this time. In the 1980s the situation changed when the International Olympic Committee decided to relax its rules on eligibility, effectively making the Games open to all. Tennis made a successful return as a demonstration event at the 1984 Olympic Games in Los Angeles and was subsequently restored to the full Games agenda for Seoul 1988.

Table Tennis grew in popularity from the late 19th century, but although the first World Championships in the sport took place in the 1920s, it was not until 1988 that the sport finally entered the Olympic Games for the first time. It enjoys enormous popularity in China and other Asian countries and Chinese players have dominated at every tournament.

Badminton had to wait well over a century for a spot in the Olympic Games. It was not until Barcelona 1992 that it was included as a full-medal sport. Ever since, competitors from Asia have dominated both men's and women's competitions and only one champion has come from outside the continent.

After winning the French Open for the fourth time and Wimbledon for the first time earlier in the year, Spain's Rafael Nadal rounded out 2008 in style when he beat Chile's Fernando Gonzalez in the final to take Tennis gold at Beijing 2008.

Badminton

Badminton was a demonstration sport at Munich 1972 but had to wait until Barcelona 1992 before making its first full-medal appearance at the Games. Competitors compete in Singles and Doubles events (for men and women) as well as Mixed Doubles. China has been the most successful nation with 30 medals, 11 of them gold.

Gao's history game

Gao Lin and her partner Zhang Jun won successive Mixed Doubles titles at the Sydney 2000 and Athens 2004 Games. Gao also won silver and bronze in the women's Doubles. She has won more Olympic Games medals in the sport (four) than any other player.

No joke for Koreans

Bang Soo Hyun, daughter of a popular Korean comedian, was deadly serious about Badminton and lost only one match in her entire Olympic Games career. That single defeat came in the final of the women's Singles in 1992, which she lost to Indonesia's Susi Susanti. Four years later, in Atlanta, she faced Susanti once more, this time at the semi-final stage, in which she avenged her Barcelona defeat. She played another Indonesian, Mia Audina, in the final and made her experience tell to win the gold medal.

↑ *Bang Soo-Hyun took the women's Singles title in 1996.*

Super star

In 2008, home favourite Dan Lin reached the men's Singles Final in Beijing without dropping a single set. A soldier in the Chinese People's Liberation Army, and number one in the world that year, he was known as 'Super Dan'. He lived up to his nickname in the final, in which he swept aside the challenge of Malaysia's Li Chong Wei to take the gold medal.

→ *Lin Dan became China's second men's Singles champion at Beijing 2008.*

Determined Danes

Denmark have been the most successful European nation in Badminton events at the Games. B. Thomas Stuer Lauridsen was the first player from outside Asia to win a medal when Badminton made its debut appearance at Barcelona 1992. He lost to the eventual winner Alan Budikusuma (Indonesia) in the semi-final. At the first tournament, both losing semi-finalists were awarded bronze medals. Subsequently a third-place play-off was introduced. At the Atlanta 1996 Games, Denmark's Poul Erik Hoyer Larsen beat defending champion Alan Budikusuma and world champion Heryanto Arbi on the way to the final, in which he beat Chinese world number one Dong Jiong to become the Games' first, and to date only, non-Asian Singles gold medallist.

Susanti keeps it in the family

Indonesia's Susi Susanti had already become a national hero for winning back-to-back All England titles when she travelled to Barcelona for the 1992 Games. There she beat Korea's Bang Su Hyun in the women's Singles Final to seal her place in her country's sporting hall of fame for ever. Hers was the first Olympic Games gold medal ever won by an Indonesian. That same day, her husband-to-be, Alan Budikusuma, overcame his fellow countryman Ardy Wiranata to win gold in the men's Singles. Their twin triumphs sparked tremendous scenes back in Jakarta when they returned home. There was a huge victory parade through the streets, led by a car carrying a giant shuttlecock. The couple each received a bonus of US$500,000 and they were married after the 1996 Games in Atlanta, though neither could quite complete the fairytale with another gold medal.

Peer Pressure

Badminton can trace its origins to early games played in India, China and Greece. Previously known as Battledore or Shuttlecock, the sport takes its name from one of the stately homes of England – Badminton in Gloucestershire, the ancestral home of the Duke of Beaufort. His Grace enthusiastically championed the sport in the 1870s, teaching visitors to his home how to play.

⬆ *Nathan Robertson and Gail Emms celebrate their Mixed Doubles semi-final victory at Athens 2004.*

Europe's best yet

For the only time in any Badminton event at the Games, three European pairs reached the last four of the Mixed Doubles in 2004. In the all-European semi-final, Nathan Robertson and Gail Emms from Great Britain beat Denmark's Jonas Rasmussen and Rikke Olsen to reach the final. They had to settle for the silver medal, though, losing to defending champions Zhang Jun and Gao Lin from China, but the British pair came within four points of the gold.

Moving success

Mia Audina has won Olympic Games medals in Badminton for two different countries. Born in Jakarta, Indonesia, she was a child prodigy at the sport. She was chosen for the 1996 Games at the tender age of 16 years 338 days and, unsurprisingly, she was the youngest player ever to enter a Badminton tournament at the Games. Even so she reached the Final of the women's Singles in Atlanta, losing to Korean Bang Su Hyeon. Audina later married a Dutchman and moved to the Netherlands, where she became a Dutch citizen. She represented her new country at Sydney 2000 and at Athens 2004, where she again reached the final. By now a comparative veteran at 24, she was beaten this time by China's Zhang Ning.

Making a mark in Munich

Badminton was included as a demonstration sport at the 1972 Games, when 25 players from 11 countries contested the four events. In an era before the sport had a formal world championship for individuals, Indonesian Rudy Hartono was considered the outstanding male player of his generation. He won the men's Singles, Japan's Noriko Nakajama won the women's Singles, and British pairing Derek Talbot and Gillian Gilks won the Mixed Doubles event. The medals awarded for the event are not considered official. It would be a further 20 years before the sport was finally included in the full programme, at the 1992 Games in Barcelona. The tournament featured only men's and women's Singles and Doubles. A Mixed Doubles event was added in 1996.

↗ *Mia Audina won medals for both Indonesia (1996) and the Netherlands (2004).*

Martin settles for silver

Denmark's Camilla Martin was the first European woman to win an individual Olympic Games medal for Badminton. Back home, she was considered the best female player of her generation and, in a land where standards are very high, she won 13 consecutive national titles. After victory at the 1999 World Championships, she travelled to Sydney 2000 as one of the favourites. She played superbly to reach the final, but was denied gold by China's Gong Zhichao.

↖ *1999 world champion Camilla Martin took the silver medal in the women's Singles event at the 2000 Games in Sydney.*

Table Tennis

Singles and Doubles events (for men and women) in Table Tennis have been contested since the 1988 Games in Seoul with Team events introduced for the first time at Beijing 2008 to replace the Doubles event. China dominate the sport's all-time medal table at the Games with 41 medals (20 of them gold).

Chinese Clean sweep

At Beijing 2008, host nation China won every Table Tennis medal available to them. China's men beat Germany in the final of the Team event, while the women won their final against Singapore to add a second gold. Ma Lin won the men's Singles title (with compatriots Wang Hao taking silver and Wang Liqin bronze); and Zhang Yining won the women's Singles event (with compatriots Wang Nan taking silver and Guo Yue bronze).

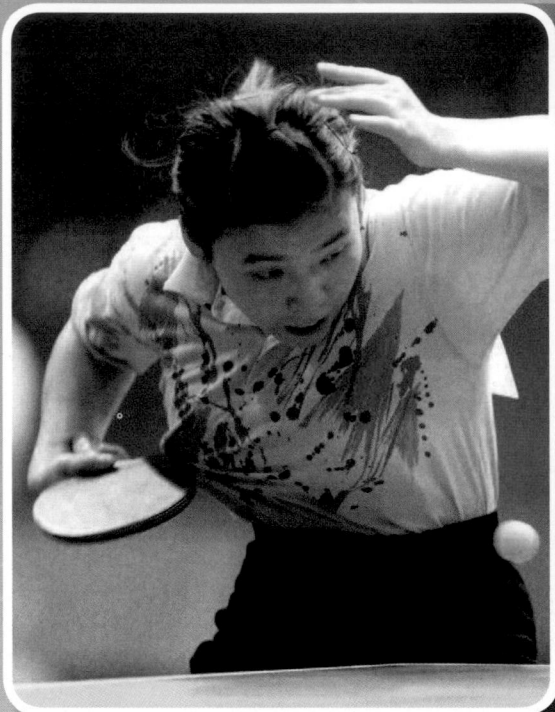

Little giant

China's Deng Yaping had always been considered too short to make the grade in international Table Tennis. A child prodigy, who won regional tournaments at the age of nine, she was originally ignored by the Chinese selectors because of her height. Eventually, though, they were forced to relent and she was picked for the national team aged only 16, by which time she had reached her adult height of 4ft ½in (1.49m). She partnered Qiao Hong to win the World Championships doubles and went on to win the singles title in 1991. Her persistence in never taking no for an answer was rewarded when she was selected for China's team for the 1992 Games in Barcelona and took gold in the women's Doubles with Qiao. Two days later, the pair faced one another in the women's Singles final and Deng won an epic encounter. She retained both her titles at the Atlanta 1996 Olympic Games, and in 2003 she was voted China's female athlete of the century and was also chosen for the IOC athletes commission.

← *China's Deng Yaping silenced those who said she was too short to play the game when she won the women's Singles and women's Doubles Table Tennis events at Barcelona 1992.*

Out of date...

On the eve of the 2004 Olympic Games in Athens, China's Table Tennis squad was thrown into turmoil by what officials described as a 'dating scandal'. Reigning Mixed Doubles champion Ma Lin began a relationship with another member of the squad. His girlfriend was dropped from the group because Chinese officials felt as though her presence would have an unsettling effect on the both the squad and its training programme. Ma himself was only spared the axe because his world ranking at the time was so high. The selectors' decision was vindicated, however, when (in partnership with Chen Qi) he went on to take gold in the men's Doubles. Four years later, in Beijing, Ma won the men's Singles event, beating compatriot Wang Hao in the Final, and was also a member of the Chinese trio that took Team gold.

King Kong

Chinese men's Doubles pairing Kong Linghui and Liu Guoliang teamed up to devastating effect at the Olympic Games at Atlanta in 1996. They lost only one game as they steamrollered their way to the gold medal. Liu also won the men's Singles at the same Games. Four years later, in Sydney, it was Kong's turn to win the men's Singles final after a tremendous struggle against Sweden's Jan Ove Waldner.

Turning the tables

It was in 1981 in the German spa town of Baden Baden that the International Olympic Committee decided to include Table Tennis on the programme for the 1988 Olympic Games. At this same meeting the 1988 Games were allocated to Seoul, South Korea.

Taken for a ride

Chinese men's Doubles pairing Lu Lin and Wang Tao very nearly did not make it to their final at the 1992 Games in Barcelona. The bus that was supposed to take them from the Olympic Village to the arena failed to arrive, so they started out on foot. Eventually they were able to hail a taxi and reached the venue in the nick of time. Their match against the German pair Steffen Fetzner and Joerg Rosskopf went the full distance before the Chinese duo took gold.

← *China's Lu Lin (left) and Wang Tao (right) celebrate after they beat Germany's Steffen Fetzner and Jörg Rosskopf in the men's Doubles final at the 1992 Games in Barcelona.*

Sporting chance

China's Jiao Zhimin won bronze in the women's Singles and silver in the women's Doubles at the 1988 Games, but it was her romance with Korean men's Doubles bronze medallist An Jae-Hyeong that hit the headlines. The pair married in 1989, even though their countries had no diplomatic ties at the time, and had a son, An Byeong-Hun, who turned out to be a brilliant golfer and won the 2009 US Amateur Championship aged only 17.

Waldner breakthrough

Sweden's Jan Ove Waldner remains the only non-Asian player to win an Olympic Games gold medal. Seeded number two for the inaugural Table Tennis tournament at the 1988 Games, he was knocked out in the quarter-finals, but proved unstoppable four years later. In the interim he had won the 1989 World Championships, and at Barcelona 1992 dropped only one game on the way to the final, where he beat Frenchman Jean-Philippe Gatien. Waldner played in the first five Table Tennis tournaments at the Games and won a silver medal at Sydney 2000, losing to China's Kong Linghui in the final. Waldner made his final Games appearance at Athens 2004, two months short of his 39th birthday.

↑ *Sweden's Jan Ove Waldner beat France's Jean-Philippe Gatien in the 1992 men's Singles final to become the event's first non-Asian winner.*

Comrade champion

Chinese star Wang Nan won two gold medals at the 2000 Olympic Games in Sydney. She won the women's Doubles and beat her doubles partner Li Ju in the Singles final. Her success brought with it some unexpected fringe benefits, such as being elected as a district representative to the Chinese Communist Party Congress. She retained her Doubles title with a new partner, Zhang Yining, at Athens 2004 and won further gold for China as part of the victorious squad in the Team event in Beijing. China's dominance of the Table Tennis competition at the 2004 Games was broken only when Korea's Ryu Seung Min took gold in the men's Singles with a dramatic win over China's Wang Hao. The match went the full distance, and even then in victory the Korean conceded that his opponent had been the better player.

← *China's Wang Nan has won four Table Tennis gold medals at the Games, one in the women's Singles (2000), two in the women's Doubles (2000 and 2004) and one in the women's Team event (2008).*

Tennis

Tennis was one of the sports contested at the inaugural modern Games in Athens in 1896 and featured at each of the first seven Games before being dropped after Paris 1924. After two appearances as a demonstration sport (in 1968 and 1984), it made a welcome return to the full-medal programme at the 1988 Games in Seoul.

Greek classic

John Pius Boland, an Irishman studying at Christ's College, Oxford, was the first man to win a Tennis title at the Olympic Games. During the Easter holidays in 1896, he accompanied a Greek friend to Athens where the first Games of the modern era were about to take place. He was persuaded to take part in the Tennis competition, despite having had little experience of tournament play. Still, he won Singles gold and then partnered the German Fritz Traun to success in the Doubles.

On target in London

Charlotte 'Lottie' Dod may have been a five-times women's Singles champion at Wimbledon, but her only appearance at the Olympic Games came in the sport of Archery. She won a silver medal in the women's Individual competition at the 1908 Games in London.

⬆ *Legendary five-time Wimbledon singles winner Lottie Dod made a surprise appearance in Archery at the 1908 Games and won silver.*

Winning for women

Great Britain provided the first female winner in Tennis at the Olympic Games. In fact Charlotte Cooper was the first woman to win any title at the Games. She beat Helene Prevost in straight sets to win Singles gold at Paris 1900. She also won gold in the Mixed Doubles, with R.F. 'Reggie' Doherty.

Tennis comeback

Exhibition and demonstration events in Tennis were held at the 1968 Olympic Games in Mexico City as the sport sought readmission to the official Games programme. But it was the demonstration event in 1984 that really paved the way for the sport's return. In Los Angeles the competition was an age-group affair (players had to be under 20): Sweden's Stefan Edberg won the men's Singles event, with West Germany's Steffi Graf winning the women's Singles.

Titanic achievement...

American Richard Norris Williams III could count himself fortunate to have taken part in the Olympic Games at all. He had been a passenger on the maiden voyage of the *Titanic* in 1912 and had swum away from the sinking ship before being rescued. He served in the military and won the Croix de Guerre in the First World War. A Wimbledon champion in the men's Doubles in 1920, he was selected for the USA team for the 1924 Games and partnered compatriot Hazel Wightman, a prolific player in the women's game, to gold in the Mixed Doubles.

➔ *Richard Norris Williams III was a Titanic survivor and a gold medallist at the 1924 Games.*

Ins and outs in London

At the 1908 Games in London, the Tennis programme featured both indoor and outdoor tournaments. The indoor competitions were held at the Queen's Club in West Kensington, London. Arthur Wentworth Gore won an all-British Final against George Caridia in straight sets. Inspired by his success, he also won Wimbledon the following year at the grand old age of 41. A stalwart of the All England Club, he had competed there every year since 1888.

Golden gamble

Great Britain's Kitty McKane reached the last four in the women's Singles in 1920 but then, amazingly, withdrew from her semi-final so as to conserve her energy to partner Winnie McNair in the women's Doubles semi-final. The Britons were up against the legendary French player Suzanne Lenglen, partnered by her compatriot Elizabeth d'Ayen. The ploy paid off as the British women won in three sets and went on to win in the final to claim the gold medal.

Sky's the limit for Henin

Before the 2004 Games, Belgium's Justine Henin was suffering from a virus, and when she arrived in Athens she had not played in 11 weeks. At the Games, however, she was extended to three sets only once, by Russia's Alexandra Myskina, the French Open champion, in the semi-finals. In the final, Henin took only 78 minutes to beat France's Amélie Mauresmo in straight sets: she celebrated by trying out her new hobby – skydiving.

➔ *Belgium's Justine Henin took the women's Singles title at Athens 2004.*

⬆ *Victory in the women's Tennis Final at Seoul 1988 saw Steffi Graf complete a memorable 'Golden Slam'.*

Graf's history lesson

1988 proved a golden year for Germany's Steffi Graf. When Tennis made its re-entry to the Games programme in Seoul, she became the first winner of the women's Singles title. She had already won the Australian, French, Wimbledon and US Open titles, the latter only a week before the Games began. Her straight sets win over Argentina's Gabriela Sabatini thus converted her 'Grand Slam' into what remains a unique 'Olympic Slam'.

Woosnam's fine moment of judgement

British tennis enjoyed a golden era in the early 1920s when Max Woosnam won the men's Doubles with Noel Turnbull at the 1920 Games. An all-round sportsman, who played first-class cricket and golf, Woosnam was in line to represent Great Britain in the Football competition, but decided to concentrate on the Tennis because the sports were scheduled too closely together. He made the right decision: Norway eliminated the British football team in the first round. Woosnam's own football career included spells at Chelsea and Manchester City, and he was capped by England at full international level.

Agassi's heritage

Andre Agassi beat Spain's Sergi Bruguera in straight sets to win the gold medal at the 1996 Games in Atlanta, but he was not the first member of his family to take part in the Olympic Games. His father Mike Emanoul Agassi had boxed for Iran in the Bantam Weight division at the 1948 Games in London and also competed in the 1952 Games in Helsinki.

⬆ *Andre Agassi beat Sergi Bruguera 6-2 6-3 6-1 to win men's Singles gold at the 1996 Games.*

Better late than never

Martina Navratilova enjoyed a glittering career, but it was not until she was 47 that she appeared in the Olympic Games, at Athens 2004. The oldest player in the tournament, she represented the United States and partnered Lisa Raymond to the quarter-finals of the women's Doubles.

Massu the master

Nicolas Massu and Fernando Gonzalez won the men's Doubles final at the 2004 Games in Athens to secure Chile's first-ever Olympic Games gold medal. In an epic final, they saved four match points against Germany's Nicolas Kiefer and Rainer Schuettler, took a fourth-set tiebreak and eventually won it in the fifth. The match ended at 2.39am. Only 13 hours later, Massu went back on court to play American Mardy Fish in the men's Singles final. He came back from two sets to one down to win another five setter and collect his second gold medal of the Games.

Chapter Eleven
Water sports

Water sports – totally separate from Aquatics – have a long history at the Olympic Games. Rowing, for example, was included in the programme for Athens in 1896 but the events had to be cancelled because of bad weather.

The first Olympic Games champions in Water sports were thus hailed in Paris in 1900, with Sailing entering the Games programme in 1932 and Canoeing in 1936. Rowing was opened up to women at Montreal in 1976 with the first Lightweight events being staged at Atlanta 1996.

Down the years the balance and identity of the events in all three have evolved – with a Windsurfer competition being incorporated into the Sailing schedule at the 1984 Games in Los Angeles, perhaps predictably.

The inclusion of Sailing at the Games meant extending the organisational challenge for Host Cities and conceding that the competition often had to be staged at venues that were often several hundred kilometers away from the Olympic Stadium. Thus the Sailing competition at London 2012 will take place on the south coast at Weymouth and Portland, some 110 miles (175km) away to the south-west of the capital.

All the surface water sports are themselves split into varied disciplines. For example, rowing with a pair of oars is sculling, while rowing with one oar is the sweep version. Canadian canoeing employs a paddle with one blade, which is switched from side to side by the canoeist sitting in a half-kneeling position, while Kayak events use a paddle with alternating strokes and blades at either end.

Rowing courses at the Games varied in length before settling down to their current standard of 2000m (1.24 miles) at the 1988 Games in Seoul. When Rowing first became an Olympic sport, at the 1900 Games in Paris, it was over a distance of 1750m (1.08 miles) on the Seine. The course at the London 1908 Games was 2414m (1.5 miles) long, on the River Thames at Henley. However, when Rowing returned to Great Britain (and to Henley) 40 years later, it was over a course 1883m (1.17 miles) in length.

Competitors leave the startline in the 2008 women's Windsurfer event held in the Qingdao International Marina in Beijing. China's Jian Yin took gold.

Canoeing and Kayaking: Slalom

Two types of boat are used in the sport: canoes, for one or two canoeists; and kayaks, for one, two or four kayakers. Slalom events were contested for the first time at the 1972 Games in Munich and, after a 20-year break, at each of four Games staged since Barcelona 1992.

East trumps west

For the 1972 Games in Munich the West German hosts spent 17 million marks (US$4m) constructing an artificial river at Augsburg. A year before the Games their East German counterparts studied the facilities and replicated them in Zwickau. And how it paid dividends: when the time came, the East Germans took gold in all four Slalom events.

Practice makes perfect

Some 24 years after the first Kayak Single event was held in Augsburg, during Munich 1972, a young man born in the city crossed the Atlantic to win gold in the event at the 1996 Olympic Games in Atlanta. Oliver Fix had first paddled on the course used at the 1972 Games when he was nine, becoming the youngest person to negotiate it. He visited the Atlanta canoeing site five times to familiarise himself with it and when he competed there in earnest he was victorious, with German rival Thomas Becker taking bronze.

Schmidt rises to the challenge

Germany's top-ranked Kayak Single competitor in the run-up to the 2000 Games was Thomas Becker, bronze medallist four years earlier and the 1997 world champion. But he was beaten in the selection races by Thomas Schmidt, who went on to defeat Britain's favourite Paul Ratcliffe – the winner of the pre-Olympic Regatta.

Elastic course

The first-ever Olympic Slalom course, built for Munich 1972, was 600 metres long and included 30 gates. When the event was next held, at the 1992 Games, it was 340m long and, in 1996, 415m long.

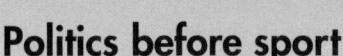

Second time lucky

Pierpaolo Ferrazzi of Italy managed only 17th place in the first run of the Kayak Singles competition at Barcelona 1992, but his second run, in which he incurred no penalties, earned him the gold with the fastest recorded time of 1:46.89.

Temporary River

The Canoe events at the Atlanta 1996 Games were staged on the Ocoee River in Tennessee – but there was a problem. The site of the course had been dry for almost 50 years and, although water had been redirected into the riverbed in 1994, it was diverted through a tunnel to a power plant to create electricity. In 1996, however, the water was released through one of the three dams into the 1-mile course for 77 days to allow for training, as well as a pre-Olympic event and the Games themselves.

➜ Michal Martikan won men's C-1 gold at Atlanta 1996 and silver in the same event at Sydney 2000.

Politics before sport

Czechoslovakia's Lukas Pollert won men's Canoe Singles gold at Barcelona 1992 when it was reintroduced to the Games after a 20-year absence. However, he said it had meant more to him to take part in the demonstrations that had led to the overthrow of Communism in his country three years earlier.

Double double

The 2000 Canoe Doubles title was won by twins – Pavel and Peter Hochschorner of Slovakia.

← *Twins Peter (back) and Pavol Hochshorner of Slovakia on their way to C-2 gold at the 2000 Games.*

Togo top man

Benjamin Boukpeti became the first athlete from Togo to win an Olympic Games medal when he won bronze in the men's Kayak Single event at Beijing 2008. Four years earlier in Athens, Boukpeti, who holds dual French-Togo citizenship, had become the first Togo athlete to reach a Games semi-final. Boukpeti marked his bronze breakthrough by breaking his paddle over his kayak in celebration.

Augsburg legacy

Like 1996 gold medallist Oliver Fix, Elisabeth Micheler was born and brought up in Augsburg, Germany. Like Fix, she also won gold, at the Barcelona 1992 Games, which involved another connection with Fix. Costa Rica's Gilda Montenegro caused many to question how she had qualified for the Games when she accumulated a grand total of 470 penalty points on her first run. Montenegro, it turned out, had not qualified. She had been working as a raft guide for the team manager who, upon learning that Costa Rica had been awarded an extra entry, offered the place to his young employee, even though she had no experience in the event. Montenegro vowed to return to the Games and to negotiate the course without missing a single gate and lived up to her word in her second run at Atlanta 1996, but still finished 28th out of 30. And the Fix connection? Montenegro married him.

Double golden

Slovakia's Elena Kaliska completed a rare Games double at Beijing 2008 as she successfully defended the women's Kayak Singles title she had won at Athens 2004.

So near, yet so far

Britain's Lynn Simpson, then the reigning women's Kayak Singles world champion, failed to live up to her billing as favourite in 1996: she missed the 11th gate during her second run and finished 23rd.

↑ *Togo's Benjamin Boukpeti celebrates his silver medal-winning performance in the K-1 at the 2008 Games.*

On camera – and on to the podium

Britain's Helen Reeves had finished fourth in the women's Kayak Singles event at Athens 2004 and was giving a TV interview when the scoreboard behind her recorded that she had been promoted to third because of a penalty registered against France's Peggy Dickens. As Reeves spoke to the interviewer, the crowd began shouting 'Bronze! Bronze!' The 23-year-old then had to wait for a quarter of an hour to see if Dickens would appeal. She did not and the bronze medal was hers.

Celebrating in style

The Czech Republic's Stepanaka Hilgertova finished the 1996 Games level on time, penalties and points with Dana Chaldek, who was also born in Czechoslovakia, but was competing for the United States. Hilgertova won because her non-counting weaker run was better than Chaldek's, during which she had capsized, missed four gates and finished last. Four years later at Sydney 2000, Hilgertova retained her title by a clear margin, finishing well clear of France's Brigitte Guibal after a faultless second run in her final that was three seconds faster than any rival. Asked if she had been motivated by the US$24,000 bonus she earned for winning, Hilgertova replied that she would have competed even if there had been no bonus, adding: 'First, I like winning, and second, as any woman, I like to be the centre of attention.'

↘ *Great Britain's Helen Reeves took the women's K-1 bronze medal at the 2004 Games in Athens.*

Canoeing and Kayaking: Sprint

Sprint events in Canoeing and Kayaking were first contested at the 1936 Games in Berlin. Men compete over 200 metres and 1000m (in canoes and kayaks with one, two or four athletes), while women compete over 200m and 500m (in kayaks only with one or two athletes).

Electrifying speed

Cliff Meidl, who represented the USA in the Kayak Four event at the 1996 Games and in the Kayak Single at Sydney 2000, was so severely electrocuted at the age of 20 – while working for a construction company he received 30,000 volts, 200 times more than is normally used for the electric chair – suffered three cardiac arrests and was unable to walk unaided for three years.

In and out

Sprinting events have been part of the Olympic Games since 1936 for men, and since 1948 for women. Kayak Single and Double races over 10,000 metres were held from 1936 to 1956, then discontinued.

Swedish flourish

The best medal haul at a single Games by one woman is the two golds and a silver amassed by Agneta Andersson of Sweden at the 1984 Games in Los Angeles. That feat was equalled at the 1988 Games in Seoul – by Germany's Fischer-Schmidt, of course.

Birgit the best

Birgit Fischer-Schmidt is the most successful canoeist at the Games, having competed over a record 24-year period between 1980 and 2004, during which time she won a record eight golds and four silvers for East Germany and Germany. Her record of eight golds is shared with Hungarian fencer Aladar Gerevich, although she achieved that total in six Games – one fewer than Gerevich.

← *Birgit Fischer-Schmidt celebrates an eighth gold at the 2004 Games.*

Little and large

Hungary's winners of the Canoe Double 500m gold at the 2000 Games in Sydney, Ferenc Novak and Imre Pulai, were known as 'The Monster and the Little Guy', as Pulai was 6ft 6in tall and weighed more than 15 stone, while Novak was 5ft 8in tall and weighed 12 stone. Because of strong winds on the day of the Final, Pulai played safe by taping his smaller partner's legs to the boat so he would not slip out.

Gert the great

The most successful male kayaker at the Games has been Sweden's Gert Fredriksson, who won six golds, one silver and one bronze from 1948 to 1960, all in the Kayak Single competition. Three golds in a single Games have been achieved by Vladimir Parfenovich, a 21-year-old PE instructor from Minsk, in the Soviet Union, in 1980, and Ian Ferguson of New Zealand four years later. Ferguson had retired after finishing seventh at the 1980 Games, but returned to the sport when the New Zealand Sports Federation offered kayakers increased financial support.

→ *Six gold medals make Gert Fredriksson the most successful kayaker in Games history.*

Triumph and tragedy

Matija Ljubek won gold and bronze medals for Yugoslavia at Montreal 1976 in the men's C-1 1000m and C-1 500m, and added two more medals in 1984 before becoming vice-president of the Croatian Olympic Committee. In 2000, however, Ljubek was shot dead while defending his mother from an estranged brother-in-law.

Silver to gold

Greg Barton, a mechanical engineer from Michigan, won the K-1 1000m event at the 1988 Games in Seoul, then lost it, then won it again – at least, that is how it seemed. Barton, who had been born with two club feet, was told immediately after his race by South Korean officials that he had narrowly beaten Australia's Grant Davies to win the gold medal. Next, the scoreboard showed him as the silver medallist, but as Davies celebrated, and Barton prepared for the Kayak Double Final, the jury of the International Canoe Federation, having studied the finish line photo, duly announced that the American had won it after all – by the slenderest of margins – 0.005 seconds, or less than a centimetre. So, in the most bizarre manner, Barton became the first US kayaker to win gold at the Games.

Comfortably numb

Clint Robinson, a 20-year-old from Queensland, worked so hard to outsprint Norway's two-time world champion Knut Holmann and earn gold in the K-1 1000m Final at the 1992 Games in Barcelona that his whole body went numb. He was also so dehydrated that it took him six hours to produce a urine sample for the standard doping test. His opponent Holmann went on to win the next two Kayak Single titles in a career that saw him take six medals in four appearances at the Games.

⬆ *Great Britain's Tim Brabants powers his way to Kayak Single 1000m gold at Beijing 2008.*

Diagnosis: Kayaking in the blood

After winning a bronze medal in the Kayak Single 1000m event at the 2000 Games in Sydney, Tim Brabants put his medical studies on hold to concentrate on training for the 2004 Games in Athens. But despite being the second fastest qualifier, he could only finish fifth in the final. Having returned to medicine for a year, Brabants renewed his full-time sporting efforts in preparation for the 2008 Games in Beijing, where, at the age of 31, he won Kayak Single 1000m gold and bronze in the Kayak Single 500m. Job done – and Brabants returned, as he thought finally, to medicine. A year later, however, he was back to full-time training once again, unable to resist the lure of a home Games in London in 2012.

Lifesaver's late flourish

Francis Amyot, who had once saved three Ottawa Rough Riders football players from drowning, took an early lead in the Canoe Single 1000m event at the 1936 Games in Berlin, only to be overtaken by Czechoslovakia's Bohuslav Karlik after 750 metres. But the 31-year-old Canadian dug deep and burst to the front in the final 50m to win the event's first-ever Olympic Games title and become Canada's only gold medallist of the Games – despite having been refused financial support from the Canadian Olympic Committee.

No Hungarian rhapsody

The weather was so bad for the Kayak Double 500m Final at the 2000 Games in Sydney that the race was delayed on three separate occasions, eventually getting underway five hours late in 40mph headwinds and choppy water. The home favourites moved up from third to first with just 50 metres to go, but the Hungarian pair of Zoltan Kammerer and Botond Storcz responded to win by around half a boat-length in a time that was 16 seconds slower than that set in the heats in balmy conditions the previous day.

Rowing

A scheduled event at the inaugural modern Games in Athens in 1896 – only for the regatta to be cancelled due to bad weather – Rowing has been contested at every Games since Paris 1900 (by men) and since Montreal 1976 (by women). The current programme involves 14 events, all of which are contested over a 2000m long course.

Records – what records?

Rowing at recent Games has been held on still water rather than rivers, but weather conditions still vary too much for official Games records to be set. The fastest average speed by a men's eight is 22.51km/h (13.98mph), recorded as the United States crew clocked 5:19.85 in the heats at the 1984 Olympic Games in Los Angeles. Since automatic timing was introduced at the 1960 Games, the narrowest winning margin in a men's event came in the 2004 Coxless Fours, in which the British crew of Matthew Pinsent, Ed Coode, James Cracknell and Steve Williams recorded 6:06.98 to beat Canada by the slender margin of 0.08 seconds.

↑ *In the background, the Great Britain Coxless Four (from left: Steve Williams, James Cracknell, Ed Coode and Matthew Pinsent) celebrate gold at Athens 2004.*

Kelly gold

Just 30 minutes after the USA's John Kelly Senior had narrowly defeated Britain's Jack Beresford in the 1920 Single Sculls Final – after which both men were so exhausted they could not shake hands – he had recovered sufficiently to add another gold medal in the Double Sculls, in the company of Paul Costello. Kelly Senior, who won a record third gold with Costello four years later, had two children who also made their mark on the world. Son John Kelly Junior won a bronze medal at Melbourne 1956, and daughter Grace Kelly became a Hollywood film star before marrying Prince Rainier of Monaco.

Confusion in Paris

At the Paris 1900 Olympic Games, France's Coxed Fours crew from Roubaix won gold despite having finished one minute slower than the third fastest crew. The reason was that dithering officials had been forced to hold two separate finals. Crews were originally told that the four places in the final would go to winners of the three heats, along with the second-placed crew in heat three, which involved four of the ten entrants. But when the losers in heats two and three recorded faster times than the heat one winner, the officials announced an extra qualifying heat – which was then cancelled because not all the crews could be contacted in time. The next idea was that the final should be between the three heat winners and the three fastest losers. But that was no good, as the course was only big enough for four boats. So the Roubaix boat, which had finished second in heat three, defeated two non-qualifiers to win gold in 7:11.00. A second final for the three heat winners saw Germany's Ruder Club win in 5:59.00, with fellow Germans from Ruder Verein taking bronze in 6:05.00.

Rowing for his life

Hugh 'Jumbo' Edwards, who won gold medals in the Coxless Pairs and Coxless Fours in the space of a single day at the 1932 Games in Los Angeles, used his prowess on the water to secure his personal safety 11 years later when, as an RAF squadron leader, he had to ditch his plane in the Atlantic Ocean and row four miles through a minefield.

↑ *John Kelly (left) claimed his second gold medal at the 1920 Games in the Double Sculls with Paul Costello (right).*

Mystery Boy

Gold in the Coxed Pairs at the 1900 Games was won by the Dutch team of Francois Brandt and Roelof Klein, who were steered to victory by ... nobody knows who. A photograph taken after the race shows the two Dutchmen standing proudly either side of the young French boy who had been asked to cox the boat at the last minute and who promptly disappeared before anyone had recorded his name. Given that he was thought to be less than ten years old, he might well have been the youngest-ever Olympic Games gold medallist. The Dutch, who were the favourites, discarded their usual cox, Hermanus Brockmann, after an unexpectedly heavy defeat in qualifying by one of the home crews, who were all using children as coxes. The Dutch decided to do the same and thus chose the mystery boy, who had been rejected by the French crews because he was too heavy. Klein, Brandt and the young 'Monsieur X' won by less than a metre.

Oldest and youngest

The oldest Rowing gold medallist in Olympic Games history was Robert Zimonyi, who coxed the United States eight at the 1964 Games in Tokyo aged 46 years 180 days. The oldest oarsman to win gold was Guy Nickalls, who was in the victorious British eight at the 1908 Games in London aged 41 years 261 days. Fellow Brit Julius Beresford was 44 years 20 days old when won silver four years later. The youngest recorded gold medallist was Giliante D'Este, who was 18 years 141 days old when he rowed for Italy in the Coxed Fours at the 1928 Games in Amsterdam. The youngest medallist oarsman was Australia's Walter Howell, who was 16 years 346 days old when he was in the bronze medal-winning eight at Melbourne 1956. The youngest medal-winning cox was France's Noel Vandernotte, who won bronze in the Pairs and Fours at Berlin 1936 at the age of 12 years 232 days. The four included his father and uncle, Fernand and Marcel.

Child's play

Benjamin Spock, a 6ft 4in student from Yale University, was in the USA eight that won gold at the 1924 Games in Paris. After graduating from medical school, Spock became a paediatrician and, in 1945, published a book – *The Common Sense Book of Baby and Child Care* – that sold more than 50 million copies in over 30 languages.

→ *Benjamin Spock (sitting third from right) in action with the USA eight at the 1924 Games in Paris.*

No go rows

The line-up of Rowing events at the Games has changed over the years. In 1996, the Coxed Pairs and Coxed Fours, which had both been a part of the programme since 1900, were discontinued. Three other events made only one appearance at a Games: the Six-Man Naval Rowing Boats (won by Italy in 1906); the 17-Man Naval Rowing Boats (won by Greece in 1906); and the men's Coxed Four with Inriggers (won by Denmark in 1912). Quadruple Sculls were introduced to the Games in 1976, and Lightweight Double Sculls and Fours became part of the programme in 1996.

↑ *A butcher by trade and a long-standing member of the Vesta Rowing Club in Putney, London, Henry Blackstaffe won gold at London 1908.*

Experience pays off

At 40, the London 1908 Single Sculls gold-medal winner Henry Blackstaffe, who worked as a butcher, was twice the age of silver medallist Alexander McCulloch, but finished more than a length ahead of his fellow Briton.

Stroke of duck

Henry 'Bobby' Pearce, winner of the Single Sculls at Amsterdam 1928, faced an unexpected challenge during his quarter-final race when he was delayed by a family of ducks that passed in front of him in single file. The Australian was still able to catch and overtake Victor Saurin of France.

↑ *The Soviet Union's Coxless Pair team of Victor Ivanov (left) and Igor Buldakov (right) in action at the Henley Regatta in 1957.*

Brotherly rows

Rowing at the Games has a strong family tradition. In Paris 1900, the winning German four contained three brothers – Oskar, Gustav and Carl Gossler, the latter being the cox. At Moscow 1980, East Germany's Landvoigt twins beat the Soviet Union's Pimenov twins in the Coxless Pairs final. At Barcelona 1992, British brothers Jonny and Greg Searle earned gold in the Coxed Pairs by defeating the defending champions, Italy's Carmine and Giuseppe Abbagnale. The Abbagnale family had come away from Seoul 1988 with not one, but two gold medals – younger brother Agostino was in the victorious Quadruple Sculls crew.

Throwing away the prize

Viktor Ivanov, an 18-year-old rower from the Soviet Union, was so thrilled at finishing second behind the United States in the Coxless Pairs at the 1956 Games in Melbourne that during the presentation ceremony he jumped up and down with joy – and dropped his silver medal into Lake Wendouree. Ivanov, who had partnered Igor Buldakov, dived into the water to search for it, but came up empty-handed. After the Games were over, however, the International Olympic Committee took pity and gave him a replacement medal.

Seven down

After failing to make the Canadian eight at the 1964 Games, George Hungerford and Roger Jackson were compensated by being allowed to enter the Coxless Pairs at six weeks' notice. The long shots won. Jackson went on to become President of the Canadian Olympic Committee and helped devise the 'Own the Podium' programme that inspired the home nation to win a record 14 gold medals at the 2010 Winter Games in Vancouver.

← *Hugh isn't the only famous member of the Laurie family; his father Ran won Coxless Pairs gold at the 1948 Games.*

Fathers and sons

Britain's Julius Beresford won silver in the Coxed Fours at the 1912 Games. In the course of the next five Games, starting in 1920, his son Jack won a total of five medals – three gold and two silver. The United States' Paul Costello won three golds in the 1920s and his son Bernard earned silver in 1956. John Kelly Senior also won three golds in the 1920s – two of them in the Double Sculls with Paul Costello – and his son John took a bronze in 1956. Guy Nickalls won gold in the British eight in 1908, and his son, Guy Junior, took silver in the 1920 and 1928 eights. Charles and Richard Burnell are the only father and son rowers in Games history to win gold medals. Charles was a member of the winning eight at Henley-on-Thames in 1908, and his son, who would go on to become rowing correspondent for *The Times* and the *Sunday Times* for 44 years, won over the same course 40 years later in the Double Sculls, partnering Bert Bushnell.

Ran the man

William 'Ran' Laurie won the Coxless Pairs event at the 1938 Henley Royal Regatta with his friend Jock Wilson while both were on leave from the Sudan, where they were serving with the British Colonial Service. The pair did not row again until, ten years later, they returned to Britain on leave to prepare for the 1948 Games in London. After six weeks' training they won at Henley again, and then proceeded to win gold medals at the Games. Laurie's son, Hugh, went on to win a rowing Blue at Cambridge and found even greater success as an actor, writer and comedian.

Redgrave the record

Immediately after he had won the Pairs gold in company with Matthew Pinsent at the 1996 Games in Atlanta, an exhausted Steve Redgrave, having just won his fourth successive gold medal at the Games, told a TV interviewer: 'If anyone sees me near a boat again, they have my permission to shoot me.' Four years later, Redgrave competed in the Fours at Sydney, collecting a record fifth consecutive gold medal and bringing his medal total to six. Redgrave, who later in 2000 was voted BBC Sports Personality of the Century, achieved his record despite discovering three years beforehand that he was diabetic, and also required treatment for colitis shortly before the 2000 Games. His 1996 partner Pinsent, with whom he had won the Pairs in 1992, earned his third gold in the Fours in 2000, and went on to add a fourth victory, also in the Fours, in 2004. Pinsent's fellow countryman Jack Beresford won one fewer gold medal, but two more silvers, as he became the first rower to win medals at five consecutive Games between 1920 and 1936. If the 1940 Games, scheduled for Tokyo, had not been prevented from taking place by the Second World War, who knows what the record would have been?

➜ *Sir Steve Redgrave poses with his five gold medals.*

↑ *New Zealand's Rob Waddell bounced back from illness to win men's Single Sculls gold at the 2000 Olympic Games in Sydney.*

Heart of gold

Rob Waddell, who rowed for New Zealand in the Coxless Fours at the 1995 World Championships, lost energy during one of their races due to atrium fibrillation, a heart condition. After withdrawing from team events, so as not to risk letting any team-mate down, and following treatment for his condition, Waddell took up Single Sculls and went on to win the gold medal at Sydney 2000.

Brothers disunited

Swiss brothers Michael and Markus Gier had spent eight years training together, and sharing an apartment in Rorschach, before competing in the Lightweight Double Sculls title at the 1996 Games. By the time they reached Atlanta they had decided to stop competing after the Games as they were irritating each other so badly. But they left with the gold medal.

Infant inspiration

With 750 metres to go in the Coxless Pairs final at the 2000 Olympic Games in Sydney, Frenchmen Michel Andrieux and Jean-Christophe Rolland shouted out their codeword for attack – 'Victor-Matthias' – before overtaking three crews to take a lead at the 1,500m mark that they never lost. Victor and Matthias were the names of their recently born sons.

Five in a row

Jack Beresford earned his place in Great Britain's Rowing team for the Antwerp 1920 Olympic Games by winning the single sculls at that year's Henley Regatta and went on to take men's Single Sculls silver at the Games. Competing in the same event at Paris 1924, however, he went one better to win his first gold medal. A switch to the men's Eights for Amsterdam 1928 yielded a silver medal, before he moved to the men's Fours at Los Angeles 1932, where he claimed his second gold. His final appearance at the Games came at Berlin 1936, when he partnered Dick Southwood to gold in the men's Double Sculls. In doing so, Beresford had become the first rower in history to win medals at five consecutive Olympic Games.

US eight's unofficial Games record

Women's Rowing was introduced in 1976 over 1,000 metres (0.62 miles), and in 1988 the course distance was standardised to that of the men at 2,000m (1.24 miles). Although varying conditions mean there are no official Games records for Rowing, the heats of the 1984 Games in Los Angeles saw the US women's eight win their heat in the fastest time ever recorded at the Games of 5:56.55 – averaging 20.19km/h (12.54mph).

➜ Silken Laumann defied injury to win bronze at the 1992 Games.

Lipa – the greatest?

Romania's Elisabeta Lipa lays claim to having been the Games' most successful rower of all time, having matched Steve Redgrave's record of five gold medals when she won at the 2004 Games in Athens, 20 years after her first victory, at Los Angeles 1984. Two additional silvers and a bronze meant that Lipa finished her Olympic Games career with a total of eight medals – more than any other rower, and two more than Redgrave's tally. Lipa's fellow countrywomen dominated the individual medal table at Athens. Doina Ignat, a member of the eight that won three straight golds, has amassed four golds and two other medals, while Georgeta Damian's victory in the Pairs at the 2008 Games in Beijing meant that she became the third rower in Olympic Games history to win five golds, having won the in Pair and Eights gold at the two previous Games. Viorica Susanu's total after the 2008 Games was four golds and a bronze, while Constanta Burcica has so far won three golds and a total of five medals in the Lightweight Double Sculls. Cox Elena Georgescu has also picked up five medals, three of them gold.

🏅 Romania's Elisabeta Lipa (second left) celebrates her fifth and final gold medal at Athens 2004.

Laumann the brave

Seventy-three days before she was scheduled to race in the women's Single Sculls at the 1992 Games in Barcelona, Canada's Silken Laumann, the reigning world champion, was involved in a shocking accident while warming up for a race in Essen, Germany. The 27-year-old's shell was rammed by that of the German Coxless Pair, Peter Holtzenbein and Cohn von Ettingshausen, and a piece of wood smashed into her lower right leg, fracturing the bone, cutting her calf muscles and causing extensive nerve and tissue damage. After helping to save her, both the German rowers fainted at the sight. Laumann was told she would need six months to recover, but after five operations, and despite having to walk with a cane and having to avoid standing up for more than quarter of an hour at a time, she achieved her target of competing at the Barcelona Games. Incredibly, she took the bronze medal. Four years later she improved to silver, when she finished behind Belarus's Ekaterian Khodotovich.

Landmark achievement

In 1986, ten years after helping the USA eight to take bronze in the inaugural women's Olympic Games Rowing event in Montreal, Anita DeFrantz became the first black woman to be selected to serve on the International Olympic Committee. She was elected on to the IOC Executive Board in 1992.

Gift of life

Four weeks to the hour after winning silver behind Australia in the Coxless Pairs at the 1996 Games in Atlanta, United States rower Missy Schwen underwent an operation to donate her kidney to her brother, Michael.

The skilful sculler

Germany's Kathrin Boron was a commanding performer in the sculls. She won gold medals in the 1992 Double Sculls (with Kerstin Köppen), the 1996 Quadruple Sculls and the 2000 Double Sculls (with Jana Thieme). Boron went on to take another gold medal in 2004, and ended her Games career in 2008 with a fifth medal, bronze in the Quadruple Sculls.

← *Germany's Kathrin Boron (left) and Jana Thieme on their way to women's Double Sculls gold at the 2000 Games in Sydney.*

Marginal victory

Since automatic timing was introduced in 1960, the narrowest winning margin in women's events came in the Single Sculls Final at Sydney 2000, when Belarus' Ekaterina Karsten, the defending champion, won gold over Bulgaria's Rumyana Neykova after they seemed to finish in a dead heat. The winning margin was determined to be one hundredth of a second – the judges' deliberations having taken three times longer than the race itself.

The odd couple strikes gold

Marnie McBean and Kathleen Heddle, known as the 'odd couple' because of their respective extrovert and introvert natures, became the first Canadians in any sport to win three gold medals at the Games as they held on for victory in the women's Double Sculls at Atlanta 1996, having won in the Coxless Pairs and Eights four years earlier in Barcelona. McBean had first sought a career in rowing aged 16 and her first move was to join local club Argonaut after finding their number in the Toronto phone directory.

Changing places

Two events from the first women's Rowing programme at the 1976 Games in Montreal have since been discontinued. Romania remain the Olympic Games' last Coxed Quadruple Sculls champions, having won at Los Angeles 1984. The German Democratic Republic won the last-ever Coxed Fours title in 1988. Four years later, at the 1992 Games in Barcelona, a Canadian quartet won the only Coxless Fours event to be run. Quadruple Sculls were introduced in 1988, and Lightweight Double Sculls in 1996.

Taxi trouble

After taking silver in the women's Pairs at her home Olympic Games in Sydney in 2000, Australia's Rachael Taylor celebrated too enthusiastically ... and ended up leaving her medal in a taxi cab. Her plight was publicised and a Sydney taxi driver returned the medal to her after finding it underneath his back seat.

↑ *Australia's Rachel Taylor (left) won women's Pairs gold at Sydney 2000 (with Kate Slatter) ... and left her medal in a taxi.*

All that glistens...

Britain's Katherine Grainger (above) earned her fifth World Championship gold medal in 2010, but has only ever won silver in the Olympic Games: in 2000 (Quadruple Sculls), 2004 (Pairs) and 2008 (Quadruple Sculls).

Chalk and cheese scullers

Marnie McBean and Kathleen Heddle, known as the 'odd couple' because of their respective extrovert and introvert natures, became the first Canadians in any sport to win three Olympic gold medals as they held on for victory in the Double Sculls at the Atlanta 1996 Games, having won in the Coxless Pairs and Eights four years earlier at the Barcelona 1992 Games.

Sailing

Since the sport's Games debut at Paris 1900, results in Sailing have been determined on the basis of aggregate scores from a series of races, with the possibility of some results being discarded. These rules have altered over the years, as have the kinds of boats involved in competition.

Elvstrom – the great Dane

Denmark's Paul Elvstrom can claim to be the most successful yachtsman in Games history after becoming the first man to achieve four successive gold medals – from 1948 to 1960. His Games career did not finish there: he competed at Mexico City 1968 in the Star class (where he was fourth); the 1972 Soling class (17th), and the Tornado class in 1984 and 1988 (where he was fourth and 15th respectively).

⬇ *Denmark's Paul Elvstrom won the first of his four gold medals in the Firefly class at the 1948 Games in London.*

Oldest and youngest

The USA's Everard Endt became the oldest gold medallist when he won the 6 Metre class in 1952 aged 59 years 112 days. The oldest winner in a single-handed race was Belgium's Leon Haybrechts, who won gold in 1924 aged 47 years 215 days. Franciscus Hin (Netherlands), who won the 12ft Dinghy event aged 14 years 163 days in 1920 with his brother Johannes is the youngest winner.

Scheidt's trap

In the 1996 Laser class, Britain's 19-year-old Ben Ainslie went into the final race in silver-medal position, trailing Brazil's Robert Scheidt by two points. As a result, there was much pre-race manoeuvring between the two as they jockeyed for position before the gun went. After four false starts, officials raised the black flag, meaning that anyone who crossed the start line early would be disqualified. As Scheidt headed for the line at the fifth attempt, he gambled that Ainslie would have to stick close to him to prevent him getting a decisive lead – and that if he crossed the line himself before the gun went, and got disqualified, the young Briton would suffer the same fate. Both crossed the line, both were disqualified – and Scheidt won gold.

⬆ *After being outsmarted by Brazil's Robert Scheidt, Great Britain's Ben Ainslie had to be content with a silver medal in the Laser class at Atlanta 1996. He would go on to win gold in 2000, 2004 and 2008.*

Ainslie's revenge

Four years after Ainslie fell into Scheidt's trap, the Sydney 2000 Laser class contest again came down to the last race, with Scheidt leading Ainslie by seven points. The only way Ainslie could win was by preventing the Brazilian from finishing 21st or better, so he harassed his opponent before the start, forcing him to commit an infraction that required a 720-degree penalty turn. Once they got underway, Ainslie blocked Scheidt's wind and repeatedly prevented him from passing, to the point where both trailed the rest of the field by 90 seconds. In his efforts to get clear, Scheidt crashed into Ainslie's boat before moving up the field to 22nd place, but he could not get any higher and, despite filing two protests, both of which were eventually rejected, as he was disqualified and the Briton awarded gold. Ainslie then put on 40lb as he moved up to the Finn class, in which he won gold in 2004 and 2008.

Take the rest of the week off

Britain's pairing of Rodney Pattison and Christopher Davies won four of their first six races in the Flying Dutchman class at Munich 1972, which meant they were certain of the gold medal without having to race on the final day. In the same class at Mexico City 1968, Pattison had partnered Iain Macdonald-Smith, scoring the lowest number of penalty points – three – in Games history. After being, they felt, unjustifiably disqualified for interference after finishing first in the opening race, they won the next five on the trot, then played safe in the last race to finish second and ended up taking gold by a margin of more than 40 points.

Two for one

The only boat to earn two gold medals at a single Games was *Scotia*, crewed by Britain's Lorne Currie and John Gretton, which won the 0.5-1 Ton and Open classes at the 1900 Games. The USA yacht *Llanoria* won the 6 Metre class in 1948 and 1952, skippered on both occasions by Herman Whiton.

Brotherly crews

Sailing has often been a family affair. In 1920, four Norwegian brothers won gold in the 12 Metre (1907 rating) class: Henrik, Jan, Ole and Kristian Ostervold. Eight years earlier, Amédée, Gaston and Jacques Thube (France), won the 6 Metre class. Sweden's Ulf, Jorgen and Peter Sundelin (5.5 Metre class) equalled the feat in 1968. The only gold medal-winning twins were Sumner and Edgar White (United States, 5.5 Metre class) in 1952.

Zeros to heroes

At Seoul 1988, Britain's Michael McIntyre and Bryn Vaile were in fourth place in the Star class going into the final race. To earn gold they needed to win it, with the US leaders, Mark Reynolds and Hal Haenel, placing no higher than sixth and Brazilians Torben Grael and Nelson Falcao no better than fifth. It was a tall order, but Fate was with the British pair. While the Brazilians finished eighth and the Americans failed to finish after their mast broke, McIntyre and Vaile duly won the race by 11 seconds. McIntyre, from Salisbury, said afterwards: 'In my wildest dreams I thought we could win – but not in any other state of mind.' It was a great victory for the Britons in what was Scotsman McIntyre's second appearance at the Olympic Games and Vaile's one and only. McIntyre had finished seventh at Los Angeles 1984 in the Finn class.

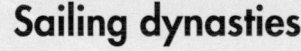 *Great Britain's Michael McIntyre (back) and Bryn Vaile (front) won the final race to take Star class gold at the 1988 Games in Seoul.*

← *Paul Smart (left) and his son Hilary (right): Star class gold medallists in 1948.*

Sailing dynasties

The 1920 Games saw the first victory by a father and son pairing when Belgium's Emile and Florimond Cornellie won the 6 Metre (1907 rating) class. Sailing's most prominent dynasty is Norway's Lunde clan. Eugen started it all off in 1924 by winning gold in the 6 Metre class; his son Peder and daughter-in-law Vibeke won silver in the 5.5 Metre class in 1952, with Vibeke's brother also aboard; and grandson Peder junior won gold in the 1960 Flying Dutchman class. That made it three generations of medallists at the Games. The 1948 Star class event saw gold go to USA sailors Paul Smart and his son Hilary, with silver being won by another father and son team, Cuba's Carlos De Cardenas Culmell and Carlos De Cardenas Junior.

Countess with the mostest

The first woman to compete in the Olympic Games was a sailor. When women's events were introduced at the 1900 Games – not in major sports – Hélène, Countess de Pourtalès, of Switzerland, became the first woman to make her mark as she crewed for her father, Count Hermann de Pourtalès, in the 1–2 Tonnes Sailing event. And they won, making the Countess, at 31, the oldest female gold medallist of the 1900 Games, and her father the oldest gold medallist of the Games at 53 years 55 days. However, as the 1900 races were handicapped, most observers do not consider them to have been part of the Olympic Games proper.

➡ *Hélène, Countess of Pourtalès, is credited with being the Games' first female starter. She won gold.*

Oldest and youngest

The oldest female gold medallist was Virginie Hériot (France), who won in the 8-Metre class at the 1928 Games aged 38 years 16 days. The oldest female medallist was Pease Glaser (United States), who took silver in the 470 class at Sydney 2000, aged 38 years 314 days. The youngest female gold medallist was Kristine Roug (Denmark), who won the Europe class at Atlanta 1996 aged 21 years 141 days. The youngest female medallist was Natalia Via Dufresne Perena (Spain), who took silver in the Europe class at Barcelona 1992.

⬅ *Virginie Hériot (left): sailing's oldest female medallist.*

Power of eight

The first woman to win a medal in Sailing at the Olympic Games was Britain's Frances Rivett-Carnac at the 1908 Games in London. She was part of the gold medal-winning crew of four sailing in the 7-Metre class. The next time a woman won a gold medal at the Games was at Antwerp 1920, when another Briton, Dorothy Wright, was also part of the victorious 7-Metre class crew. Another eight years would pass before the next female medallist, France's Virginie Hériot, at the Amsterdam 1928 Games. The eight-year cycle for women winning medals continued when Sweden's Dagmar Salen of Sweden was part of the bronze-medal crew of five in the 6-Metre class at the 1936 Games in Berlin. After the Second World War interrupted the Olympic Games, there were no women medallists until the 1952 Games in Helsinki. This time two women went home with medals: Norway's Vibeker Lunde won the silver medal as part of the crew of three in the 5.5-Metre class andthe United States' Emelyn Whiton was one of six crew members who took the gold medal in the 6-Metre class.

Family endeavour

Paul Elvstrom, who had claimed four gold medals in the Firefly class (1948) and Finn class (1952, 1956 and 1960), came out of retirement to race in the Tornado class, a two-man catamaran, at the 1984 Games in Los Angeles. Only this was a one-man, one-woman catamaran, as he was joined by his daughter, Inge Trine. Despite being the people's choice, the Danish father and daughter team missed out on a medal by one place in an event that was unexpectedly won by the New Zealand pairing of Rex Sellers, a lobster fisherman, and Christopher Timms. Four years later, at the age of 60, Elvstrom returned to the Tornado class at the 1988 Games in Seoul, during which he and his daughter finished a disappointing 15th.

From four to the fore

Shirley Robertson missed out on a medal in the Europe class by just two points at Atlanta 1996. Four years later, in Sydney, she was in with a shout for gold with just two races remaining, needing to finish fourth or better in either. When she could only manage 16th place in the first of them, the pressure was on to finish ahead of Holland's Margriet Matthijsse, winner of the penultimate race. The Dutchwoman won the last race too, but Robertson finished in third place to secure gold. At the next Games, at Athens in 2004, the Scotswoman skippered Britain to gold in the newly established Yngling class.

Golden coach

Guided by their coach, Viktor Kobalenko, the Ukraine pairing of Ruslana Taran and Olena Panholchik, 470 class bronze medallists at the 1996 Games, won three consecutive world and European titles. But when their coach moved to Australia their form began to falter – and that of the Australian pair, Jenny Armstrong and Belinda Stowell, started to improve under his guidance. The Ukraine pair won another bronze at Sydney 2000, while the gold went to Armstrong and Stowell – who had originally come from New Zealand and Zimbabwe respectively.

Mending broken hopes

The 470 class for women was staged for the first time at Seoul 1988 and Alison Jolly and Lynne Jewell (USA) went into the final race needing only a 14th-place finish or better to secure gold. In treacherous weather, half-way through the course they were hit by a large wave, which broke the wire connecting their jib to the halyard, leaving the jib sail sagging and taking them from fourth to 15th. 'There goes the gold,' said Jolly. 'We've got to fight!' replied Jewell. Despite 30 knots of wind and ten-foot waves, Jewell managed to repair the jib with a piece of spare twine and the pair managed to secure gold by recovering to ninth place.

On the up

In the Sailing competitions at both Athens 2004 and Beijing 2008, women represented 35 per cent of the competing athletes (139 out of 400). That represented a 32 per cent increase in women's participation since the 2000 Games in Sydney (95 out of 402).

Yngling, Yngling, gone...

Sarah Ayton was a member of the British crew that won the Yngling class – an event for a three-person keel boat – when it was introduced to the Olympic Games in 2004. Her partners in Athens were skipper Shirley Robertson and Sarah Webb. Four years later in Beijing, Ayton was skipper of a British crew that won Yngling gold again, this time partnered by Webb and newcomer Pippa Wilson. Having won the world title as well, the British trio were looking forward to completing a hat-trick in their home Games in 2012 but, in 2009, the International Federation dropped Yngling from the Games programme.

⬆ *From left to right: Shirley Robertson, Sarah Webb and Sarah Ayton celebrate their Yngling victory at Athens 2004.*

Sensini supreme

A total of 90 medals have been won by women sailors at the Olympic Games, but Italy's Alessandra Sensini is the only woman sailor to have won four medals – one gold (in 2000), one silver (in 2008) and two bronzes (in 1996 and 2004).

⬅ *Italy's Alessandra Sensini powers to Mistral bronze at Athens 2004.*

Windsurfer (RS:X)

Windsurfer (RS:X) is a class that combines the elements of sailing and surfing and is often referred to as sailboarding as it takes place on a board with a sail on it. In competitions at the Games, participants all use the same standard equipment.

Breezing in

The Windsurfer class for men was first contested at the Los Angeles 1984 and the women's event became part of the Games programme eight years later at Barcelona 1992. Different styles of board have been used at different Games. For the inaugural event at Long Beach in Los Angeles, a Windglider was used – a board 12 feet 9 inches long and 25½in wide that carried a sail of 70sq ft. At Seoul 1988 and Barcelona 1992, the Lechner Division II board was chosen – a 12ft long, round-bottomed sailboard with a 78.6sq ft sail. In 1996, 2000 and 2004, the Mistral board was used, a 13ft 11in long board made of fibreglass with a sail of 7.4sq m. Beijing 2008 saw the introduction of the Neil Pryde RS:X board.

Safer at sea

At the 1988 Games in Seoul, heavy winds gusting up to 25 knots on the fifth day of racing created waves almost two metres in height, and only 19 of the 43 men starters finished. Conditions favoured heavier windsurfers, but the gold went to New Zealand's Bruce Kendall, who weighed just over 10 stone. Kendall, aged 24, had encountered more difficulties on dry land, having grazed his hand badly after falling off his skateboard while listening to rock music on his Walkman. New Zealand team officials banned him from further skateboarding until after the Games were over.

Herminator-style

Christoph Sieber, Austria's unexpected winner of the event at the 2000 Games in Sydney, credited his success to the winter weight-training training he had undertaken in the snow with the Austrian skiing legend Hermann Maier.

⬆ *Christoph Sieber held off Charles Espinola (Argentina, silver) and Aaron McIntosh (New Zealand, bronze) to take Windsurfing gold in 2000.*

Going Dutch

The first Windsurfer class gold medallist at the Olympic Games was Holland's Stephan van den Berg, who held off the competition from home contender Randall Scott Steele off Long Beach, California, in 1984. Van den Berg was favourite to win, having been world champion for the three previous years. This was Holland's first Sailing gold since Berlin 1936, when Daniel Kagchelland had won the Finn class at Kiel. Eight years later, Van den Berg competed at the 1992 Games in Barcelona, finishing seventh.

Rubbish luck

Michael Gebhardt (USA) took Windsurfer class silver at Barcelona 1992 and might have won gold had it not been for a stray rubbish bag. There had been complaints before the competition got underway that the course at the Parc de Mar venue was not fit for purpose because of the amount of refuse floating in it. On the last lap of his seventh race, a bag became caught on the end of Gebhardt's board. By the time he had disentangled himself from it, the American had been passed by six rivals.

Back to the drawing board

The originator of the first sailboard is generally believed to have been an American named Newman Darby who, as a 20-year-old in 1948, had the idea of mounting a hand-held sail on to a small catamaran. Darby, however, did not patent his idea. The first patent on a windsurfing boat was taken out by two Californians, Jim Drake and Hoyle Schweitzer, who named their design the Windsurfer. Fittingly, the Windsurfer class event was contested for the first time at the 1984 Olympic Games in Los Angeles.

Sister power

Four years after her brother, Bruce, had won gold for New Zealand in the Windsurfer competition at the 1988 Games in Seoul, Barbara Kendall did likewise at Barcelona 1992 to become the first female Olympic Games champion in her event. Remarkably, seven months before the Games got underway, Kendall had been thrown from a power boat, the propeller of which had severed a tendon in her arm and broke the scaphoid bone in her wrist. China's Zhang Xiaodong finished runner-up to Kendall to become the first Asian athlete to win a Sailing medal at the Games. Kendall went on to become the first New Zealand woman to compete at five Games, finishing second in 1996, third in 2000, fifth in 2004 and sixth in 2008, before retiring in 2010.

Close encounter

Endra Ha-Tiff, of the Seychelles, almost did not make it to the start line at the 2000 Games in Sydney, having narrowly escaped with her life after a close encounter with a ferry while training in Sydney Harbour. Luckily it left her with nothing worse than a scraped knee.

First and last?

When Hong Kong's Lee Lai-Shan won Windsurfer class gold at Atlanta 1996, four years after the disappointment of finishing in 11th place in Barcelona, she became her country's first Olympic Games medallist since their entry to the Games in 1952. So dominant was Lai-Shan that she did not need to take part in the ninth and final race.

Israeli first

At Athens 2004, Gal Fridman became the first Israeli champion at the Olympic Games when he won gold four years after taking bronze in Sydney. Fittingly, 'gal' is the Hebrew word for 'wave'. Fridman dedicated his gold medal to the memory of the 11 Israeli athletes who died after being seized by members of the Black September organisation during the 1972 Games in Munich. Shahar Zubari maintained Israeli momentum by finishing second in the final race at Beijing 2008 to take the bronze medal, with the gold going to New Zealand's Tom Ashley and the silver to France's Julien Bontemps.

↑ *After taking Windsurfer class bronze at Atlanta 1996, Gal Fridman struck gold at Athens 2004 to become Israel's first-ever gold medallist.*

Home Heroine

Yin Jian (who had finished second at the previous Games in Athens) provided China with a home champion at Beijing 2008 as she held off the challenge of the 2000 champion Alessandra Sensini of Italy, and won four of the event's ten races (including the first three) to take gold in the Windsurfer class. Bryony Shaw finished third to win Britain's first Windsurfer class medal at the Games and celebrated the feat by breaking down in tears.

→ *Having picked up a silver medal in the Windsurfer class at Athens 2004, China's Yin Jian thrilled the home crowd when she took gold at Beijing 2008.*

Chapter Twelve
Target sports

Target sports have been an integral part of the modern Games from the outset. Interest in rifle shooting had increased across Europe and North America throughout the 19th century, and Baron Pierre de Coubertin, founder of the modern Olympic Movement, was himself a former French pistol champion, so it is little wonder that Shooting was one of the nine events contested at the inaugural Athens 1896 Games. At the time, the Shooting competition consisted of five events – two using a rifle and three with a pistol. The first event, the Military Rifle, was won by Greece's Pantelis Karasevdas. The second event, for Military Pistols, was dominated by two American brothers, John and Sumner Paine, who became the first siblings to finish first and second in the same event.

The history of Archery as a competitive sport long pre-dates the modern Olympic Games and reputedly goes back to the 17th century. Even so, the sport was blighted for many years by a lack of governance and made its first appearance at the Olympic Games at Paris in 1900 – six events were contested, with France and Belgium picking up three gold medals each. Continued confusion over the interpretation of Archery's rules led to its disappearance from the Games' agenda for 52 years, before it was finally reintroduced at the 1972 Games in Munich. Currently, Archery has a global appeal and 83 nations have competed in the recurve discipline, with gold medallists hailing from no fewer than four different continents.

The Ukraine's Viktor Ruban takes aim during the men's Individual Archery Final at the 2008 Olympic Games in Beijing. In a memorable contest, he beat South Korea's Park Kyung-Mo 113–112 to win the gold medal.

Archery

The use of a bow to fire arrows dates back to the time of Genghis Khan and his Mongol Empire in the 13th century and has been the weapon of choice for countless armies throughout the ages. As a sport, archery is believed to have begun as an Anglo-French event, so it was fitting that the inaugural Archery event at the Games took place at Paris 1900.

Team after team

Archery as a team sport was added to the Games agenda at Seoul 1988 and has been dominated by South Korea's women's Archery team. From 1984 to 2008 they won 16 gold medals and retained their unbeatable tag with further gold in Beijing. At Sydney 2000, the country's archers, inspired by Seo Hyang-Soon, won three of the four events. The team put their success down to a healthy combination of preparation, scientific training – and the right DNA! World record holder Yoon Ok-hee claimed that Korean women were dexterous due to heightened sensitivity in their fingers.

↑ *New Zealand's Neroli Fairhall made history at Los Angeles 1984 when she became the first paraplegic to appear in the Olympic Games.*

Accidental outsider

There are countless examples of Olympians becoming movie stars. However, in Archery the reverse was the case when Hollywood actress Geena Davis took part in the qualifying for Sydney 2000. Davis competed in the semi-finals of the United States trials, but ultimately finished 24th and missed out. She said: 'This was a once-in-a-lifetime opportunity to be exposed to this amount of stress and level of competition. I just focus on my technique and not worry about the result.'

Fantastic Fairhall

The 1984 Games in Los Angeles saw one of the ultimate examples of inspirational endeavour. New Zealand athlete Neroli Fairhall had been paralysed from the waist down in a motorbike accident. Subsequently she took up archery and became the first wheelchair-bound athlete to compete at the Summer Games, finishing 35th overall. A national champion for many years, Fairhall won medals and held titles at the Paralympic Games, IPC-Archery World Championships and many international tournaments and was awarded the MBE.

↑ *Geena Davis, winner of the Best Supporting Actress Oscar in 1988, took part in the US trials for the 2000 Games but missed out on selection.*

Taking a time-out

Archery maintained a low-key presence at the 1904, 1908 and 1920 Olympic Games. However, there was no international consensus about the rules of the sport and differing interpretations were used by successive host countries, with the result that Archery was banished from the Games altogether. The emergence of the Fédération Internationale de Tir à l'Arc, in 1931, finally gave the sport much-needed governance and, more importantly, a standard set of rules. This paved the way for Archery's return to the Games at Munich 1972, four decades later, and only then as an Individual competition. It took a further 16 years before a Team competition was contested for the first time.

The most golden arrow

Archery's highest-profile moment came at the climax of the Opening Ceremony at the 1992 Games in Barcelona. Billions of eyes around the world were captivated by the spectacular lighting of the Olympic Flame by an arrow fired from the bow of Spanish Paralympic archer Antonio Rebollo. He said later: 'There were no nerves: I was practically a robot, I focused on my positioning and reaching the target. Later people described to me how they saw it, what they felt, their emotions. That is what made me realise what such a moment actually meant.'

➜ *Antonio Rebollo, a two-time Paralympic bronze medallist, lights the Olympic Flame in spectacular fashion during the Opening Ceremony at Barcelona 1992.*

Always on target

In the pantheon of archers at the Games, Belgium's Hubert Van Innis arguably ranks highest of them all. He won six gold medals, despite competing at only two Games. At the 1900 Games in Paris, Van Innis struck gold twice, after which 20 years passed before his next appearance. At Antwerp 1920, he showed he had lost none of his control when he won another four gold medals. After his successes in 1920, Archery was banished from the Olympic Games during his lifetime, but in 1933, at the age of 67, he was still a team winner at the World Championships.

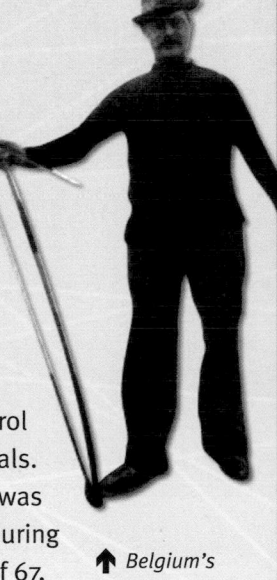

⬆ *Belgium's Hubert Van Innis is a six-time gold-medal winner.*

Meeting in St Louis

Archery at the 1904 Games in St Louis was effectively a US national amateur championship, as not a single professional or foreign archer competed. Events in the men's competition were dominated by Boston's G. Phillip Bryant, who won both of the Individual competitions, while the men's Team event saw Reverend Galen Carter Spencer win a gold medal aged 64. He remains the USA's oldest gold medallist at the Games. The silver medal went to an even older competitor, Samuel Duvall, who, at 68, is the USA's oldest-ever medallist at the Games.

Captivating Koreans

Of the 83 nations to have competed in Archery competitions at Olympic Games the most successful has been South Korea, with a haul of 16 gold medals and an overall tally of 30 medals. The United States are not far behind, with a total of 14 golds and 30 medals. However, the true magnitude of the Korean achievement lies in the fact that all their medals have been won since Archery was re-admitted to the Games programme in 1972.

Golden years

Age has proved no barrier to women archers. At the 1908 Olympic Games in London, Britain's Sybil Fenton Newall (known as Queenie Newall) won the gold medal at the age of 53. Newall's score of 688 points gave her a 46-point victory over second-place finisher Lottie Dod. She remains the oldest woman ever to have won a gold medal at the Games.

⬇ *Fifty-three-year-old Queenie Newall showed the younger competitors how it was done when she took Archery gold at London 1908.*

Shooting

Shooting was contested at the first modern Games in 1896 and, with the exception of 1904 and 1928, has been a feature at every Games since. Shooting today comprises nine events: 10m Air Pistol; 10m Air Rifle; 25m Rapid Fire Pistol; 50m Pistol; 50m Rifle Prone; 50m Rifle 3 Positions; Double Trap; Skeet; and Trap.

Opening shots

Shooting was one of the nine events contested at the inaugural Olympic Games in Athens, in 1896. At those Games, five Sport Shooting events were contested. These took place at the newly constructed shooting range at Kallithea. They were organised and prepared by the Sub-Committee for Shooting. Some 61 shooters from seven nations competed in the five events: Military Rifle, Free Rifle, 25m Military Pistol, 25m Rapid Fire Pistol and Free Pistol. The host nation claimed three golds, with the United States bagging the other two.

Mixed results

Barcelona 1992 was a landmark Olympic Games for shooting equality as China's Zhang Shan took the gold medal in the mixed-gender Skeet competition, becoming the first woman to win a mixed event. Female shooters had been admitted to the Olympic Games only at Mexico City 1968 and it was not until 1984 that separate shooting events for women were introduced, in addition to mixed events. The International Shooting Union subsequently prohibited women from shooting against men.

⬆ *Zhang Shan created a slice of history at Barcelona 1992 when she claimed Skeet Shooting gold to become the first woman in history to win a mixed event.*

Family business

When Sweden's Oscar Swahn won silver in the Running Deer Double Shot Team event, at the 1920 Olympic Games in Antwerp, he became the oldest person to win a medal at the Games. The 72-year-old had already won gold and bronze medals at the 1908 and 1912 Games, with his success at the latter, in Sweden, at the age of 64, making him the oldest gold medallist ever. His appearance in 1920 broke a further record: he became the oldest athlete ever to compete in the Summer Games. His gold medal-winning son Alfred, was by his side at every team event he competed in at Antwerp.

⬇ *(Left to right) Alf Swahn, Ake Lundberg, Oscar Swahn and Per Olof Arvidsson won Running Deer Double Shot silver for Sweden at the 1920 Games.*

Pigeon relief

The Shooting contests at the 1900 Games in Paris were mired in controversy. Live pigeons were used as moving targets and it was reported that as many as 300 were shot dead. Clay pigeons were introduced in time for the following Games. The controversy did not stop there, however. Out of the 6,351 shooters listed, 96 per cent were from France. Also, values were compromised at the 1900 Games because prize money was awarded to virtually every winner in the Shooting events.

Shooting star

Carl Townsend Osburn holds the distinction of being the most successful competitor in Shooting at the Games in history. Until Michael Phelps's record-breaking performance in the swimming pool, Osburn was the all-time leading male medal winner for the United States in any sport at the Games, with a tally of 11. Osburn competed between 1912 and 1924 while serving in the US Navy, where he attained the rank of Commander. His shooting prowess saw him dominate the Shooting competition at the Antwerp 1920 Games, in which he claimed no fewer than six medals, four of which were gold. Such was his dominance, he would probably have added even more medals had the 1916 Games not been cancelled.

Teenage talent

Atlanta 1996 was the stage that produced the Olympic Games' youngest Shooting gold medallist: American Kimberly Rhode, who won the Double Trap event at the tender age of 17. She won a second gold medal at Athens 2004, but the elimination of Double Trap Shooting from the Games roster for women saw her focus on the Skeet. Having won the 2007 World Cup, during which she set a world record of 98 hits (73 in qualification and a perfect 25 in the final), Rhode won silver in Beijing before she became a television presenter.

➜ *Shooting's youngest champion: the United States' Kimberly Rhode.*

Deer hunters

The 1908 Olympic Games in London included the Running Deer competition for the first time. Instead of using real deer, however, the organisers used cardboard cut-outs shaped like deer. The target made ten runs of 75 feet (23 metres) and the shooter fired two shots during each run. The runs lasted roughly four seconds each and the target was located 110 yards (100m) from the shooter. There were three concentric circles on the target, with the smallest counting for four points, the middle for three and the outermost for two. The Running Deer competition was still to feature as a Shooting event as recently as the Melbourne 1956 Games.

⬇ *Hungary's Károly Takáks won gold medals shooting with his right hand and, following an accident, with his left to leave his unique mark on the history of the Games.*

Baron's choice

Shooting owes its place on the modern Olympic Games programme partly to the event's founder, Frenchman Baron Pierre de Coubertin. The nobleman was a former French pistol champion and supported the inclusion of four pistol and two high-power rifle events on the inaugural 1896 Games programme.

Pick a number

The number of Shooting events at the Summer Games has varied. Technology and ethics have dictated changes in the sport and when Shooting was reintroduced in 1932, it consisted of only two events. The number had gone up to a record 17 at the 2000 and 2004 Games. At Athens 2004, three shooting disciplines (Rifle, Pistol and Shotgun) saw participants competing for 51 medals in ten men's and seven women's events. Four years later, in Beijing, competition was limited to 15 events, with a clear distinction between men's and women's tournaments.

Magyar miracle

One of the most extraordinary of all Shooting champions at the Games was Hungary's Károly Takács, the first shooter to win two gold medals in the 25m Rapid Fire Pistol event. Having joined the Hungarian Army, Takács became an outstanding pistol shooter, but in 1938 an accident with a hand grenade resulted in him losing his right hand and his shooting career appeared to be at an end. However, his determination saw him learn to shoot with his left hand and, remarkably, he won the national championships the following spring, before the Second World War curtailed the Olympic Movement. At the 1948 Games in London, the 38-year-old Takács shocked the world by claiming gold, a feat he repeated at Helsinki 1952. He is the first physically disabled athlete known to have competed in the Olympic Games and has been recognised as one of the 'Olympic heroes' by the International Olympic Committee.

Chapter Thirteen
Weightlifting

Weightlifting is one of the basic sports at the Games, reflected in the third part of the Olympic Motto – 'Citius, altius, fortius' (faster, higher, stronger). The sport has been part of the Games programme since Athens 1896 and has produced some of the most colourful moments in the event's history.

The fascination of Weightlifting lies not just in the demonstration of physical prowess but also in the tactics, which are intriguing but easy to understand. Every competitor has three attempts at two movements: the snatch and the clean and jerk – a third, the press, was discarded after the 1972 Games.

In the snatch the bar is lifted overhead in one movement; in the clean and jerk it is pulled into the top of the chest, usually with the competitor squatting beneath the weight to receive it, and then jerked overhead, invariably with one leg going forward and the other back for support.

The best performances on the two lifts are then aggregated, with the competitor who has recorded the highest total adjudged the winner.

Key to the sport's tactics is the fact that once a weight has been selected, the competitor cannot go down. If the athlete fails in an attempt, he must either retake the lift using the same weight again or increase it. If two competitors have the same total, the man or woman with the lighter bodyweight wins.

There are eight bodyweight divisions for men and seven for women. Women's Weightlifting was first contested at Sydney 2000 and has been dominated by China.

Germany's Matthias Steiner lifted a mighty 258 kilograms with his final clean and jerk lift to win the men's +105kg Weightlifting competition (by just 1kg over Russia's Evgeny Chigishev) at the 2008 Games in Beijing.

Men's Weightlifting

The first two men's Weightlifting competitions at Athens 1896 did not feature any weight limits, which were introduced for the first time in 1920, have been modified several times over the years and, since 2000, feature eight categories from 56kg to +105kg.

Countries with most medals in men's Weightlifting

	gold	silver	bronze	total
1. Soviet Union	39	21	2	62
2. United States	15	16	10	41
3. Bulgaria	12	16	8	36
4. China	13	10	8	31
5. Poland	4	5	19	28

Beating the system

In 1932, France's Louis Hostin, runner-up in 1928, took the light-heavyweight title in Los Angeles, finishing 5 kilograms ahead of Denmark's Svend Olsen. Hostin continued to improve and was the clear favourite for Berlin 1936. There he led his main rival, Germany's Eugen Deutsch, by 5kg on the press, and on the snatch he raised 117.5kg, with Deutsch failing to raise 110kg three times. The Germans then protested that one of Deutsch's attempts had been valid and the Jury of Appeal, under considerable pressure, allowed one effort to be ratified. The British Olympic Association's official report noted: 'This was keenly resented by many present.' However, Hostin held on for his second successive victory.

The strongest man

Charles Rigoulot was one of France's most famous figures during the 1920s, not because he won the light-heavyweight title at the 1924 Games but because of his career afterwards. In 1925, he was challenged by a professional French strongman, Ernest Cadine, a gold medallist at Antwerp 1920, for the title of 'The World's Strongest Man'. Rigoulot won. Subsequently he became a professional wrestler, continued to train with weights, raced cars for Peugeot and was imprisoned in a concentration camp during the Second World War for hitting a German officer.

↑ *Charles Rigoulet became a huge celebrity in the 1920s.*

Bowling them over in Bond...

Harold Sakata was one of the few weightlifters to achieve international fame, but not because of his exploits in the sport. He finished second in the light-heavyweights at the 1948 Games, became a professional wrestler and went on to become the Canadian tag team champion. However, his greatest role was still to come: he played the role of Oddjob in the Bond film *Goldfinger*.

← *Harold Sakata in action at the 1948 Olympic Games in London.*

Family support

Khadr El Touni was a decisive winner of the 1936 middleweight title, setting a world record with a lift of 387.5 kilograms. At London 1948, he signed himself out of a London hospital, to which he had been admitted, to take part in the competition and could only finish fourth. His last major victory came when he won the world title in 1950. He died six years later after electrocuting himself during a domestic repair.

Bars to prison bars

The USA's John Davis reigned supreme among weightlifters for 15 years. He won his first world title at light heavyweight in 1938, aged 17. After the war, he won two gold medals at the Games and five world super heavyweight titles, even though, at only 100 kilograms, he was much lighter than many of his opponents. In 1950, Davis lifted the famous Apollon railway axle, which had defied many people over the years, although he needed four attempts to do so because his small hands were not suited to grasping the thick bar.

Fast food route to gold

The bespectacled American Norbert Schemansky was the first weightlifter to win four medals at the Games, as he moved between the mid-heavyweight and heavyweight divisions from London 1948 to Tokyo 1964, when he finished third at the age of 40. His career, in which he took three world titles, was interrupted by serious back injuries. 'Skee' was not helped by a diet that owed little to healthy nutrients. When once asked of what it consisted, he replied: 'Hamburgers. Pizza. Beer.'

↖ Norbert Schemansky took 90kg gold at Helsinki 1952.

Answer to prayer

Mohamed Nassiri was Iran's first-ever Weightlifting Olympic gold medallist. A devout Muslim, before each lift he would turn his back on the spectators, pray and then call out to Imam Ali, the original leader of the Shia branch of Islam. After finishing third in the 1966 World Championships, he was set for his career-defining moment at Mexico City 1968. He managed to lift 150 kilograms in his final clean and jerk – 9kg more than the world bantamweight record – to win gold. At the 1972 Games he won the silver medal, and in 1976 the bronze.

Conquering not just asthma

Born in Sacramento of Japanese extraction, Tamio 'Tommy' Kono was an asthmatic child, but, having been introduced to Weightlifting in a relocation camp during the Second World War, he became perhaps the greatest competitor the sport has ever known. Between 1952 and 1959, he won two Olympic and six world titles, in the lightweight and light heavyweight categories.

Cold War weights

When the Soviet Union competed for the first time at the Olympic Games in 1952, the Cold War was at its peak. This gave a special edge to the rivalry between the United States and the Soviets, and nowhere was this keener than in the Weightlifting competition. The light heavyweight class in 1952 was perhaps the most controversial in the history of the sport, with Trofim Lomakin and Arkady Vorobyev trying to take away the title from the American Stan Stanczyk. There were constant protests from both sides and two judges resigned after their decisions were reversed. Lomakin eventually won, with Stanczyk second, but Vorobyev just failed with his last clean and jerk when he tried a world record lift of 170 kilograms. He got the bar to arms' length, but the sudden roar from the crowd applauding his feat seemed to unsettle him and he dropped the weight.

Winning gambles

Born in Israel and the son of a Brooklyn rabbi, Issy Berger won the featherweight crown at Melbourne 1956 and then the world title in Stockholm in 1958. He was renowned for placing wagers on lifts and was nicknamed 'Betcha' Berger. One weight that he twice failed to raise, despite impressive performances in the gym, was the 152.5 kilograms he needed to retain his Olympic Games title in 1960, leaving the Soviet Union's Yevgeny Minayev, the only man in the entire competition to complete all nine attempts, as the champion.

Martin the master

Louis Martin, who was born in Kingston, Jamaica, but who went on to represent Great Britain, was his adopted country's greatest-ever weightlifter, winning four world titles and mid-Heavyweight silver and bronze medals at the Olympic Games, at Rome 1960 and Tokyo 1964 respectively. His last chance for gold came in Mexico City in 1968, but it was not to be. Trailing going into the clean and jerk, he went for 192.5kg in a bid to get the bronze medal. Three times he got up with the bar. Three times he jerked it overhead. Three times he failed.

→ Louis Martin won bronze at Rome 1960 and silver at Tokyo 1964 in the -90kg category.

Women's Weightlifting

Women's Weightlifting made its debut at the 2000 Olympic Games in Sydney and features seven weight categories: 48kg, 53kg, 58kg, 63kg, 69kg, 75kg and +75kg. Chinese competitors have been the dominant force, winning 11 of the 21 gold medals contested (with Thailand the next best with two).

The sweet smell of success

When women's Weightlifting was introduced to the Games programme at Sydney 2000, the organisers enterprisingly gave red carnations to all the female competitors and spectators. Few deserved it more than Soraya Jimenez Mendivil. The 23-year-old Mexican produced the performance of a lifetime – she managed to jerk an impressive 127.5 kilograms (15kg more than her best performance at the previous year's World Championships) – to take the 58kg gold medal from North Korea's Ri Song-Hui, who failed her second jerk attempt because she ran out of time. When asked afterwards whether females should compete in Weightlifting, Mendivil replied decisively: 'This is a sport for women. All sports are for women.'

← *Celebration time for Soraya Jimenez Mendivil after an impressive final clean and jerk lift took her to gold at the 2000 Games in Sydney.*

Cao Lei powers to gold

China dominated the women's Weightlifting competition at the Beijing 2008 Games winning four of the seven gold medals on offer, and the star of the show was Cao Lei. A former junior world champion and the reigning senior world champion (having taken the title in both 2006 and 2007), the 24-year-old dominated the 75kg category, setting new Olympic Games records in both the snatch and clean and jerk disciplines (with lifts of 128kg and 154kg respectively). Her total score of 282kg was also a new Games record. She may have failed with her final world record attempt (159kg in the clean and jerk), but it mattered not: she had lifted a combined 16kg more than her closest competitor (Kazakhstan's Alla Vazhenina) to win gold.

↑ *Cao Lei dominated the 75kg category at Beijing 2008.*

If at first...

After being the first person to train at the US Olympic Center in Colorado in three different sports, Tara Nott-Cunningham finally competed at the Games in Weightlifting. The 1.54-metre tall Texan was originally a gymnast, but had failed to qualify for the Games. Then she tried volleyball, basketball and finally football, in which she played internationally, but was not picked by the United States for Atlanta 1996. She took up weightlifting for fitness and became Pan American champion in 1999. In Sydney, she finished second in the 48kg category – becoming the first American to win a Weightlifting medal since 1960 – and was subsequently elevated to the gold medal position.

Strongest and longest

Confusion reigned briefly at Beijing 2008, when a seemingly unknown Thai weightlifter won the 53kg class – the bantamweights. Jaroenrattanatarakoo Prapawadee also had the distinction of having the longest name of all the competitors in the Games. However, after she had raised a total of 221 kilograms to claim gold, the truth emerged. The winner revealed that, following a run of bad luck, including not being picked for the previous Games, she had consulted a fortune-teller and was told she would be successful at the 2008 Games if she changed her name from Kuntatean Junpim, by which she had been known earlier when she won senior and junior world titles.

➔ *A change of name brought a change of fortune for Thailand's Jaroenrattanatarakoo Prapawadee when she won gold at Beijing 2008.*

Countries with most medals in women's Weightlifting

		gold	silver	bronze	total
1.	China	11	1	0	12
2.	Thailand	2	0	5	7
3.	Russia	0	4	3	7
4.	North Korea	1	1	1	3
5.	Indonesia	0	2	2	4

Liu Chunhong

The performance of Chen Yanqing at Beijing 2008 was emulated by Chinese team-mate Liu Chunhong, who won her second light heavyweight crown at the Games. Russia's Oxana Slivenko, the world record-holder in snatch, had been expected to challenge Liu, but the Chinese competitor set new Games and world records – not bothering with her final clean and jerk to win the title by 31 kilograms, with a total of 286kg. The official magazine of the International Weightlifting Federation suggested she was a worthy contender to be considered the best woman lifter of all time.

More weight

The supreme super heavyweight at Beijing 2008 was South Korea's Jang Mi-Ran, who added an Olympic Games gold medal to her six world crowns. She had begun weightlifting aged 16, and in 2008 won the gold medal by 49 kilograms, setting new world records with both her snatch lift and her overall total.

Now you see her...

Beijing 2008 witnessed one of the outstanding Weightlifting feats in history, when China's Chen Yanqing retained her Olympic Games title to become the first woman in history to win two gold medals in the Games. This was the climax of an international career that had begun 11 years earlier, in 1997, when she won the world middleweight title. Despite winning the lightweight crown two years later, she was not picked for the 2000 Games in Sydney, but came back at Athens 2004 to win her first Olympic Games gold medal. However, after the Asian Games in Doha she had another period away, taking a BSc in psychology, before returning successfully once again.

➔ *China's Chen Yanqing won the 58kg Weightlifting category at Beijing 2008 to become the first woman in history to defend her title at the Games.*

Chapter Fourteen
Defunct Olympic sports

Throughout the long history of the Olympic Games, the programme of events has constantly evolved. While some sports have grown in popularity and strength, others have naturally fallen by the wayside.

Certain sports were dropped from the itinerary because of a general desire for more events in which women could compete, while others, such as rugby, were dropped in part to make way for a greater number of individual events. Some of these defunct sports, such as Basque pelota or roquet, had their roots deeply set in a host nation's traditions and these events tended to be routinely won by competitors from the host nation.

Other sports have evolved through technology: thus Shooting may have lost several events over the years but remains an important part of competition at the Games today. Athletics has equally evolved through time, and the use of metric measurements has had an undoubted impact on distances run, jumped or thrown and, of course, on subsequent Olympic Games and world records.

Some sports that have not been included for many Games are either poised for a return or are under discussion for the future; these include popular worldwide sports such as golf and rugby, both of which will be back in the programme at the 2016 Games in Rio.

Yet every defunct sport had its moment in the limelight, when it was the focus of attention around the world and in which every individual gold medallist sealed his or her personal mark in history.

Two teams battle it out during the Tug of War competition at Antwerp 1920. After four previous outings (in 1900, 1904, 1908 and 1912), it was the event's final outing at the Olympic Games.

Defunct athletics events

Numerous athletic events have come and gone at the Olympic Games over the years. Some have evolved and are now contested over different distances – metric as opposed to imperial; others, such as Both-Hands Throwing or standing-jump events, only made the briefest of appearances.

Ray of light

American athlete Ray Ewry was one of the first superstars of the modern Olympic Games. Not content with winning the gold medal in the Standing Long Jump on four occasions, Ewry doubled up with gold in the Standing High Jump at the same four Games, setting world records for the Standing High Jump (1.65 metres) and the Standing Long Jump (3.47m). Ewry retired after the London 1908 Games, but another American, Platt Adams, claimed gold in the Standing High Jump at the 1912 Games in Stockholm, giving the US a perfect winning record as this was the last Games to feature this sport.

⬇ *Ray Ewry leaps to gold in the Standing High Jump at London 1908.*

Stand-out superstar

Although the Standing Long Jump ended its association with the Olympic Games almost a century ago, it remains an athletic discipline for some of the world's fittest individuals. The event, which was first included at the 1900 Olympic Games and for the last time in 1912, was dominated throughout its 12 years by the United States. It was open only to men, and American Ray Ewry was a true master, winning gold at four consecutive Games between 1900 and 1908, including the Intercalated Games of 1906 in Athens. Of the 15 medals available during the event's lifetime at the Games, no fewer then 12 were won by Americans, and even today the Standing Long Jump is one of the events contested at the annual NFL combine.

⬆ *Ray Ewry was the king of standing-jump events, winning eight golds.*

Make that three

The 1900 Games featured the men's Standing Triple Jump, which was predictably won by American Ray Ewry, who won all three of the standing jump competitions in Paris. All three standing jumps clearly required special technique, and notably all of the competitors in the Standing Triple Jump also went on to compete in the regular Triple Jump, with the exception of the three medallists. Ewry defended his Standing Triple Jump was title at St Louis 1904, before it disappeared from the Games roster.

Crossed out

Cross Country is a popular feature of competitive endurance running, but the last time it featured at an Olympic Games was at Paris in 1924. That year, as Finland's Paavo Nurmi recorded his second consecutive gold medal, more than half of the field of 38 runners failed to finish as a result of unseasonably hot weather and poisonous fumes from a nearby factory.

➡ *Paavo Nurmi (right) heads to Cross Country gold at Paris 1924.*

Right on!

Finland has a rich pedigree in the men's Javelin competition at the Games, and Stockholm 1912 was no exception. What was different there, however, was the appearance, on this one occasion only, of the 'men's Javelin throw, both hands' event. In the scheduled final, the three qualifiers were meant to have three further throws with each hand, with the best of each hand being totalled. In the event, all three finalists were Finnish and elected not to contest a final, which meant that the gold medal went to Julius Saaristo for his winning right-handed throw of 61 metres, which broke the Games record set by Eric Lemming in winning the single-arm Javelin throw three days earlier.

⬇ *Julius Saaristo took Both-Hands Javelin gold at Stockholm 1912.*

Cops on the beat

At St Louis 1904 the men's 56lb-weight Throw event was one of only two track and field events not won by an American. This was the first of only two occasions that the sport was included, and the competition comprised of six athletes from the US and Canada, with Etienne Desmarteas, a Montreal policeman, defeating favourite John Flanagan. The men's 56lb-weight Throw reappeared at the Antwerp 1920 Games and was won by Patrick McDonald, who was as a police officer in Times Square.

Walk-out

London 1908 played host to the men's 10 Miles Walk, the only time the event took place at a Games. The race was a triumph for the home nation as Great Britain took a clean sweep of the medals, with George Larner winning the gold and following up in the 3,500-metre race. Having already set nine world records, Larner found that training interfered with his police duties and had previously retired from the sport, returning to competition just three months before striking gold.

➡ *George Larner led a clean sweep of British medallists in the 10-mile Walk at London 1908.*

American advantage

The 1904 Games featured a men's Four Miles Team Race, which took place at Francis Field, St Louis. A variation of the 5,000m team event, which had taken place four years earlier, the competition was a straight match race between two teams, comprised of five athletes. Nine of the competitors were American, with one Frenchman completing the line-up. The United States team were victorious and Americans filled the first eight places, with Arthur Newton.

Mixing it up

The Medley Relay remains a familiar term at the Olympic Games – in the swimming pool. However, at the 1908 Games in London the men's Medley Relay was very much a part of the track and field events. The race was run over 1,600 metres by teams of four athletes, but it had a twist: the runners competed at different distances. The first two runners covered 200m, the third ran 400m and the final runner ran 800m. Seven nations participated, with the United States comfortably winning the gold medal ahead of Germany and Hungary. Although subsequently dropped from the Games, the event's track legacy remains as popular as ever: the 4 x 400m Relay.

Troubled Triathlon

The Athetics Triathlon has only appeared at the Games on one occasion, at St Louis in 1904. Perhaps the confusion surrounding it precluded further competitions, as its status was disputed. An event comprising of the Long Jump, Shot Put and 100-Yard Dash, it was deemed part of the Athletics programme by the International Olympic Committee, but other sources listed the triathlon among the gymnastic activities. Gymnasts competed, rather than athletes, resulting in a clean sweep of medals for the United States.

Defunct ball games

The list of ball games that once formed part of the Games roster is a long one, from mainstream sports such as cricket, golf and rugby, to less well-known regional sports, such as roque and the Basque pelota.

Single wicket

Paris 1900 was the setting for the curious, original appearance of cricket at the Games. The competition was not formally recognised as such at the time and the competing teams, Great Britain and France, did not even know they were participating in the event. The British side was a touring club team, the Devon and Somerset Wanderers, while the French team, the French Athletic Club Union, consisted mainly of British expatriates. Great Britain won the match and the team were awarded silver medals, with the French side receiving bronze medals. The event was formally recognised as an Olympic Games contest at Stockholm 1912, when the medals were changed to gold and silver. Cricket had originally been pencilled in as an event for the inaugural modern Games in 1896 and was even included in the provisional programme. However, the competition was cancelled when there were too few entries. For the Paris 1900 Games the plan was to feature four teams, but Belgium and the Netherlands withdrew from the contest when their co-hosting bids fell through. The eventual competition featured just Great Britain and France, and by mutual agreement the sides consisted of 12 players rather than the traditional 11-a-side.

← Great Britain beat France in the Games' only ever Cricket Final at Paris in 1900.

Lyon heart

Golf is set to return to the Games – but in Rio de Janeiro in 2016, not at London 2012. Until now it has featured only twice at the Summer Games, more than a century ago. Paris 1900 struck an early blow for equality as it featured tournaments for both men and women. The men's tournament consisted of 36 holes of matchplay, and the women's tournament of nine holes of strokeplay. American Charles Sands took the gold medal in the men's event, while Margaret Ives Abbott led a clean sweep of the women's medals for the US team. The last time golf featured at the Games was in 1904 in St Louis. This time only men competed and the field of 77 players comprised of 74 Americans and three Canadians. The team event resulted in all three team medals going to the United States, but the individual tournament had a rather different outcome, with 46-year-old Canadian George Lyon winning the gold medal. Lyon might have added further victory in 1908, but a dispute saw British golfers boycott their 'home' Games, and this was followed by the withdrawal of the US golfers, leaving Lyon as the sole entrant. He declined the offer of the gold medal on the grounds that it had not been won fairly in competition.

↑ Canada's George Lyon beat Chandler Egan (United States) 3&2 in the Final in St Louis in 1904 to become the Games' last Golf gold medallist. The sport will make a return to the Games in 2016.

Back with a difference

Rugby has not featured as a sport at the Games for two generations, but in the formative years of the modern Olympic Games it was included regularly, except in 1912. Pierre de Coubertin, architect of the Games, was also responsible for establishing rugby in France. On Rugby's first appearance in 1900, the gold medal went to the French, who emerged as the overall winners in a round-robin tournament with Great Britain and Germany. The sport will return to the Olympic Games in Rio de Janeiro in 2016 – in the seven-a-side rather than the traditional 15-a-side format.

Royal and ancient

Real Tennis, the ancient, indoor ancestor of Lawn Tennis, is also known as Royal Tennis, in the US as Court Tennis and in France as Jeu de Paume. It was under the latter name (which originally referred to a game played with the hand rather than a racquet) that the sport made its one appearance (as a medal event) at the 1908 Olympic Games in London. Real Tennis, like Lawn Tennis, is played over a net, but with a curious-looking racquet and in an enclosed court that has features as complex as the game's rules and scoring system. An outdoor version had previously been played as a demonstration sport at Paris 1900, and the 1924 Games, again in Paris, saw the sport return as an exhibition event. In 1908, the world famous Queen's Club in London played host to an event contested by 11 players from Great Britain and the United States. The youngest contestant, Jay Gould II, just 19, won the gold medal for the US.

Basque speciality

In 1900, Paris put on the only official Basque Pelota tournament ever held at the Games, although the sport, also known as Jai Alai, has been a demonstration sport three times (in 1924, 1968 and 1992). Regarded as the fastest sport in the world, pelota has its origins in the Basque region. In 1900, the men-only tournament involved just two teams, with the Spanish pair of Villota and Amezola defeating the French team.

Doubling up

Few Olympians can lay claim to having won gold medals in two different sports. That distinction was achieved by Sydney Middleton, a member of the victorious Australasia Rugby team (comprised of Australians and New Zealanders), that defeated Great Britain to win the London 1908 Rugby gold medal. Four years later, with Rugby not included in the Games itinerary, Middleton won a second gold medal as a rower. The Australasia team of 1908 also included Danny Carroll, who, at the Antwerp 1920 Games, won another Rugby gold medal, this time for the United States. The participation of the US in Rugby at the Olympic Games began with victory in Antwerp. Middleton's impressive exploits were bettered by Morris Kirksey, who, alongside his Rugby victory, won a second gold medal in the men's 4 x 100m Relay and a silver in the men's 100m Dash. The US team won the Rugby gold medal again in 1924, winning the infamous Final against the host nation in Paris, where a pitch invasion led to the medal ceremony taking place with police protection. This was the last time Rugby appeared at the Olympic Games.

⬇ *France on the attack against Romania at the 1924 Olympic Games in Paris – the last time Rugby featured at the Games.*

Roquet that fizzled out

At the time of its inclusion as a sport at the Games, at St Louis 1904, roquet was hailed as the 'Game of the Century'. Its subsequent decline has been almost terminal, and today it is only played by a handful of people in the United States. The sport is a variation on croquet, played on a hard, smooth surface as opposed to a lawn. Unsurprisingly, all four competing players in 1904 were American, with Charles Jacobus winning the gold medal.

⬆ *Roquet only made one appearance at the Games: at St Louis in 1904.*

Jail break

Perhaps the only sport contested at the Games that was formed in a prison was rackets, which appeared just once – at London 1908. A game not unlike squash, but much faster and played with a small, hard ball in a much bigger court, rackets originated in the 18th century in the King's Bench and Fleet debtors prisons, as a game in which a ball was hit against a wall, first with hands and then with racquets. It was then taken up by the public schools and developed in an enclosed court. The tournament at the 1908 Games featured two men-only events, singles and doubles, both dominated by Great Britain. Evan Noel beat Henry Leaf in the Final to take Singles gold, before combining with Leaf to win bronze in the Doubles.

Other defunct events

Some sports at the Games have become defunct through the simple passing of time – as weight categories in various sports became standardised, for example. Others, however, such as rope climbing, motorboat racing, equestrian long jump or polo, fell by the wayside as organisers tried to find room for other events, particularly those for women.

Chucked out

Polo has been included in five Olympic Games (1900, 1908, 1920, 1924, 1936) and made its last appearance at Berlin 1936. It first appeared at the 1900 Games in Paris, just 24 years after it had become an accepted sport in Great Britain and the United States. With world-class players in short supply, the top players from the US, England, Spain, France and Mexico formed four mixed teams. The gold medal was won by the Foxhunters, who included the outstanding player of the era, the American Foxhall Keene. Polo returned to the Games in London in 1908, and Great Britain won the gold medal at both these Games and at the next opportunity, in 1920 in Antwerp. Then, in 1924, Argentina served notice of its burgeoning reputation in the sport, winning gold at its first attempt in Paris. In 1936, the Argentina team was so strong that it was undefeated in the play-offs and trounced England 11–0 in the final. It was the last Polo match played at the Games and, fittingly, it was contested by the sport's only two gold medal-winning nations.

Long gone

While Equestrian sports remain on the Olympic Games agenda, events such as the Equestrian Long Jump have passed into history. The 1900 Games in Paris played host to the only such competition, with 17 competitors. The Belgian rider Constant van Langendonck, on his horse Extra Dry, took the gold medal with a jump of 25ft ¼in. Italian Giovanni Trissino, on Oreste, took the silver medal, but gained revenge on Van Langendonck as joint gold medallist in the Horse High Jump competition, in which his rival won the bronze. When Equestrian sports returned to the Games in 1912, both events had been discontinued. Before 1952, Equestrian competition was limited to male cavalry officers, but Helsinki proved a watershed. Not only women, but also civilians, were permitted to enter.

Blown away

The Olympic Games' flirtation with motorised competition was brief. Featured as a demonstration sport in 1900, motorboat racing was only once permitted as an official sport at the Games. At London 1908 there were three events, all raced over five laps of eight nautical miles. Owing to strong gales, only one boat finished in each of the three classes, with the French boat *Camille* winning gold in the Class A competition, when the Duke of Westminster's boat *Wolseley Siddeley* ran aground, and the British *Gyrinus* triumphing in both the Class B (under 60 feet) and Class C (6.5- to 8 metre) events.

↑ *Motorboat racing made only one appearance at the Games: in 1908, when contestants raced around the Isle of Wight off England's south coast.*

↖ *Argentina score one of their unanswered 11 goals in the 1936 Polo Final against Great Britain. It was the last time the sport was contested at the Games.*

All-round medallists

Lacrosse devotees hope that this North American-born sport may one day make a return to the Olympic Games after an absence of more than a century. Lacrosse has been on the Games programme twice, in 1904 and 1908, and holds a special distinction in that every competing nation has won a medal. In 1904, two Canadian teams challenged a local team from St Louis, with the Shamrock Lacrosse Team of Winnipeg winning gold. The 1908 Games saw Canada retain the gold medal, defeating the only other team in the competition, Great Britain. Lacrosse also featured as a demonstration sport at the 1928, 1932 and 1948 Games.

Americans spiked!

Nowadays mostly seen at summer fetes, Tug of War was once considered a serious sport at the Games, and at London 1908 it was the subject of controversy. After a match between Great Britain and the United States the defeated Americans protested that their opponents had gained an unfair advantage by wearing spiked footwear. The protest was rejected and the American team withdrew, gifting gold and silver medals to Great Britain. Tug of War was contested by teams of eight individuals whose object was to win by pulling the opposition a distance of 6 feet (1.8 metres); if no such drama had occurred after five minutes, the side who had pulled their opponents the furthest triumphed. A combined team of Swedes and Danes won the first Tug of War gold medal at the 1900 Games in Paris, and the sport remained on the agenda until 1920.

⬇ *The Great Britain team – made up of the City of London Police team – took Tug of War gold at the 1908 Games in London.*

Start and finish

Solo Synchronised Swimming was short-lived as a sport at the Games. The event made its debut at the Los Angeles 1984 Games, with America's Tracie Ruiz claiming the gold medal from Canada's Carolyn Waldo, who would win gold four years later in Seoul. After American Kristen Babb-Sprague won gold at Barcelona 1992, the organisers dropped the sport on the basis that a solo sport, by definition, could not be synchronised.

⬅ *Canada's Carolyn Waldo wins gold at Seoul in 1988.*

Gold ribbon event

Club Swinging was a forerunner to Rhythmic Gymnastics. The event, which involved swinging a club festooned with ribbons around the body and head, was held twice, at the St Louis 1904 and Los Angeles 1932 Games. The Club Swinging competition was dominated both times by the United States, who won all six medals contested. The 1932 Games provided a story very much in tune with the times. As the Great Depression continued, an unemployed American named George Roth won the gold medal in front of a crowd of 60,000. Minutes later, he was seen walking out of the stadium to hitchhike home.

Tied up in knots

The men's Gymnastics programme at Athens 1896 featured eight events, including Rope Climbing. This sport required contestants to climb a 14-metre rope, with marks awarded for time and style – host nation Greece claimed gold and silver. In subsequent contests a shorter rope was used (usually 8m long) and contestants were judged purely on time. The event appeared on the Olympic Games programme on five occasions, the last of which was at Los Angeles 1932.

Event for dummies

The Duelling Pistol event was not exactly about pistols at dawn, though it did see the deployment of mannequins dressed in frock coats as targets. Competitors fired from distances of 20 metres and 30m, and the dummy had a bull's eye located on the throat. The event first took place at the 1906 Intercalated Games, but was not officially recognised by the IOC. It reappeared once, however, at Stockholm 1912, with France's Léon Moreaux winning the gold over 20m and Greece's Konstantinos Skarlatos over 30m.

Deep but short

Sport at the Olympic Games entered a new dimension with the Diving competition at St Louis 1904, when the Plunge for Distance event made its one and only appearance. The United States was guaranteed a clean sweep of the medals as all five competitors came from the host nation. Essentially this event was a diving long jump, with competitors diving into the pool from a standing position. Their performance was measured in one of two ways: either as their recorded distance after 60 seconds, or as the distance to the point at which they broke the surface if that event happened before 60 seconds had elapsed. Participants were prohibited from propelling themselves underwater, making William Dickey's winning effort of 19.05 metres a remarkable feat.

Strong stuff

The Weightlifting competition at the 1904 Olympic Games in St Louis provided an early incarnation of today's World's Strongest Man contest, in the shape of the All Around Dumbbell event. The event took place over two days, with competitors performing five different types of lift on each day. Disciplines included tossing one dumbbell in one hand from the ground to arm's length above the shoulders in one motion, without stopping at the shoulder, and jerking up one dumbbell with one hand from the shoulder to arm's length above the shoulder. Judges and the referee awarded up to 25 points after ten rounds. American Oscar Osthoff won the gold medal for the host nation.

← *The United States' Frederick Winters on his way to the silver medal in the Weightlifting All-Around Dumbbell competition at St Louis 1904. It was the only occasion the event was staged at the Games.*

Anyone for Croquet?

Croquet made its Olympic Games debut at Paris 1900, where three events were contested: the doubles, one-ball singles and two-ball singles. Nine of the ten participants were French (a single Belgian competitor also took part), which predictably resulted in the host nation winning every medal, while, uniquely at the time, the competition was mixed-sex. Madame Filleaul Brohy and Mademoiselle Marie Ohnier thus became the first ever female Olympians during the course of the 1900 Croquet competition.

Obstacle race

Australia's proud Swimming record at the Olympic Games was enhanced in unusual fashion at the Paris 1900 Games. The event in question was the only ever Olympic 200m Swimming Obstacle Course race. Frederick Lane had already won the straightforward 200m Freestyle event but he had to employ a mixture of very different skills second time out. The event, which took place in the Seine, saw competitors challenged to climb over a pole, scramble over a row of boats and then swim beneath another row of boats. Lane made sure he could clamber over the boats quickly by aiming, astutely, for the stern.

Winning tumble

American gymnast Rowland 'Flip' Wolfe made his mark on Olympic Games history in two distinct ways. Firstly, in Los Angeles in 1932, he became the only ever winner of a gold medal in the Tumbling event, which was never included at the Games again. For good measure, his age at the time, 17 years and 307 days, made him the youngest ever Gymnastics champion. Wolfe then studied for a degree in chemistry and was later involved in the Manhattan Project, to build an atomic bomb.

Naval ratings

Athens 1896 saw one unique specialist event in the Swimming. In addition to the normal 100m Freestyle, the Games saw a 100m Freestyle event open only to Greek Navy sailors. The winning swimmer was Ioannis Malokinis, but his winning time was almost a full minute slower than that of the winner of the open race.

Great Dane

Although the Firefly class Sailing event only featured at the 1948 Games in London, it launched the career of one of the great Olympians. The event, which by the following Games was renamed the Finn class, marked the debut and the first of four consecutive gold medals for Dane Paul Elvstrom, at the age of 20. Remarkably, he continued to compete at the Olympic Games up to Seoul in 1988, appearing in eight separate Games, spanning 40 years. His final two appearances in the Tornado class resulted in further records as his boat was crewed by his daughter Trine, making the pair the first father and daughter team to appear at the Games.

One-hand wonders

Weightlifting has seen its share of changes at the Games. One of the early events was the One-Hand Lift competition. The event, similar to the modern snatch, was included in the inaugural 1896 Games. Participants were permitted to lift weights with only one hand at a time, but had to perform lifts with each hand, the winner being the one with the best combined score. In Athens, Britain's Launceston Elliott was able to take advantage of an injury to his Danish rival Viggo Jensen to claim gold. The event was also held at the 1906 Intercalated Games in Athens, where Austrian Josef Steinbach was victorious, but thereafter the event was dropped from the Games programme.

↑ *Sweden's Erik Adlerz (the 1912 High Diving champion) performs a silver medal-winning dive at the 1920 Games in Antwerp.*

Taking a dive

Sweden dominated men's High Diving competition before it evolved into 10m Platform Diving. They recorded a clean sweep of the medals at the 1912 Games in Stockholm, when the sport was officially recognised for the first time. The Scandinavians would also win every medal at the 1920 Games in Antwerp, before Australian Dick Eve provided a shock gold medal victory at the 1924 Games in Paris. Eve's efforts 'were marked by extreme grace, alertness, and crispness', according to one report, but his win was unexpected given his lack of international competition at home. Acrobatic moves were prohibited in the event, which permitted only straight dives (five in the competition) off the platform. It was discontinued and merged with 'fancy high diving' to create 10m Platform Diving.

Index

Picture credits

The publishers would like to thank the following sources for their kind permission to reproduce the pictures in this book. The page numbers for each of the photographs are listed below, giving the page on which they appear in the book and any location indicator (C-centre, T-top, B-bottom, L-left, R-right).

Action Images: 80B, 109B, 114; /Carlos Barria/Reuters: 108B, 109R; / Mike Blake/Reuters: 79B; /Kin Cheung/Reuters: 190B; /Claro Cortez/ Reuters: 25B; /Nir Elias/Reuters: 86T; /Mike Finn-Kelcey/Reuters: 171B; /Caren Firouz/Reuters: 123T, 123B; /Stuart Franklin: 17BR; /Zainal Abd Halim/Reuters: 175L; /Yves Herman/Reuters: 204-205; /Jim Hollander/ Reuters: 4R, 127T; /Kim Kyung-Hoon/Reuters: 159B, 160T; /Jerry Lampen/Reuters: 16B; /Nigel Marple/Reuters: 195B; /Tony Marshall/ Sporting Pictures: 77B; /Dylan Martinez/Reuters: 23R, 81T; /Toby Melville/Reuters: 191R; /Jason O'Brien: 4BCR; /Susan Ogrocki/Reuters: 217T; /Kai Pfaffenbach/Reuters: 76B; /Oleg Popov/Reuters: 209B; / Jason Reed/Reuters: 83L; /Reuters: 163T, 170B, 175B, 196; /Sporting Pictures: 150T; /Ruben Sprich/Reuters: 93B; /Crispin Thruston/Sporting Pictures: 39B; /Topham: 47BR, 62R, 140TR; /Rick Wilking/Reuters: 48B; /Tim Wimborne/Reuters: 183R

Corbis: /Bettmann: 51T; /Underwood & Underwood: 138L, 139L, 178B

Getty Images: 5BL, 14TR, 15T, 37B, 54T, 56T, 70B, 95TR, 98B, 116C, 140L, 142; /AFP: 31R, 33L, 46T, 49B, 52R, 65B, 75T, 120-121, 130R, 158TR; / Odd Andersen/AFP: 53B, 103BL; /Nicolas Asfouri/AFP: 20; /Frank Barratt: 18L; /Natalie Behring/Bloomberg: 141; /Al Bello: 35, 39R; / Hamish Blair: 105B; /Bloomberg: 21T; /Shaun Botterill: 59B; /Clive Brunskill: 132L; /Simon Bruty: 193T; /Martin Bureau/AFP: 26-27; /Matt Campbell/AFP: 200B; /David Cannon: 4C, 13B, 55B, 101T, 118T, 190C; / Central Press: 12B, 23L, 61T, 64T, 68B, 88T, 95BR, 207B; /Rich Clarkson/ Time & Life Pictures: 28B, 106B; /Chris Cole: 177T, 177R; /Michael Cooper: 19B; /Ralf Crane/Time & Life Pictures: 70R; /Creutzmann/AFP: 130L; /Mark Dadswell: 99T; /James Drake/Sports Illustrated: 53T; /Tony Duffy: 15B, 33T, 34T, 38, 39T, 50B, 52L, 56B, 57B, 67T, 73T, 73B, 84L, 85L; /Emmanuel Dunand/AFP: 102; /Don Emmert/AFP: 33B, 180-181; / Tony Feder: 75BL; /Eric Feferberg/AFP: 139TR; /Al Fenn/Time & Life Pictures: 59T; /Jonathan Ferrey: 110-111; /Julian Finney: 44-45, 112T; / Focus on Sport: 32B, 40B; /Stu Forster: 71R, 89BL, 169B; /Fox Photos: 22B, 188R; /Romeo Gacad/AFP: 88B; /Gamma-Keystone: 31T, 194L, 206L, 216B; /Michel Gangne/AFP: 176; /Daniel Garcia/AFP: 119BR; / Lluis Gene/AFP: 128-129, 137T; /Ron Gerelli: 63B; /John Gichigi: 46L; / George Gobet/AFP: 165B; /Jim Gray/Keystone: 162T; /Jeff Gross: 21B; / Valery Hache/AFP: 65T; /Alexander Hassenstein/Bongarts: 78T, 101B, 203T; /Julian Herbert: 125T; /Patrick Hertzog/AFP: 155TR; /Mike Hewitt: Front Endpaper, 47L, 49T; /Goh Chai Hin/AFP: Back Endpaper; /Hulton Archive: 10B, 40T, 42C, 90T, 157; /IOC Olympic Museum: 124T, 158L, 164B, 210-211, 212B, 213L, 216R; /Alexander Joe/ AFP: 107B; /Trevor Jones: 126R; /Mark Kauffman/Time & Life Pictures: 16TR; /Keystone: 16L, 30L, 74TR, 150B, 151T; /Michael Kienzier/ Bongarts: 191T; /Toshifumi Kitamura/AFP: 74L, 175TR; /Heinz Kluetmeier/Sports Illustrated: 28L; /Patrick Kovarik/AFP: 103T, 115L; / Robert Laberge: 186L; /Nick Laham: 87TL; /Lake County Museum: 168L;

/David Leah/Mexsport: 41TL; /Kevin Levine: 25TR; /Marco Longari/AFP: 161T; /Bob Martin: 85TR, 132T; /Darren McNamara: 98T; /Aris Messinis/ AFP: 22T; /Damien Meyer/AFP: 118B; /Olivier Morin/AFP: 6; /Gray Mortimore: 50T; /New York Daily News Archive: 36B, 145T; /Kazuhiro Nogi/AFP: 133B, 137B, 144C, 145B; /Mustafa Ozer/AFP: 96-97; /PNA Rota: 207T; /Peter Parks/AFP: 172-173; /Pascal Pavani/AFP: 80T; /Doug Pensinger: 108R, 115T; /Paul Popper/Popperfoto: 57T; /Popperfoto: 11T, 28TR, 36R, 48T, 60R, 61B, 71T, 126B, 156BL, 162B, 164T, 169T, 192T, 215B, 218, 219; /Mike Powell: 69T, 72T, 82T, 119TR, 119BL, 143B, 153T; / Steve Powell: 76T, 95BL; /Adam Pretty: 89T, 112L, 160B, 166-167; /Gary M Prior: 189B; /Mark Ralston/AFP: 43B; /Andreas Rentz: 41BL; /Rolls Press/Popperfoto: 66B, 138B; /Manpreet Romana/AFP: 153B; /Quinn Rooney: 107T; /Martin Rose/Bongarts: 42B; /Vladimir Rys/Bongarts: 198-199; /STF/AFP: 152B; /Jewel Samad/AFP: 91B; /Sankei Archive: 134L; /Ezra Shaw: 5BR, 161B, 177B; /Christophe Simon/AFP: 85BR; / Javier Soriano/AFP: 55T; /Cameron Spencer: 105R; /Jamie Squire: 19T, 170R; /Michael Steele: 60L, 78B, 208L; /Billy Stickland: 86B; /Henri Szwarc/Bongarts: 143T; /Bob Thomas: 5C, 5BCL, 5BCR, 29T, 34B, 87R, 116L, 136B, 149L, 159T, 179TL, 200T, 203B; /Bob Thomas/Popperfoto: 10T, 100L, 178L; /Tony Tomsic/Time & Life Pictures: 163B; /Topical Press Agency: 14B, 104L, 187R, 201B, 212L, 213B; /Pedro Ugarte/AFP: 72L; / Phil Walter: 113L, 125B; /Ian Walton: 83B; /William West/AFP: 18R; / Nick Wilson: 25L, 191B; /Andrew Wong: 8-9

Press Association Images: 32R, 63T, 68R, 212T; /AP: 12T, 29B, 58T, 64B, 84T, 92C, 94L, 127B, 132B, 148L, 155L, 165T, 188T, 193B, 214C; /ABACA: 179TR; /Bernat Armangue/AP: 197B; /Matthew Ashton: 115B; /A. Bibard/Panoramic: 124B; /Bildbyran: 202B; /Luca Bruno/AP: 4BC; / Zhang Chen/Landov: 174B; /Paul Chiasson/The Canadian Press: 208T; /ChinaFotoPress: 51B; /DPA: 32T, 37T, 43T, 62L, 94TR, 135, 148B; /David Davies: 183B, 195T, 197T; /Wang Dingchang/Landov: 41R; /Matt Dunham/AP: 24B, 134B; /Empics Sport: 69B, 104R, 113B, 156TR, 186B, 187B, 202R; /John Giles: 67T, 117; /David Guttenfelder/AP: 184L; /Ma Hailin/Landov: 11B; /Petr David Josek/AP: 103BR; /Thomas Kienzle/AP: 93T; /Peter Kneffel/DPA: 24T; /Lehtikuva: 168B; /Yang Lei/Landov: 209T; /Tony Marshall: 89BR, 99B, 171T, 183TL; /Andrew Milligan: 113B, 146-147; /Dominique Mollard/AP: 201T; /Don Morley: 136L, 152T; /Anja Niedringhaus/AP: 87BL; /Phil O'Brien: 182L; /S&G and Barratts: 5L, 13T, 14L, 17L, 54B, 79L, 149T, 154, 184B, 192L, 206B, 217B; /Amy Sancetta/ AP: 144B; /Lucas Schifres/ABACA: 17R; /Schimer Sportfoto/DPA: 66T; / Neal Simpson: 77T, 81T, 91T, 189T; /Topham Picturepoint: 58B, 122, 131T, 131B, 155R, 214B; /Fernando Vergara/AP: 4BR; /John Walton: 82B; /Aubrey Washington: 100B, 182B; /Wu Wei/Landov: 151B; /Kathy Willens/AP: 5BC; /Valeria Witters: 90B, 174T, 179B; /Liu Yu/Landov: 30B

Private Collection: 133T, 194T, 201C, 215R

Topfoto.co.uk: /RIA Novosti: 92B, 106T

Every effort has been made to acknowledge correctly and contact the source and/or copyright holder of each picture and Carlton Books Limited apologises for any unintentional errors or omissions that will be corrected in future editions of this book.

➔ Back endpaper: The Closing Ceremony at the Beijing 2008 Games.